Music and

MW00812636

Music and the Paranormal

An Encyclopedic Dictionary

MELVYN J. WILLIN

McFarland & Company, Inc., Publishers

Jefferson, North Carolina

LIBRARY OF CONGRESS CATALOGUING-IN-PUBLICATION DATA

Names: Willin, Melvyn J., author.
Title: Music and the paranormal : an encyclopedic dictionary /
Melvyn J. Willin.
Description: Jefferson, North Carolina : McFarland & Company,
Inc., Publishers, 2022. | Includes bibliographical references and index.
Identifiers: LCCN 2021061110 |
ISBN 9781476685984 (paperback : acid free paper) ∞ |
ISBN 9781476644714 (ebook)
Subjects: LCSH: Music—Psychological aspects—Encyclopedias. |
Musicians—Psychology—Encyclopedias. | Parapsychology—Encyclopedias. |
Curiosities and wonders—Encyclopedias. | BISAC: MUSIC /
Reference | BODY, MIND & SPIRIT / Parapsychology / General
Classification: LCC ML102.P79 W55 2022 | DDC 306.4842/03—dc23
LC record available at https://lccn.loc.gov/2021061110

BRITISH LIBRARY CATALOGUING DATA ARE AVAILABLE

ISBN (print) 978-1-4766-8598-4
ISBN (ebook) 978-1-4766-4471-4

On the cover: The Davenport brothers circa 1869 Boston,
W. White and company (Library of Congress/Flickr);
stereoscope of Florizel von Reuter, ca. 1911, Stereostopic Co.
(Wikimedia Commons/Public Domain)

Printed in the United States of America

*McFarland & Company, Inc., Publishers
Box 611, Jefferson, North Carolina 28640
www.mcfarlandpub.com*

Table of Contents

Acknowledgments

There is always a risk with acknowledgments of omitting people who should have been named and have not been for a variety of reasons. If this has occurred here, then please accept my genuine apologies. The Society for Psychical Research has been supportive of my research into paranormal matters for many years now and I have frequently used their excellent library which is admirably maintained by Karen Patel. The works of David Tame, Joscelyn Godwin and Scott Rogo were particularly helpful in the preparation of this book. My editor David Alff gave me advice throughout the project and Karen Patel deserves a special mention for all her endeavors in tracking down the illustrations and photographs.

Preface

The subject of this encyclopedia is music, but not in its commonplace understanding since it will be researched from a paranormal angle but encompassing the abnormal and the anomalous and furthermore what may have been viewed as such in bygone eras. Mainstream books about music tend to provide historical details of composers and their works, instruments, theoretical analysis, psychological and philosophical perceptions, etc., which will not be the main theme here. I shall not be listing the countless thousands of musical compositions that have been inspired by often literary supernatural themes—ghosts, vampires, demons, witches, etc. Instead, the work will consist of references exploring where music has been manifested, perceived, composed, performed or written about outside of its normal presence or realm. It will be as comprehensive as possible but with the limitation that new cases and information are always arising which may escape the author's eye or ear and some examples may be omitted when they are from single sources that may be spurious! The geographical areas researched will concentrate on the UK, the United States and Europe, but other countries will be included where appropriate. The amount of space available is often an issue, but readers should be able to expand their knowledge if desired by using the notes as well as the appendices and extensive bibliography. As to what constitutes music, as opposed to sound, I have included bells, but not doorbells and servants' bells. The human voice has been included when singing or chanting, but not when speaking, screaming, or whispering except when other musical phenomena were present. Extraneous sounds such as creaking doors, howling wind, and possible animal or bird sounds have generally been omitted. There are, of course, many problems to be encountered in using words which are subject to multiple interpretations—"supernatural," "paranormal," "anomalous," "occult," "esoteric" can all suggest different experiences according to how and where they are used and by whom. What is normal changes according to time and place as well as people's own preconceptions and prejudices. For the purpose of this work, I shall use such words sparingly and ask the reader to accept that the motivation for being included in the book is that the areas under discussion are generally thought to be outside of people's normal experiences.

Another problem is deciding whether or not to include examples from mythology or folklore. I have mainly avoided such material since, although such stories have relevance in an understanding of religions or archetypal concepts, they are not generally accepted as being indicative of actual events in twenty-first-century culture. Examples have been included when it was thought that some members of contemporary society might still trust the veracity of the communications, or it seemed wise to incorporate them because of their possible interest to the reader.

Gerard van der Leeuw (1890–1950), the Dutch historian and philosopher, wrote, "Music represents the great struggle of reaching the wholly other, which it can never express" (cited in Sharpe, p. 1912). Furthermore, "the effect of music on the emotions is so mysterious as to seem magical. There is no logical explanation why a particular combination of musical notes, whether in the form of a tune or of a simple chord, can affect the heart. Nothing in nature has perhaps so persistently resisted explanation" (Parker, p. 51). Since music is arguably the most intangible of the arts and since the paranormal, in all its manifestations, continues to intrigue people, the placing of these two subjects together seems long overdue. My own career in music as both a teacher and performer was infiltrated throughout my life with anomalies that intrigued me and my fellow musicians. Nobody seemed to be able to explain why some people appeared to be able to compose music or perform beyond their normal ability which, in some cases, they attributed to the deceased. Nobody seemed to be able to explain why music was sometimes heard when there was no obvious, or even un-obvious, source of the sound. Nobody seemed to explain why a number of people heard music when they were close to death which they remembered when they were resuscitated. Nobody seemed able to explain how intrusive operations could be conducted on people without anesthetic, but by using music to eliminate the pain. Nobody seemed able to explain why autistic people often possessed phenomenal musical abilities. The list of questions continues. I decided to undertake research into these and other related musical anomalies over a period of many years which culminated in two doctorates being awarded by Sheffield University and Bristol University, both in the UK. Previous pure music degrees were awarded by London University and Surrey University and a graduate diploma from the Royal Academy of Music, London. For more than thirty years I have been a member and then council member of the Society for Psychical Research (SPR) and more recently the archive liaison officer. During this time, I have been directly involved with the archiving of the Society's manuscripts collection stored at Cambridge University Library. The audio-visual archive is held at my own premises in Essex, England. The SPR archive contains a wealth of information about the alleged paranormal in all its many guises.

The printed sources for my extensive research are many and varied, but I have not found a single book that has brought the multiple strands together. The American parapsychologist D. Scott Rogo wrote two books providing information on what he called "transcendental music" (see Rogo, 1970; 1972) which provided considerable information about some people's hallucinatory experiences. Joscelyn Godwin has written extensively (see Godwin, 1987; 1989; 1992; 1995) about music and the occult and the English musical medium Rosemary Brown also wrote several books about her alleged musical dictations from composers such as Liszt, Beethoven and Chopin, but none of these fascinating works have explored the overall subject in such depth and clarity as I shall be attempting here. An earlier work of my own, *Music, Witchcraft and the Paranormal* (see Willin, 2005), outlined my original academic study of the material. I shall also be able to present my own case histories taken from interviewing a wide range of people and visiting sites where music has allegedly been heard from unknown sources. The end result will be a reference work that can be used to explore the academic study of music and the paranormal in a comprehensive alphabetical order as well as be of interest to the general public.

Parker, Derek, and Julia (1992). *The Power of Magic.* London: Mitchell Beazley.
Sharpe, Eric J. (1970). "Music." *Man, Myth and Magic.* Vol. 5. London: Purnell.

THE ENCYCLOPEDIA

Names and words in **bold** refer to other main entries

Abbas Hall

Abbas Hall is a country house situated in Great Cornard, Suffolk, in England, which dates from the thirteenth century and extended in the Elizabethan period. Paranormal events have been reported there including harpsichord music which is produced when nobody could be responsible for it. It has been heard by a Mrs. Palding who also felt "a strong supernatural presence in the house, but it is not evil" (*Two Worlds,* September 15, 1951).

Abell, Arthur M.

Arthur M. Abell (1868–1958) was an American music critic and author working for the *Musical Courier* and the *New York Times.* He is mainly remembered for his book of reminiscences, *Talks with Great Composers,* which included **Brahms**, Bruch, **Richard Strauss, Puccini** and Grieg (Abell, 1955). He described from his own first-hand accounts how the composers believed they were influenced by external powers to achieve their masterpieces which, in some cases, were inspired by "God Almighty." **Brahms** revealed that "I immediately feel vibrations that thrill my whole being.... These are the Spirit illuminating the soul-power within, and in this exalted state, I see clearly what is obscure in my ordinary moods; then I feel capable of drawing **inspiration** from above, as **Beethoven** did" (Abell, 1955, p. 5). Abell also drew attention to the composers' discussions about being in a "semi-trance" condition when they were composing. He admitted that his own grandmother had witnessed the medium **Daniel Dunglas Home** levitating and making a **piano** play without anyone at the keys. Brahms believed that some of the powers displayed by **Blind Tom** were comparable to Home's exploits and further dialogues between the men concerned Tartini's most famous **violin** solo *The Devil's Trill Sonata.* Abell's recollections were not solely devoted to Brahms and his

5

conversations with Puccini prompted "the music of this opera [*Madama Butterfly*] was dictated to me by God; I was merely instrumental in putting it on paper and communicating it to the public" (Abell, p. 117) and Strauss told him that his gift was a "mandate from God" (Abell, p. 100). Bruch mentioned the importance of **dreams** to him, and **Wagner** was quoted as believing himself to be lying at the bottom of the Rhine when from his entranced imagination the opening music of *Das Rheingold* came to him. Abell provided a wealth of evidence from composers that their works originated from sources beyond themselves, namely paranormal.

Abell, Arthur M. (1955). *Talks with Great Composers*. London: Psychic Book Club.

Further information about Abell can be found in the New York Public Library Archives and Manuscripts. Arthur M. Abell papers. 1829–1976 inclusive [bulk 1905–1958].

Aberdovey

The "Bells of Aberdovey" appear in a number of different legends which have been repeated in poems, songs and written accounts. The tales concern land that was engulfed by the sea in the Cardigan Bay off the coast of Wales, which occurred when the protective sluice gates were not closed by the watchman Seithenin. Usually, no date is supplied for this event. Many of the local inhabitants and the buildings were swept away in the deluge which was commemorated in the poems *Boddi Maes Gwyddno* ("The Drowning of the Land of Gwyddno") and *Clychau Cantre'r Gwaelod* ("The Bells of Cantre'r Gwaelod") by the bard John James Williams (1869–1954). There is a well-known song *The Bells of Aberdovey* which is believed to have been written by the English composer Charles Dibdin (1745–1814) for his comic opera *Liberty Hall* in 1785. There are many instances of **sunken bells** to be found throughout literature describing sea and lake-based musical phenomena (Willin, 1999). Whatever the origin of this story it is still believed that occasionally the bells of a submerged church can be heard chiming in the distance (Underwood, pp. 12–13).

Underwood, Peter (1971). *Gazetteer of British Ghosts*. London: Souvenir Press.

Abergeldie Castle

Abergeldie Castle in Aberdeenshire, Scotland, stands on the banks of the River Dee and was built during the sixteenth century. It is only a few miles away from the famous royal residence Balmoral Castle. A serving girl there named Kittie Rankie was reputedly burned for **witchcraft** on a nearby hill overlooking the castle having previously been imprisoned in the castle cellars. In these same cellars unaccounted screams and the ringing of bells have been heard, notably when misfortune was about to happen to a member of the Gordon clan who were the perpetrators of her execution (Spencer, p. 135).

Spencer, John, and Anne (1992). *The Encyclopaedia of Ghosts and Spirits*. London: Book Club Associates.

Aboriginal Death Song

There is an example in the literature of an aboriginal death song which was, and possibly still is, used as a method of execution in aboriginal tribes in Australia. The case was printed in *The Times* in Darwin, Australia, throughout April 1956. Nineteen-year-old Lya Wulumu was "sung to death" by Aborigine women of the Gubabmwingu tribe after committing an offense against tribal laws. He could not swallow or breathe and was flown to Darwin Hospital and placed in an iron lung. Doctors could not find anything wrong with him despite tests for poison and X-rays, but Wulumu insisted that he wanted to live and after further treatment he made a recovery. It was the first recorded example of an Aborigine surviving the "death song," since this and the better-known bone-pointing ceremony are usually fatal. It has not been possible to find audio examples of the actual song used.

Another case was reported in *The Sunday Express* (November 16, 1975) when "an eerie wailing chant went on for three days" in an attempt to kill the Queensland premier Jon Bjelke Petersen—a counter curse was put in place by a witch referred to as "Circe" which offset the original death song.

"Fight to save young aborigine's life." 1956. *The Times*, Darwin; Sydney. April 13–22. Cited in Coote Lake, E.F. (1956). "Folk Life and Traditions." *Folklore* 67, no. 3 (September): 175–178.

Acoustics

It is beyond the remit of this volume to present an in-depth study of the aspects of acoustics that could be applied to all of the phenomena contained herein. These would encompass the neuroscience of music and the brain's cognitive processes in interpreting what is heard as well as discussions as to how the resonance of places can affect the resulting sounds be they musical or otherwise. Infrasound has been investigated by Steven Parsons (Parsons, pp. 83–105) and Vic Tandy (2000; 2002) as a possible contributor to anomalous experiences that were previously described as paranormal, but these studies are more involved with sound than music. "Measurements of resonant frequencies have been carried out at Newgrange, for example, and have shown that resonance occurs between 95 and 112 Hertz, peaking at around 110 Hz (the male baritone range). This suggests that such places may have been used for ritual **chant**ing ... the bottle-shaped passage and chamber design of prehistoric graves produces a very low frequency resonance indeed (roughly 4 Hz). This resonance could have been set up by drumming and would doubtless have had a significant effect upon those experiencing it" (Ennis, p. 17). For the reader who wishes to pursue acoustics from a purely musical stance which combines various fields such as physics, psychophysics and theory one should study the German pioneer Hermann von Helmholz (1821–1894) who introduced its study in his ground-breaking book *On the Sensations of Tone as a Physiological Basis for the Theory of Music* (Helmholz, 1895). For more recent studies *Music and the Brain* edited by Macdonald Critchley and R.A. Henson (1977) provide invaluable material and the work of John Reid and David Elkington has explored how amplified sound can produce images that might correspond to the environment where the specific instruments would be played (cited in Amerland, pp. 28–29). *Stone Age Soundtracks* by Paul Devereux (2001) explores the subject of acoustic archaeology in considerable depth.

Amerland, David (2002). "The Sound of Magic." *Prediction* (February): 28–29.
Ennis, Giles (2002). "Sacred Breath, Sacred Chant." *Pagan Dawn* 142 (Spring).
Parsons, Stephen, and Callum Cooper (2015). *Paracoustics. Sound & the Paranormal*. Hove: White Crow.
Tandy, Vic (2000). "Something in the Cellar." *Journal of the Society for Psychical Research* 64, 129–140.
Tandy, Vic (2002). "A Litmus Test for Infrasound." *Journal of the Society for Psychical Research* 66, 167–174.

Agrippa, Henry Cornelius

Henry Cornelius Agrippa (1486–1535) was a German scholar and writer on occult matters. His three books of occult philosophy (*De Occulta Philosophia libri III*) encompass a study of esoteric philosophy and **magic** which includes the importance of music in accessing hidden knowledge. The full three volumes first appeared in Cologne in 1533. Chapter twenty-four, in *Book II*, discusses the power of music harmony drawing on the works of Pliny, Plato, Iamblichus and others. The outbreak of **tarantism** is mentioned and an intriguing stone in Megaris, a state in ancient Greece, which "makes a sound like a **harp** every time the string of a harp is struck;

so great is the power of music, that it appeaseth the mind, raiseth the spirit, stirreth up soldiers to fight, and refresheth the weary, calls back them that are desparate, refreshes travelers" (Agrippa, p. 333).

Agrippa, Henry Cornelius (1998). *Three Books of Occult Philosophy*. Ed. Donald Tyson. Trans. James Freake. St. Paul: Llewellyn.

Alcatraz Prison

The notorious Alcatraz Prison seems an unlikely setting for paranormal activity and especially that of a musical nature, but there are documented stories attached to it and notably concerning the convicted gangster Al Capone (1899–1947) who was imprisoned there from 1934 to 1939. He took up playing the banjo and the mandola (a large mandolin) and joined in a prison band called "The Rock Islanders." He wrote to his son "'boasting that he could play over 500 songs.' Capone even wrote a love song, 'Madonna Mia,' that was published posthumously in 2009" (www.smithsonianmag. com). He used to practice in the shower room and it has been reported by a park ranger "in recent years" that he heard banjo music coming from there and that "other visitors and employees have reported hearing the sound of a banjo coming from the prison walls" (www.liveabout.com).

"This Letter Tells What Al Capone Was Up to in Alcatraz." www.smithsonianmag.com.
"The Ghost of Al Capone?" www.liveabout.com.

Al-Farabi

Al-Farabi (aka Alfarabi/Abou-Nasr-Mohammed-Ibn-Tarkaw) was born in Asia Minor and was prominent in the first half on the tenth century. Though of Turkish ancestry he spent most of his life in Baghdad where he wrote a book about the philosophy of music titled *Kitab al-Musiqa*. The treatise was controversial at the time since it opposed the Pythagorean theory of the **music of the spheres** and promoted the concept of sound being connected with "atmospheric vibrations" (Spence, p. 14). Another thesis "discussed the therapeutic effects of music on the soul" (Haque, p. 363). On a visit to the Sultan of Syria it was alleged that his playing of the lute was so astonishing that "the gravest sages could not but **dance** to it ... and at last with a gentle lullaby he put the court to sleep" (Spence, p. 14).

Haque, Amber (2004). "Psychology from Islamic Perspective: Contributions of Early Muslim Scholars and Challenges to Contemporary Muslim Psychologists." *Journal of Religion and Health* 43, no. 4: 357–377.
Spence, Lewis (1994). *The Encyclopedia of the Occult*. London: Bracken Books.

Aliens and UFOs

When UFOs have been heard by people they have usually been described as "humming" or making a "sonic boom" rather than actual music being emitted (Randles and Warrington, 1980). The concept of music and alien contact became prominent after the American science-fiction film *Close Encounters of the Third Kind* (1977) used the five-note theme that was used so effectively by the composer John Williams. However, ever since the surge of interest in aliens and UFOs in the nineteen fifties and sixties, rock musicians in particular have taken an interest in the subject. The record producer Joe Meek (1929–1967) and creator of the popular hit song "Telstar" was obsessed with the occult and the idea that extra-terrestrials and dead musicians might make contact with him. The idea of making contact with aliens with music was pursued in 2001 with "The First Theremin Concert for Extraterrestrials" organized by the Russian scientist Alexander L. Zaitsev (www.thereminworld.com/Article/13825/2001-tams-first-theremin-concert-to-space-aliens-featured-ly). The theremin is an instrument operated without touch but using electronic high-frequency signals. It is often used in TV programs and films for special effects (Honigman, pp. 30–32).

Many famous names have freely admitted to both personal experiences as well as a general belief in the existence of UFOs and alien contact, which include Elvis Presley, Jimi Hendrix, David Bowie and Kate Bush. The Canadian band Klaatu formed in 1973 named themselves after an alien who visits Earth in the film *The Day the Earth Stood Still*. One of their hits was "Calling Occupants of Interplanetary Craft" (1976). A UFO landing platform was built on a site at the first Glastonbury Music Festival in 1970 and one of Mick Jagger's homes "housed a UFO detector" (Roberts, p. 36). A UFO experience led to a belief in greater creativity as was the case with Ian McCulloch from the band Echo and the Bunnymen (cited in Roberts, p. 36). The investigator Jenny Randles believes that the increase in using song lyrics about these experiences might be caused by a psychic manifestation and the ex-rock musician Julian Cope drew comparisons between UFO landings with crop and stone circles (Roberts, p. 38). In a far more extreme context the Birmingham, Alabama-born jazz composer Hermann Blount (1914–1993) changed his name to Sun Ra (the ancient Egyptian sun god) and claimed he was from Saturn and had been directed to speak to the world through his music after what appeared to be an alien abduction (Simmons, pp. 34–35).

Honigman, Andrew (2000). "Sound of Mystery: The Theremin." *Fate* (January): 30–32.
Randles, Jenny, and Peter Warrington (1980). *UFOs. A British Viewpoint*. London: BCA.
Roberts, Andy (1996). "Rocking the Alien." *Fortean Times* 88 (July).
Simmons, Ian (2009). "Mothership Connections." *Fortean Times* 244 (January): 30–35.

All Saints Church

In May 1950 several residents of the village of Cressing in Essex, England, testified that they had heard "weird symphonies on the organ in the dark behind the locked doors of the thirteenth-century church" (Payne, p. 15). Members of the local fire brigade held several all-night vigils, but they witnessed nothing paranormal. However, the locals continued to believe that music was being played there from an unknown source.

Payne, Jessie K. (1995). *A Ghost Hunter's Guide to Essex.* Norfolk: Ian Henry.

Altered States of Consciousness (ASCs)

The literature researching and discussing altered states of consciousness is vast and it will only be possible to touch on the subject here. (The bibliography should be consulted for further study.) The expression refers to the state of mind that is achieved when internal or external measures are put into effect with subsequent changes in perception and thought processes. The alternate words "trance" and "**possession**" are sometimes used, but the latter implies being taken over in either a religious or demonic manner which is narrower than is generally suggested. Composers have frequently spoken about writing their music in such a state and performers can similarly lose themselves when playing or singing (Willin, 2005). Gilbert Rouget "outlines the fundamental distinctions between trance and ecstasy, **shaman**ism and spirit possession, and communal and emotional trance" (Rouget, back cover) in his authoritative book *Music and Trance*, whereas June Boyce-Tillman draws attention to the "alliance of **drugs**, music and **dance** to produce this [transcendence]" within Western society which she believes leads to exploitation (Ralls-MacLeod and Harvey, p. 147).

Experiments have been conducted within the academic study of **para-psychology** to research whether extra sensory perception (ESP) can be enhanced by the use of ASCs in what are called "**ganzfeld**" experiments. One such large-scale study was undertaken by the author (Willin, 1996a, 1996b) using music as the target for attempted telepathy to be manifested between different pairs of people. Although the results were classified statistically as only displaying a chance outcome, during the course of the one hundred and twenty trials several pairs of people scored considerably above chance in their results which indicated that a degree of musically prompted telepathy might have occurred during their ASCs.

Music is used in some rituals to achieve ASCs in order to allow contact with whichever entity is required and appropriate to the **religion** or belief system followed. The Arab nations have associated music and trance very closely and the ecstatic states (*wajd*) achieved by **Sufi** dancers would not seem to be possible without the hypnotic music that is performed to accompany them. It is said that music "has mystical power to draw out the deepest emotions, but also, when coordinated with symbolic words and rhythmical movements, has power over man's will" (Trimingham, p. 195). It is also an integral part of **shamans**' rituals and in **witchcraft** ceremonies "**chant**s and tunes that have deep meaning and power in them ... can transport us into altered states of consciousness" (Hill, cited in Magliocco and Tannen, p. 176). ASCs have frequently been mentioned in private correspondence with the author as being enhanced by the use of music in witchcraft gatherings to attain communication with the deities chosen. The opening of Philip Glass' film music *Koyaanisqatsi* was felt to be conducive to Samhain rituals and Carolyn Hillyer's Winter Blessing from the CD *Riven Inside* was also a popular choice. The very subjective experience of music means that every individual will respond differently to different pieces or types of music. A transcendent ASC might be achieved by one person listening to, for instance, Samuel Barber's *Adagio for Strings* whereas someone else may find it either boring or conjuring up images from the violent war movie *Platoon* that included the same music. Therefore, it cannot be stated that any particular piece of music is guaranteed to produce an ASC whoever hears it.

Hill, Anne, cited in Sabina Magliocco and Holly Tannen (1998). "The Real Old-Time Religion: Towards an Aesthetics of Neo-Pagan Song." *The Journal of the Folklore Studies Association of Canada* 20, no. 1: 175–201.

Ralls-MacLeod, Karen, and Graham Harvey, eds. (2000). *Indigenous Religious Musics*. Aldershot: Ashgate.

Rouget, Gilbert (1985). *Music and Trance: A Theory of the Relations between Music and Possession*. Chicago: University of Chicago Press.

Trimingham, J. Spencer (1973). *The Sufi Orders in Islam*. London: Oxford University Press.

Amdusias

Although strictly speaking the demon Amdusias should not be included in this work since it is unlikely that the music he produces is likely to be heard in this life, the unusual nature of the phenomena perhaps deserves a brief mention. From a list of seventy-two demons listed in the *Ars Goetia*, which is part of the anonymous grimoire *The Lesser Key of Solomon*, Duke Amdusias is claimed to be the demon in hell producing harsh discordant music to torture the souls therein. He is depicted as human but with the head of a unicorn and claws instead of hands and feet. A **trumpet** is usually shown close by with which he presumably makes the terrible din associated with him.

Further details about Amdusias can be discovered in the *Pseudomonarchia Daemonum* (Johann Weyer, 1583) and the *Dictionnaire Infernal* (Colin de Plancy, 1863).

Amherst Mystery

In 1878 an eighteen-year-old girl called Esther Cox was living with her sister's family in an overcrowded house in Amherst, Nova Scotia, Canada, when she seemingly attracted poltergeist activity. It was manifested through bodily swellings, flying objects such as pillows, bedclothes, knives, rappings and other auditory phenomena. The sound of **trumpet** music was also heard sounding throughout the house and finally a silver trumpet was discovered which did not belong to any of the family: "A trumpet was heard in the house all day. The sound came from within the atmosphere—I can give no other description of its effect on our sense of hearing. It was evidently a small trumpet, judging by its tone, and was at times very close to the ears of all" (Hubbell, p. 123). The following year a stage magician Walter Hubbell stayed with the family and believed the occurrences to be real, but after the words "Esther, you are mine to kill" appeared on the wall above her head she was sent away to stay with friends. After incidences of theft and finally arson, for which she was convicted, the occurrences stopped. The psychical researcher Hereward Carrington later interviewed Esther and spoke to people who had witnessed the events that had happened around her and in 1919 Walter Franklin Prince, the American founder of the Boston Society for Psychical Research, wrote an account in the *Proceedings of the American Society for Psychical Research* which concluded that "there was no question of fraud" (cited in Wilson, p. 58). Hubbell subsequently published a book about the whole affair which went through many editions.

Hubbell, Walter (1916). *The Great Amherst Mystery: A True Narrative of the Supernatural.* New York: Brentano's.
Wilson, Colin (1981). *Poltergeist! A Study in Destructive Haunting.* London: New English Library.

Amityville

The Amityville Horror (1977) became a best-selling book after George Lutz claimed that his house was haunted by numerous terrifying paranormal phenomena including demons, ghosts and poltergeist activity, and numerous sensational horror films were subsequently made of the story. It was claimed that the events described had actually happened, but skeptics generally believed it was a giant **hoax**. The house itself had been the scene in 1974 of the mass murder by Ronald DeFeo of his family. DeFeo's lawyer claimed that "the whole 'horror' was cooked up around the Lutzes' kitchen table over several bottles of wine. He asserted that after approaching them with the idea, the Lutzes went on their own, and he sued for a share of the book and movie profits" (Guiley, p. 8). The Lutzes claimed that martial music was heard in the house in the middle of the night which stopped when it was investigated. "While outside the house, Lutz heard a band playing within, accompanied by the stamping of feet.... The noises stopped when he entered" (Paul, p. 168).

Guiley, Rosemary Ellen (1994). *The Guinness Encyclopedia of Ghosts and Spirits*. Enfield: Guinness.
Paul, Philip (1985). *Some Unseen Power: Diary of a Ghost-Hunter*. London: Robert Hale.

Amusia

"'Amusia' is a collective term denoting the loss or impairment of musical capacity that may occur as a consequence of brain disease. The impairment may take a variety of forms" (Benton, p. 378). The disabilities might include the loss of ability to sing, read or write musical notation, play an instrument or recognize familiar tunes and it has been argued that temporal lobe malfunctions might be responsible for these conditions (Benton, pp. 392–394). However, auditory **hallucinations** may also occur during such seizures which could be a possible source of music being heard when none is actually present. **Wilder Penfield** and Theodore Rasmussen wrote extensively about such occurrences when parts of the brain were electronically stimulated in *The Cerebral Cortex of Man* (1952) and the term "musicogenic **epilepsy**" has been coined to describe auditory hallucinations. Oliver Sacks devotes a complete chapter to the subject in his book *Musicophilia* (2007) as does Steven Mithen in *The Singing Neanderthals* (2005).

Benton, Arthur L., in Macdonald Critchley and R.A. Henson, eds. (1977). "The Amusias." *Music and the Brain*. London: Heinemann.

Angel

The Angel in Lymington, Hampshire, England, is an old coaching inn that was originally called the George Inn. It has a long tradition of being haunted but a written statement by a past manager Mr. M.E. McKinley verified an incident witnessed by his sister-in-law in 1966 when she was kept awake by loud **piano** playing when staying there when there was not a piano in the building (Playfair, pp. 81–82). Correspondence with the manager in 1997 by the author revealed that "two geriatric spinsters claim to have bore witness to a piano playing itself a merry little ditty in the style of Noel Coward" (private correspondence).

Playfair, Guy Lyon (1985a). *The Haunted Pub Guide*. London: Harrap.

Angels

Angelic music has been written about in numerous sources during a period of hundreds of years. An early treatise describing the church modes in the ninth century was the *Musica Disciplina* written by Aurelian of Réôme. After expounding on theoretical matters derived from **Boethius** and others, Aurelian mentioned instances of hearing angelic music: "there was a certain monk of the monastery of St Victor.... Holding vigil by night before the porch of the church, he heard a choir of angels singing the responsory ... one night coming out of his own house adjoining the wall of St Alban's basilica, he heard a harmonious choir of angels singing the word 'Alleluia' with Psalm 148 up to the end of the Psalter" (cited in Godwin, p. 96). Angelic choirs from antiquity are also to be found in Isaac Ben Solomon Ibn Sahula's Hebrew texts *Mishna* Yoma, where "nine angels who sing by night sing down on all those who can sing" (cited in Godwin, p. 61). The German mystic Heinrich Seuse, also known as **Henry Suso** (c. 1295–1366), wrote about hearing music from an angelic source outside of himself: "it seemed to him in a vision that he heard angelic strains and sweet heavenly melody; and this filled him with such gladness that he forgot all his sufferings" (cited in Godwin, p. 112).

A degree of caution is necessary in referring to such ancient manuscripts, since faulty translation may have suggested external origins for the music when it was not intended, and the authors may have externalized what was part of their deeply held beliefs. Numerous saints including St. Chad, St. Joseph of Copertino, St. Veronica and St. Guthlac either heard celestial music or it was heard by others at their **deathbeds** (Rogo, pp. 86–88). In more recent times, although perhaps not meaning to be taken literally, Thomas Carlyle wrote: "Music is well said to be the speech of angels; in fact, nothing among the utterances allowed to man is felt to be so divine. It brings us near to the infinite" (cited in Hopler). In electronic voice phenomena (EVP) experiments the Italian researcher **Marcello Bacci** believes that he has recorded angelic voices on his equipment (private correspondence). It is perhaps not surprising with the number of references to angels singing or playing musical instruments in art and song, that people will believe that they have genuinely heard these messengers communicating with them through music. In the late twentieth-century individuals were still claiming to hear "angelic choirs" as the author can vouch from the correspondence he has received from them.

Godwin, Joscelyn (1987b). *Music, Mysticism and Magic*. London: Arkana.
Hopler, Whitney (2018). "How Angels Communicate Through Music." Learn Religions, Feb. 11. learnreligions.com/how-angels-communicate-through-music-123829.
Rogo, D. Scott (1970). *NAD*. New York: University Books.

Contemporary stained glass illustration of angels singing and playing musical instruments (Zvonimir Atletic/Shutterstock.com).

Animals

Mythology has its fair share of stories perpetrating the musical powers of animals and their connections with human beings and one such example is the story of Arion and the dolphin. The animal kingdom has influenced humans throughout the history of music through composers' attempts to copy their sounds and notably with bird song. Charles Darwin stated in his *The Descent of Man*: "Thus musical tones became firmly associated with some of the strongest passions an animal is capable of feeling" (cited in Diserens p. 2). In 1967 whale song began to be thought of in terms other than as a messaging language and the "songs" of the humpback whales in particular, through their far-ranging melodies, have been an **inspiration** to such composers as George Crumb and Paul Winter. It has also been reported that whales have changed their song patterns "implying a cultural transmission and evolution" (*Fortean Times*, 2001a, p. 8). In 1983 the French composer François-Bernard Mâche "began to explore the idea that animals might also make music for reasons more than practical communication. In his book *Music, Myth and Nature* he formalized the concept by coining the word 'zoomusicology'" (Fischer & Cory, p. 24). This concept opens up a completely new way of listening to the sounds that animals make and exploring them in musical terms in much the same way that one might analyze human music through melody, harmony, timbre, rhythm etc. Further attention was drawn to this notion by Leonard Williams (the father of the famous classical guitarist John Williams) in his exploration of the origins of primitive music—*The Dancing Chimpanzee* (1980). Fiona Middleton became fascinated by the effect her **violin** playing seemed to have on the seals that inhabited the waters around her island dwelling of Islay in Scotland: "When one seal pup was in my house I once played her a jig instead of the slow music I usually play. It was really funny to see her whole body speed up and shake to the music" (Cook, p. 49). However, a warning must be sounded of succumbing to anthropomorphism especially when animals seem to respond to human music when, in fact, they may be reacting to different stimuli possibly through their other heightened senses. An example of this may well be the so-called **snake charmers**' music not affecting the snake but rather his rhythmic swaying to entice it out of the basket and the production of a treat when a pet animal hears a certain piece of music may not involve the animal's appreciation of the piece being heard. Obviously, the more studies that are conducted the closer one will be to understanding these impressions. As long ago as 1879 the Scottish physician and botanist William Lauder Lindsay (1829–1880) published a breakdown of how music affected twelve hundred and fifty animal species:

- As a gentle calmative in states of irritation or excitement.
- As a mild excitant in conditions of depression.
- As a dangerous irritant in certain morbid states of mind or body, including the part it plays in the development of insanity.
- As a stimulant to work of an uncongenial kind—to endurance, perseverance, strength, and energy in ordinary domestic life, of courage, and ardor in the war-horse or elephant.
- As a means of refinement in animals whom man thinks it worth his while to subject methodically to its power... [Lindsay, p. 308].

The Hungarian astrologer Szendrey Jutka has spoken publically about her cat, Nina, who evidently loves music and moves in time to the rhythm when she plays the **piano**. She further claimed that Nina "moved her ears rhythmically and purred during the sailor's song and **dance** from *The Flying Dutchman*" (Iosif, p. 35). Perhaps the most bizarre story concerns the research claiming that "an elephant could distinguish twelve musical tones, remember simple melodies, even when played on different instruments, and recall melodies eighteen months later" and this was in addition to a different report relating to a band of elephants in Thailand that have been given music training and have produced an album of their music (cited in *Fortean Times*, 2001b, p. 12). Work being highlighted in *Animal Music Sound and Song in the Natural World* (Fischer & Cory) is bringing this research into the twenty-first century and it is claimed that further discoveries are expected.

Cook, Fidelma (1995). "Sealed with a kiss." *Mail on Sunday*, October 22.
Diserens, Charles M. (1926). *The Influence of Music on Behavior*. Princeton: Princeton University Press.
Fischer, T., and L. Cory (2015). *Animal Music*. London: Strange Attractor Press.
Fortean Times (2001a). "Whales Change Tune…." 144 (March): 8.
Fortean Times (2001b). "Pachyderm Boogie." 148 (July): 12.
Iosif, Boczor (2000). "The Cat with an Ear for Music." *Fate* (May): 35.
Lindsay, William Lauder (1879). *Mind in the Lower Animals in Health and Disease*. 2 vols. London: C. Kegan Paul.
Williams, Leonard (1980). *The Dancing Chimpanzee*. London: Allison & Busby.

Anstey

The village of Anstey in Hertfordshire, England was the scene of what was probably a legend rather than a factual event that occurred "at least two centuries ago" (Blatchley) when "George," a blind **fiddle** player, left the local inn The Chequers having consumed too much alcohol and decided to explore a local cave and tunnel commonly referred to as the *Devil's Hole*. He entered the cave with his dog and continued to play his fiddle which could be heard by the attendant customers from the inn. After a while "the unearthly sound of an unknown fiddle tune rose from beneath" (Blatchley) and after a discordant sound there was silence. George's dog returned from the tunnel in a disheveled state, but George was never seen again.

In reality a fiddler by the name of "George" was alive in the parish at the time in question, but he was recorded as having been buried in the local churchyard. The Chequers has been re-named The Blind Fiddler and songs by Fairport Convention and Litha have celebrated the alleged event.

Blatchley, N. (n.d.) hertsmemories.org.uk/content/herts-history/towns-and-villages/anstey/blind-fiddler-anstey.

Arriola, Pepito

José "Pepito" Rodríguez Carballeira (aka Pepito Arriola) (1896–1954) was a Spanish child prodigy pianist and allegedly a fine **violin**ist. There are inevitably conflicting details about child **prodigies** and Arriola was no different in this respect. One source claims that he played for Arthur Nikisch, the conductor of the *Gewandhaus* Orchestra in Leipzig, when he was four, having already played for his mother since he was two and a half years old (kevinwoolsey.com/article-library/the-story-of-a-wonder-child). The same source claimed that he played at the Royal Albert Hall and for the kaiser of Germany. The imminent psychologist Charles Richet wrote in the *Revue Métaphysique* that "in 1900, in Paris, during the exhibition, I presented to a meeting of psychologists a child of three years and three months, Pepito Arriola, a Spaniard, who played the **piano** amazingly, composed marches, waltzes, habaneras, minuets, and played twenty or more difficult pieces from memory. In the meeting hall a hundred people heard him and applauded. Later I had this tiny little pianist come to my house, and there the precocious prodigy performed twice during the day, once in the evening in front of various people when he played the piano, my own piano, in the absence of his mother" (cited in Barrington, p. 9). It was claimed by Dr. John H. Gower, a correspondent to the Society for Psychical Research, that Arriola could also produce "**automatic writing**" and that "his piano playing is so remarkable that a psychic explanation of some kind seems to me to be about necessary" (Gower, p. 60).

Barrington, Mary Rose (2005). "Archive No. 56: A Flawed Critique—Herr Albert Moll and the Clairvoyance of Kahn by Prof. Charles Richet from the *Revue Metaphysique*, 1926/3, pp. 215–218." *The Paranormal Review of the Society for Psychical Research* 33 (January): 7–9.
Gower, John H. (1913). *The Journal of the Society for Psychical Research* 16 (April).

Aubert, Georges

There are surprisingly few details known about the musical medium Georges Aubert apart from what is presented in his brief autobiography *La médiumnité spirite de Georges Aubert exposée par lui-même avec les expériences faites sur lui par les savants de l'Institut Général Psychologie de février à mai 1905*. It describes the three stages he went through as a medium, namely his initial experiences; his physical manifestations; and his **musical medium**ship and experiments made in Paris at the Institute of General Psychology. He informs the reader that he was born into a musical family, but that he nevertheless obtained a science degree in 1896. He was, however, influenced by friends who were very musical, and he received basic music theory and **piano** lessons. After a period of table-turning, rapping and poltergeist activity he believed himself to be taken over by a spirit which impelled him to play in the style of numerous composers including **Bach, Beethoven, Berlioz, Chopin, Liszt, Mozart**, Schubert and **Schumann.**

Altogether his musical mediumship lasted from 1891 to 1904 after which time he was investigated at the Institute for several months. During this time, he underwent grueling tests such as being asked to play a Mozart-like sonata while blindfolded and with two phonographs playing the march from Verdi's *Aida* in one ear and *Marche Indienne* by Sellenick in the other. On another occasion he had to read out loud a philosophical work while continuing to play, and the researcher Yourievitch thrust a needle into his left hand in the "midst of a brilliant piece" (*Annals of Psychic Science*, p. 131) which had no adverse effects on his playing. Aubert believed that this proved that he was unconscious of what he was doing and that an external intelligence had taken him over.

The Annals of Psychic Science. 1906. Vol. 3: 131.

Autism

People who are diagnosed with autism when it is particularly manifested in musical ways are often referred to as "musical **savants**." An early example was the American slave **Blind Tom** who exhibited phenomenal capabilities in the 1860s and since then many further individuals have come to light who have displayed what some people believe to be "supernatural abilities" (private conversation). There are books by Darold Treffert (1989), Leon K. Miller (1989) and an extensive study by Adam Ockelford about a blind musical savant Derek Paravicini (2007). The English savant Stephen Wiltshire, who was well known for his visual capabilities, also developed extreme musical gifts at the age of sixteen (Sacks, p. 154). One is reminded of the power of music to influence such people by Anthony Storr's quotation from Sacks' book *The Man Who Mistook His Wife for a Hat*, when a musician "could only dress himself, eat a meal, or have a bath, if he did so whilst singing" (Storr, p. 37). The music of the Welsh rock band Catatonia was said to have cured an autistic boy Christopher Howells from his inability to speak when he "burst into song" after listening to their hit single "Mulder and Scully" (*Fortean Times*, p. 11). Maintaining a focus on the musical aspects of autism and not its medical analysis, it would seem that musical savants have resources which are considerably beyond ordinary people. Their ability to copy other people's performances and improvise in a multitude of styles and genres can be truly awe-inspiring based on the author's own encounters of them and many other experts.

Fortean Times (2001). "Music Breaks the Silence." 148 (July): 11.
Miller, Leon K. (1989). *Musical Savants: Exceptional Skill in the Mentally Retarded*. Mahwah: Lawrence Erlbaum.
Ockelford, Adam (2007). *In the Key of Genius: The Extraordinary Life of Derek Paravicini*. London: Hutchinson.
Sacks, Oliver (2007). *Musicophilia*. London: Picador.
Storr, Anthony (1992). *Music and the Mind*. London: HarperCollins.
Treffert, Darold A. (1989). *Extraordinary People*. London: Bantam Press.

Automatic Writing

The history of psychical research contains hundreds of examples of people who have displayed the ability to write or paint beyond their normal ability and without seemingly using conscious effort. Their lives can appear to be normal in every other way other than they usually believe that the source of their **inspiration** is through dictation by a dead composer, author, artist or poet. A fine example from the literary world would be the American Pearl Curran (1883–1937). She possessed some musical talents but had an otherwise average education and intelligence level. Yet, after some dabbling with a Ouija board she seemed to be taken over by an English woman called Patience Worth from the period between 1649 and 1694, who may have lived in the county of Dorset. In the identity of Patience Worth, Curran quickly wrote a large number of novels in an antiquated language that revealed an in-depth knowledge of subjects that she had never studied herself. The psychologist Luiz Antonio Gasparetto (1949–2018) produced art works from departed artists and painters in a similarly dramatic way using just his fingers and both hands at once but insisting that classical music was played while he worked. Hélène Smith, whose real name was Catherine-Elise Müller (1861–1929), was a famous Swiss medium who claimed to communicate with **Martian**s through automatic writing!

Interesting though these and many others are the focus must return to the musical automatists, limiting this to those who physically wrote their music down rather than solely performing it as was the case, for instance, with **Georges Aubert, Florizel von Reuter, Jesse Shepard** and **Leo May**. Once again there are a large number of **mediums** to explore. The most famous example was the English musical medium **Rosemary Brown** (1916–2001) who produced hundreds of compositions. In addition to researching Brown the author conducted a number of case studies of mediums claiming automatic musical abilities, but pseudonyms will be used when needed to protect their identities. One such English lady believed herself to be controlled by the Russian composer Pyotr Ilyich **Tchaikovsky**. Unfortunately, the music was not provided with harmony, and neither was the rhythm, but just a string of notes on a keyboard printout. A leading expert on Tchaikovsky's music found it to be "appalling" (private correspondence). Another correspondent believed that she was being inspired by Ivor Novello as well as **Edward Elgar**. The **piano** score of Novello's music that she produced was pleasant to play, but more in line with a pastiche of his musical idioms which she, as a competent musician herself, could have written without Novello's input. Initially of more interest was the promise of a full score of a symphony by Arnold Bax which was being dictated from the spirit world to a chartered accountant ("M") living in the south of England. The author visited M. and was leant a copy of the full score to show to a Bax expert, Anthony Payne. He found the score most interesting and confirmed, to his knowledge, that M. had not plagiarized any of Bax's known works. Payne believed that the symphony had, at the very least, been written by someone who was well versed in the music of Bax (private correspondence). However, it is important to stress that M. had received training in composition at Trinity College of Music, **London** and admitted that he had always been obsessed with Bax's music. He probably knew that Bax had a predilection for mystical scenarios, and it is therefore difficult to verify whether he had been dictated to by the spirit of the dead composer or whether his own subconscious mind was at work. Of greater veracity perhaps was a **Beethoven** piano sonata that was allegedly dictated to T., who lived on the Isle of Wight, since he only had a very basic musical knowledge. He did not subscribe to **Spiritualism** particularly but wondered where the source of his inspiration might be coming from if it wasn't from Beethoven himself. T. was unable to play the sonata himself, since it was too difficult, and the services of a professional pianist were employed. Both he and the other experts that the music was sent to agreed that although it was pleasant to listen to and probably beyond the composing capability of T., nevertheless, it did not show the development of form or harmonic ideas that Beethoven's music possesses. It would seem from past and present sources, such as various editions of the *Grove Dictionary of Music*, that **musical mediums**, despite the claims of the Spiritualist establishment, have not yet achieved a high enough standard of composition to be acclaimed by professional musicians without extenuating circumstances being predominant (Willin, 2005).

Willin, Melvyn J. (2005). *Music, Witchcraft and the Paranormal*. Ely: Melrose Press.

Ava Nursing Home

Ava Nursing Home can be found in Leicester, England. In 1978 a nursing auxiliary Ann Pratt was working a night duty shift when she heard **piano** music on the premises which surprised her since there was no piano there and nobody had a radio playing. The classical piece was the same each time she heard it on several other occasions, and it always heralded the death of a resident. One of her colleagues confirmed that she too had heard the music (Bell, pp. 51–52).

Bell, David (1992). *Leicestershire Ghosts & Legends*. Newbury: Countryside.

Bacci, Marcello (1927–)

Marcello Bacci, the electronic voice phenomena (EVP) visionary, is held in such esteem that the first 2006 installment of the *Journal for the Investigation of Instrumental Transcommunication Phenomena* (*ITC Journal*) was dedicated to him. For more than forty years his EVP studio at Grosseto in Italy has been a very active center for the transmission of EVP as well as discovering music phenomena from allegedly unknown electronic sources. Bacci tunes his radio to the short-wave band, in a frequency ranging between 7 and 9 MHz, which is a zone he believes is clear from normal radio transmissions. Although his work is mainly centered on spoken voices being perceived via his old valve radio, on at least one occasion a female sounding choir has been recorded quite clearly singing in an unknown language for several minutes. The Televisione Svizzera Italiana Mysteries Channel produced an informative documentary *Documentario sulle esperienze metafoniche di Marcello Bacci* in 2015 with English subtitles which was uploaded to YouTube. The video provides a variety of testimonials from people who genuinely believe that their loved ones are speaking to them from beyond the grave.

youtube.com/watch?v=Dj3FErg4l7g.

Bach, Johann S.

It is not surprising that one of "classical" music's best-known and admired composers would be attached to reports about the man and his music in the realm of the paranormal. Johann Sebastian Bach (1685–1750) was named by the musical medium **Rosemary Brown** as one of her contacts from the spirit world. He was also identified as one of Leonora **Piper**'s leading spirit guides who had in turn been the guide of a blind psychic healer called J.R. Cocke who had influenced her journey into **medium**ship. The child **prodigy Pepito Arriola** was witnessed producing **automatic writing** during which time the signature of "J. S. **Bach**" was produced (Gower, p. 60) and the psychical researcher Vernon Harrison wrote, "I have myself heard in the **dream** state a brilliant, and correct, performance of Bach's famous D minor Toccata and Fugue, played on a large three-manual instrument by some unseen agency. No physical sounds were produced and I do not know whence came the music" (Harrison, p. 470). Finally, perhaps mention should be made of the story of Bach being asked by the insomniac Russian envoy Count Kayserling to compose music to help him sleep. Thus came about the possibly fictitious story of the composition of the *Goldberg*

Variations BWV 986 which promptly put Kayserling to sleep when played by Johann Goldberg on the harpsichord.

The concert pianist Rosalyn Tureck (1913–2003) suffered a loss of consciousness when she was practicing a Bach prelude and fugue in the 1930s, and when she regained her normal waking state, she "realized a whole new concept to the structure and meaning of playing Bach" (*Mystifying Mind*, p. 108) which she subsequently put into practice for the rest of her life. She found it impossible to return to the world of music she had known before.

Gower, John H. (1913) *Journal of Society for Psychical Research* 16 (April): 60.
Harrison, Vernon (1974). *Journal of the Society for Psychical Research* 47, no. 761: 470.
The Mystifying Mind. (1991). "Bachanalia." Alexandria: Time-Life Books.

Backster, Cleve

Cleve Backster (aka Grover Cleveland Backster, Jr.) (1924–2013) was born in New Jersey and will best be remembered for his polygraph experiments with **plant** perception, despite being an interrogation officer for the CIA for the first part of his career. His work started in 1966 and he reported experimental results two years later suggesting that there is primary perception in plant life which in modern parlance is usually called extra sensory perception (ESP) (Backster, 1968). It is believed that he was inspired by the research of Jagadis Chandra Bose who suggested that "plants react to music and light" (Williams, p. 25) and his own work led to further research into the subject specifically using music as the connection in ESP.

Backster, Cleve (1968). "Evidence of a Primary Perception in Plant Life." *International Journal of Parapsychology* 10, no. 4 (Winter): 329–348.
Williams, William F. (2000). *Encyclopedia of Pseudoscience.* New York: Facts on File.

Balcomie Castle

Balcomie Castle is situated near Crail in the East Neuk of Fife, Scotland and it possibly dates back to the fourteenth century. Tradition informs one that a whistle (fife) player annoyed the person in charge of troops that were garrisoned there by his continuous playing. He was thrown into the dungeons where he died. It is said that his ghost walks the castle and that "the sound of his whistle has often been heard around the castle" (Brooks, p. 211).

Brooks, J.A. (1990). *Britain's Haunted Heritage.* Norwich: Jarrold.

Barcaldine House

Barcaldine House situated in Strathclyde, Scotland, is a sixteenth-century mansion that was restored by the Campbell Clan in 1896 and is currently used as a hotel. Allegedly a "Blue Lady" of unknown identity, accompanied by similarly unknown music, haunts the establishment (Underwood, pp. 144–145). The owners contacted the author in 1996 with details of "a **piano** being played by a lady dressed in blue" (Willin, p. 123). They named the ghost "Harriet" and mentioned that none of the Campbells had met her yet.

Underwood, Peter (1993). *The Ghosthunters Almanac*. Orpington: Eric Dobby.
Willin, Melvyn J. (2005). *Music, Witchcraft and the Paranormal*. Ely: Melrose.

Baring, Maurice

Maurice Baring (1874–1945) was an Englishman known for his literary works and notable wartime service for which he was awarded the OBE in 1918. He witnessed music of an unknown origin in the company of a friend who also heard singing. On investigation they remained perplexed and were not able to explain the event: "empty though it was, the singing went on, such curious singing too; strange, alien, confused, tinkly ... unreal with a kind of burr in it as if you were listening to voices on a telephone that is out of order. We walked through the singing and heard it behind us still going on; and in the bedroom we found our friend asleep. There was nobody outside; and the ghost did not turn out to be rats, mice or a gramophone" (cited in Haynes, p. 47).

Haynes, Renée (1976). *The Seeing Eye, the Seeing I*. London: Hutchinson.

Baroque Rhythm

Georgi Lozanov (1926–2012) was a Bulgarian scientist who developed and promoted the concept of increased learning capability through relaxation and the use of slow Baroque music. He found that suitable music being played at sixty beats a minute had the effect of slowing down the heartbeat, brain waves and blood pressure which increased the ability to remember facts and figures (Hoffman, p. 13). Concerti grossi have been mentioned as causing "considerable internal activity" and these rhythms have a "deeply penetrating suggestive effect" (Bancroft, pp. 45–47). Don Campbell reiterates this: "Slower Baroque music (**Bach**, **Handel**, Vivaldi,

Corelli) imparts a sense of stability, order, predictability, and safety and creates a mentally stimulating environment for study or work" (Campbell, p. 78). Lozanov's "suggestopedia" as it has come to be known as has been fostered particularly in Austria and Norway. In 1977 the medical researcher Dr. Michele Clements discovered that playing a Vivaldi allegro movement at about seventy-two crotchets to the minute helped the birth of a baby that an obstetrician could not deliver (cited in Playfair, p. 55).

Bancroft, W. Jane (1976). *Suggestology and Suggestopedia: The Theory of the Lozanov Method.* U.S. Department of Health, Education and Welfare.
Campbell, Don (1997). *The Mozart Effect.* London: Hodder & Stoughton.
Hoffman, Janalea (1995). *Rhythmic Medicine.* Leawood: Jamillan Press.
Playfair, Guy Lyon (1985b). *If This Be Magic.* London: Cape.

Barrett, William

Sir William Fletcher Barrett (1844–1925) was one of the main founders of the Society for Psychical Research (SPR) in 1882. He was an English physicist and psychical researcher and held the Chair of Physics at the Royal College of Science in Dublin. He was particularly interested in the experiences of the dying and his collection of such cases, **Death-Bed** *Visions* was published posthumously in 1926. Apart from visual examples the book also contains examples of "music heard at the time of death by the dying or by persons present at a death-bed" (Barrett, p. 96). In modern parlance these events are often referred to as **near-death experiences** (NDEs) when the individual survives death.

Barrett quoted one such case from the second volume of the substantial SPR survey **Phantasms of the Living** (Gurney, Myers, Podmore, 1886) concerning multiple witnesses of music at the time of the death of an Eton master's mother in 1881. The music was described as "low, soft music, exceedingly sweet, as of three girls' voices" and "very low, sweet singing" (Barrett, pp. 96–97). Further testimonies were:

> Just after dear Mrs. L.'s death between 2 and 3 a.m., I heard a most sweet and singular strain of singing.... All in the room (except Mr. L.) heard it, and the medical attendant, who was still with us, went to the window, as I did, and looked out, but there was nobody. It was a bright and beautiful night. It was as if several voices were singing in perfect unison a most sweet melody which died away in the distance. Two persons had gone from the room to fetch something and were coming upstairs at the back of the house and heard the singing and stopped saying "What is that singing?" They could not, naturally, have heard any sound from outside the windows in the front of the house from where they were at the back.

[Dr. G. was also in attendance and wrote]:

... we heard a few bars of lovely music, not unlike that from an Aeolian harp—and it filled the air for a few seconds. I went to the window and looked out, thinking there must be someone outside, but could see no one though it was quite light and clear... [Barrett, pp. 97–98].

From the several deathbed experiences that Barrett mentions, another is worth quoting since it originates from the writer and preacher John Bunyan (1628–1688) who related that as a man was dying "the woman that looked to him thought she heard music, and that the sweetest that ever she heard in her life, which also continued until he gave up the ghost. Now, when his soul departed from him the music seemed to withdraw, and to go further and further off from the house, and so it went until the sound was quite gone out of hearing" (Bunyan, pp. 653–654).

Barrett, William (1926). *Death-Bed Visions*. London: Methuen.
Bunyan, John (1855). *Works*. Ed. George Offor. Vol. 3: 653–654. Cited in Barrett (1926). *Death-Bed Visions*. London: Methuen.

Battlefields

There are quite a large number of allegedly haunted battlefields in the literature which can be found as far back as the writer Pausanius describing the ghostly sounds of battle at Marathon in Greece (cited in Innes, p. 11). In the sixteenth century there were reports of "ghostly battles" with **trumpets**, **drums** and rattles (cited in Tomlinson, p. 156). Further examples can be found from the English Civil War in the seventeenth century when re-enactments of battles such as Naseby (1645) have been recorded (Forman, p. 1341). Although ghostly sounds are frequently reported, notably clashing weapons and the screams of the wounded and dying, there is generally a lack of music heard in the heat of the battles. One possible exception was the "very loud sound of drums used in war" (cited in Inglis, p. 50) which were heard by John Calvin in December 1562 when there were no such instruments nearby, but the Battle of Dreux was taking place far away. However, there was much more evidence for the sounds of battle including drums from the Battle of Edgehill in 1642 when the Royalist troops of Charles I clashed with Oliver Cromwell's army. A month after the bloody confrontation shepherds reported seeing and hearing a re-enactment of the battle, news of which came to the King's knowledge whereupon he sent a Royal Commission to investigate the phenomena. They too witnessed the events previously spoken of. Two early pamphlets, *A Great Wonder in Heaven...* and *The New Yeares Wonder* (1642), described the apparitional and auditory events that allegedly occurred two months after the battle, but the scholars Peter McCue and Alan Gauld have cast doubt on their veracity (McCue and Gauld, pp. 78–94).

Forman, Joan (1982). "Old Soldiers Never Die." *The Unexplained* 68. London: Orbis.
Inglis, Brian (1985). *The Paranormal*. London: Guild.
Innes, Brian (1996). *The Catalogue of Ghost Sightings*. Leicester: Brown Packaging.
McCue, Peter, and Alan Gauld (2005). "Edgehill and Souter Fell: A Critical Examination of Two English 'Phantom Army' Cases." *Journal of the Society for Psychical Research* 69.2, no. 879: 78–94.
Tomlinson, Gary. (1993). *Music in Renaissance Magic*. Chicago: University of Chicago Press.

Bayham Abbey

The thirteenth-century ruins of Bayham Abbey are situated near Lamberhurst in Kent, England. It suffered under the Dissolution of the Monasteries by Henry VIII and was finally taken over by English Heritage in the twentieth century. The ruins of the abbey are said to be "haunted by a group of white monks, **chanting** and the ringing of **bells** has been heard, and sometimes the fragrance of incense has been noticed" (www.mysteriousbritain.co.uk).

Bayless, Raymond

Raymond Gordon Bayles (1920–2004) was an American landscape painter and psychical researcher. He co-authored books with D. Scott **Rogo** and undertook pioneering work in the field of EVP. He had musical experiences of an anomalous nature which he initially believed to be a radio playing, but he soon realized that this was not possible: "It seemed to be produced by vast numbers of players, singers.... I cannot say that the music was vocal or that it was instrumental; it was on an inconceivably higher level than such distinction, and all that can be said is that it was incredibly beautiful, clearly superhuman, and could not possibly originate from earthly instruments and voices" (Rogo, pp. 97–98). Bayless also provided details of his friend Attila von Sealay who had a similar mystical experience when sometime in the 1930s he "began to hear faint music.... It seemed to be in my head. I just stood still and the music welled up into my consciousness.... I became overwhelmed by it.... I just stood there and the tears came into my eyes and I think that I became entranced for at least ten minutes" (Rogo, p. 98).

Rogo, D. Scott (1990). *Beyond Reality*. Northamptonshire: Aquarian Press.

Beauchief Hall

Beauchief Hall was built in the seventeenth century and is situated on the outskirts of Sheffield, England and has had a variety of different occupiers and uses. It has been reported (Salim, p. 28) that mysterious **piano** music has been heard in a top room which was empty at the time.

Salim, Valerie (1983). *A Ghost Hunter's Guide to Sheffield*. Sheffield: Sheaf.

Beaulieu Abbey

Beaulieu Abbey in Hampshire, England is well represented in literary references to "ghostly" monks **chant**ing. In the latter part of the twentieth century the sister of Lord Montague, the Honorable Mrs. Elizabeth Varley, heard chanting there: "I was sitting by the window of my room quite late at night when I heard it. It was very clear and quite loud enough for me to pick up the notes of the chant ... when I sang the tune the next day to someone staying in the house, they recognized it as **Gregorian chant**" (cited in Brooks, pp. 42–42). In 1959, Michael Sedgwick, the curator of the motor museum housed in the grounds, claimed also to have heard distinctive chanting. He initially believed it to be a radio but could not identify the

Part of the ruins of Beaulieu Abbey where ghostly monks have been heard chanting (Mick Harper/Shutterstock.com).

source. He experienced these sounds on a second occasion. They were also heard by the wife of the film director Fred Zimmerman, during the filming of *A Man for All Seasons* at the house (cited in Willin, 2015). The famous inventor Guglielmo Marconi (1874–1937) visited the family and was particularly intrigued with Mrs. Varley's experience (St. Aubyn and Hanbury, pp. 64–65). The author attended an all-night investigation of the abbey in 1994, but the only auditory phenomena recorded was the whirling of an electric fan in the lavatory.

Brooks, J.A. (1990). *Britain's Haunted Heritage*. Norwich: Jarrold.
St. Aubyn, Astrid, and Zahra Hanbury (1996). *Ghostly Encounters*. London: Robson.
Willin, M. (2015). "Beaulieu Abbey." *Psi Encyclopedia*. London: The Society for Psychical Research. psi-encyclopedia.spr.ac.uk/articles/beaulieu-abbey.

Beethoven, Ludwig van

It is not surprising that the name of Beethoven (1770–1827) appears in many connections with music and anomalous phenomena, since he is one of the few composers whose name is familiar to most people. His music is held in the highest esteem by people who have studied it in depth: "Beethoven, then, was a musical avatar, born to initiate new and higher vibrations of thought and feeling in the hearts of the people of his own day, of our day, and of untold centuries to come" (Tame, p. 14). The concert pianist **John Lill** spoke at length about his contact with the spirit of Beethoven during an extended recorded interview with the author in February 1996. In addition to dictating part of a tenth symphony to Lill, Beethoven was also a channeling composer for **Rosemary Brown** and other less well-known **musical mediums**. **Cyril Scott**, the composer and occultist, believed that Beethoven's music seemed to have an effect on the subconscious mind which went beyond the sounds which were "heard by the ears" (Scott, p. 68). Beethoven was asked by Louis Schlösser in 1823 where the source of his **inspiration** came from. His reply was: "That I cannot say with any degree of certainty: they come to me uninvited, directly or indirectly. I could almost grasp them in my hands, out in Nature's open, in the woods, during my promenades, in the silence of the night, at earliest dawn. They are roused by moods which in the poet's case are transmuted into words, and in mine into tones that sound, roar and storm until at last they take shape for me as notes" (cited in Crabbe, p. 87). He told Elizabeth Brentano that "music is the one incorporeal entrance into the higher worlds of knowledge which comprehends mankind, but which mankind cannot comprehend" (cited in Wilson, p. 324).

The transcommunication researcher Sarah Wilson Estep (1926–2008) believed that Beethoven contacted her directly through electronic voice phenomena and that he also sent her music as proof. Professional musicians were not able to identify the music, but she believed that part of the music was from his famous "Moonlight Sonata" opus 27, no. 2 (Estep, pp. 113–117). In 1982 she established the American Association of Electronic Voice Phenomena "to provide objective evidence that we survive death in an individual conscious state" (cited in Brunke, p. 80).

Brunke, Dawn Baumann (1996). "An Interview with Sarah Estep." *Fate* (May): 78–80.
Crabbe, John (1982). *Beethoven's Empire of the Mind.* Berkshire: Lovell Baines.
Estep, Sarah Wilson (1988). *Voices of Eternity.* New York: Fawcett.
Scott, Cyril (1958). *Music. Its Secret Influence Throughout the Ages.* London: Aquarian Press.
Tame, David (1994). *Beethoven and the Spiritual Path.* Wheaton: Quest.
Wilson, Colin (1988). *Beyond the Occult.* London: Transworld.

Bells

Bells have been associated with anomalous phenomena for many centuries and in many **religions**. They are frequently mentioned in the book of Exodus in the **Bible** and are worn by **shamans** and the **fairy** folk to oppose evil spirits. Bells are rung to call the faithful to church; to dispel storms; to protect crops and **animals** and in many other respects (Maple, pp. 238–240). Bells have been used for their **healing** ability, as found in Sir John Sinclair's *Statistical Account of Scotland* (1778) where he remarked that in St. Fillan's Chapel, Perth, there was a bell which could cure depressions and madness. They have been rung in **séances** to prove the presence of spirits and the Necromantic Bell of Giradius was used to summon the dead according to instructions in France in the eighteenth century (Guiley, p. 18). A ship's bell represents its very soul and many bells have been associated with hauntings including **Minsden Chapel, St. Albans Abbey**, and **Great Leighs. Sunken bells** have been heard off many coastlines and in lakes and rivers notably in Cornwall and Norfolk, England, both of which have extensive coastlines where erosion has destroyed pre-existing villages (Willin, pp. 179–182).

Maple, Eric (1970). "Bells." *Man, Myth and Magic.* Vol. 1. London: Purnell.
Guiley, Rosemary Ellen (1999). *The Encyclopedia of Witches and Witchcraft.* New York: Checkmark.
Willin, Melvyn J. (1999). *Paramusicology: An Investigation of Music and Paranormal Phenomena.* PhD thesis. Music Department. University of Sheffield.

Berlioz, Hector

Louis Hector Berlioz (1803–1869) was born in France and originally studied medicine before turning to music. He was named by both

Rosemary Brown and **Jesse Shepard** as a composer who channeled them with music works from beyond the grave and his *Symphonie Fantastique* was frequently chosen in the **ganzfeld** experiments undertaken by the author in 1996 (Willin, pp. 32–33). He was scornful of the spiritualist table-turning craze that engulfed Europe in the 1850s and wrote scathingly of the accounts that **Beethoven**'s spirit was present in **séances**: "The poor spirits, we must admit, are very obedient. Beethoven, whilst he was on earth, would not have put himself out of the way ... even if the Emperor of Austria had sent to beg him urgently to come" (cited in Crabbe, p. 90). His agnostic beliefs did not stop him from composing many supernaturally themed works, notably the *Symphonie fantastique* with its eerie witches' Sabbath.

Crabbe, John (1980). *Hector Berlioz: Rational Romantic*. London: Kahn & Averill.
Willin, Melvyn J. (2005). *Music, Witchcraft and the Paranormal*. Ely: Melrose Press.

Bible

"Psychic activity occurs in the Bible from its first pages to its last" (Martin, p. 22). The book of Genesis 4:21 provides the reader with the "father" of music in the person of Jubal, descendant of Cain, whose name originally signified a ram's horn (*shofar*) or **trumpet** (Reik, p. 222). This holds true of whichever version one reads and in whichever translation. Although one can encounter ESP, **channeling**, **dreams**, **magic** and other forms of divination in the Bible, the place of music in these paranormal phenomena is more limited. There are, of course, difficulties, in deciding whether the music described is meant to be interpreted literally or metaphorically, but, with this caveat in place, the following might be included as such:

> Joshua 6:4–20   Seven **trumpet**s of rams' horns were blown around the walls of Jericho which, in accompaniment to a great shout, the walls fell down.
>
> 1 Samuel 16:23   "...when the evil spirit from God was upon Saul, that David took an **harp**, and played with his hand: so Saul was refreshed, and was well, and the evil spirit departed from him."
>
> 2 Kings 3:15   "But now bring me a minstrel. And it came to pass, when the minstrel played, that the hand of the Lord came upon him."
>
> 2 Chronicles 5:12–13   "...having cymbals and psalteries and harps ... and with them an hundred and twenty priests sounding with trumpets ... that then the house was filled with a cloud...."
>
> Acts 16: 25–26   "...Paul and Silas prayed, and sang praises unto God.... And suddenly there was a great earthquake ... all the doors were opened and every one's bands were loosed."

The fall of Jericho is often quoted as a miraculous event involving music, but it has been suggested that an earthquake in the region may have been responsible as a "timely event" which Joshua may have been expecting (North, p. 119). The trumpets are particularly popular in the Bible as can be seen in the references to them notably throughout Revelation where they are used for divine announcements proclaiming miraculous events. They are also used as a signal for plagues and devastation (cited in Tenney, p. 2381). Other references to trumpets can be found in Zechariah 9:14 where God blows the trumpet himself and sometimes in the hands of the **angels**. Sometimes the trumpet is referred to as a "trump" as at the return of Jesus Christ to the earth in I Thessalonians 4:16 and in 1 Corinthians 15:52 where both trump and trumpet are used in the same verse. The paranormality of all these events, with accompanying music, depends on one's own personal belief system as to its legitimacy.

The Bible has also been cited in references to a comparison between the architectural proportions of the temple of Solomon (I Kings 6:2; 6:17) and the basic ratios of musical harmony which were later proposed by **Pythagoras** using ratios which can be converted into the perfect intervals of fourth, fifth and octave (Strachan, pp. 31–32). The *De re aedificatoria*, consisting of ten books of architecture, written by Leon Battista Alberti (1404–1472) drew direct comparisons between the proportions of architecture and music. (For an overview of "Heavenly Music" in Judaism and Christianity in the Bible and elsewhere see Chapman, pp. 93–105).

Chapman, Colin (1990). *Shadows of the Supernatural.* Oxford: Lion.
Martin, Ted (1997). *Psychic and Paranormal Phenomena in the Bible.* Nashville: Psychicspace. com.
North, Anthony (1996). *The Paranormal.* London: Blandford.
Reik, Theodor (1958). *Ritual.* New York: International Universities Press.
Revelation 1:10; 4:1; 8:2; 8:13; 9:14; 18:22.
Strachan, Gordon (1992/3). "The Temple of Solomon and the Cosmic Music." *The Occult Observer* II, no. 3 (Winter): 30–33.
Tenney, M.C. (1970). "Revelation." *Man, Myth and Magic.* London: Purnell.

Billingham Manor

Billingham Manor is situated on the Isle of Wight, just off the coast of England and was built in the first half of the seventeenth century. In more recent times it was owned by the novelist and playwright J.B. Priestley who was particularly interested in psychical research and a member of the Society for Psychical Research. He was reported to have not witnessed anything paranormal while living there (Steedman and Anker, p. 23). However, in the late 1970s the owners Mr. and Mrs. Forbes related that "the scent of lilies …

pervades the hall and music room…. It seems to be summoned by music….
Play a pop song or a **Mozart piano** concerto and a guest may well murmur,
'What's that lovely smell?'" (Steedman and Anker, p. 25). They have also
reported the sound of **piano** music being heard when the house is empty.

Steedman, Gay, and Ray Anker (1977). *Ghosts of the Isle of Wight*. Newport: Saunders.

Binham Priory

The Priory Church of St. Mary and the Holy Cross at Binham in Norfolk, England, was founded in the eleventh century as a Benedictine priory. It is known locally as "Binham Priory" and has attracted many legends
to it during a long history of turmoil as well as well-documented reports of
spectral monks being seen by reliable witnesses. Its anomalous music connection concerns a secret underground tunnel that allegedly linked the priory with the famous religious shrine at Walsingham. In a story similar to
the **Anstey** manifestation a **fiddler** was said to have entered the tunnel with
his dog, but after a while his playing stopped and only the dog returned
(Jeffery, p. 52).

Jeffery, Peter (1988). *East Anglian Ghosts, Legends and Lore*. Gillingham: The Old Orchard
    Press.

Bird Cage Theatre

The Bird Cage Theatre in Tombstone, Arizona, was "a combination
brothel, gambling hall, theatre, and saloon. Back in the 1880s, it was a favorite night spot for many of the West's most legendary characters, including
Wyatt Earp, Doc Holliday, and Bat Masterson" (Davis, p. 16). It closed down
for an extended period, but in 1921 music was reported from inside the
building prior to its re-opening in 1934 which has continued to be heard as
well as poltergeist activity. Tourists have reported the mysterious singing by
a woman of "old-time music" and the song "Red River Valley" was allegedly
heard by two employees when no one else was present (Davis, p. 19).

Davis, Carolyn (2000). "The Old Bird Cage Theatre." *Fate* (March): 16–19.

Bispham, David Scull

David Scull Bispham (1857–1921) was an American professional baritone singer who related parts of his life in the autobiographical *A Quaker*

Singer's Recollections (1920). Therein he revealed that during a planchette (early ouija board device) demonstration by his friend Baron Rudbeck he received a message telling him to concentrate on and prepare several operatic roles from Verdi and **Wagner** rather than continuing with his previous concert work. "Astonished, Bispham felt he would be wise to learn the parts—even Beckmesser, for which he felt himself unsuited" (Inglis 1987, pp. 195–196). In what can only be described as a series of extraordinary coincidences a number of illnesses and postponements led to him being asked to sing these roles soon after and, because of his preparations, he was able to perform them to great acclaim (Inglis 1985, pp. 221–222).

Inglis, Brian (1985). *The Paranormal*. London: Guild.
Inglis, Brian (1987). *The Unknown Guest—The Mystery of Intuition*. London: Chatto & Windus.

Black Horse

The Black Horse public house in White Roding, Essex, England is a sixteenth-century building that it is claimed once had a **pian**o-playing phantom, even though there was not a piano in the establishment. A cavalier was allegedly killed in the area, and it is believed that his spirit may be responsible for the phenomenon (Payne, p. 62).

Payne, Jessie (1995). *A Ghost Hunter's Guide to Essex*. Norfolk: Ian Henry.

Blind Tom

Blind Tom (Wiggins) was the blind son of a slave who was bought at an auction in Georgia in 1850 by one Colonel Bethune and he was re-named Thomas Greene Bethune (cited in Treffert, p. 16). The Colonel was amazed to find Tom, at the age of about four years, was able to play a **Mozart piano** sonata which he had learnt by listening to the Colonel's daughter practicing. Tom's repertoire soon expanded to include works by **Beethoven**, Mendelssohn, **Bach**, **Chopin** and many others which allowed the Colonel to promote, though it might be said to exploit, Tom's talent through concert tours (Treffert, p. 17). He played at the White House before President James Buchanan followed by further concert tours of Europe and the United States. Wherever he went he was tested to ensure his talents were genuine. In 1862 he was told to play the second part of a fourteen-page original which he had not heard before, while the composer played the treble: "Tom sat beside the composer and played the first note to the last in the secondo part. Following that he fairly shoved the man from his seat and proceeded to play the treble with more brilliancy and power than its composer" (Treffert, p. 18). Unlike many musical **savants**, Tom continued to play until the age of fifty-three, but after the death of the Colonel he became despondent and died in 1908.

Treffert, Darold A. (1989). *Extraordinary People*. London: Bantam Press.

Bodiam Castle

Bodiam Castle, East Sussex, England, was built in the fourteenth century and attracted the interest of the famous psychical investigator Harry Price who gave a lecture to the Ghost Club in the 1920s concerning haunted Sussex including the castle. "Another feature of this haunt is the music ... which can always be heard on Easter Sunday by those whose ears are attuned to 'psychic music' [and] foreign-sounding songs" (Underwood, p. 32). The author received a letter from the administrator of the castle denying any knowledge of recent "ghostly" music being heard there (private correspondence).

Underwood, Peter (1984). *This Haunted Isle*. London: Harrap.

Boethius

Anicius Manlius Torquatus Severinus Boethius (c. 480–524) was born in Rome and wrote treatises, one of which, *De Institione Musica*, "did have an incalculable effect on the general estimation of music as an influence on the Soul and as a reflection of the cosmic harmony, his dicta being repeated again and again by Medieval and Renaissance writers" (Godwin, p. 44). Furthermore, Boethius' writings seemed to support Plato's doctrine that "the soul of the universe is united by a musical concord" (cited in Godwin, p. 45). It is hardly surprising that the influence of his work on the West during the Middle Ages promoted the power of music over the mind and body in what might be called paranormal ways: "[He] gave a thorough yet accessible statement of the Pythagorean-Platonic view that individual souls (musica humana) could be re-tuned to cosmic harmony (musica mundane) through the intermediary of appropriate musica instrumentalis.... Boethius also conveniently gathered the best anecdotes illustrating the power of musica instrumentalis to influence both somatic and psychic ailments.... *De musica* remained on some university syllabuses until the nineteenth century" (cited in Hordern, p. 103).

Godwin, Joscelin (1987b). *Music, Mysticism and Magic*. London: Arkana.
Hordern, Peregrine (2000). *Music as Medicine*. Aldershot: Ashgate.

Bolton Abbey

Bolton Abbey, near Skipton in Yorkshire, England, was founded by the Order of Augustinian Monks in the twelfth century. The ruins are attached to a more recent building. Numerous firsthand accounts of hauntings have been recorded from there including the organ which has been heard to sound when no one was playing it (Linahan, p. 187). During an investigation the author heard and recorded **Gregorian chant** from an unknown source which soon became identified as the cleaning lady admitted that she like to play such music when she was working there!

Linahan, Liz (1997). *The North of England Ghost Trail*. London: Constable.

Bonny, Helen

Although strictly speaking not paranormal, the "Guided Imagery and Music (G.I.M.)" work of Helen Bonny (1921–2010) has certainly guided people into an **altered state of consciousness** which has allowed them to have experiences which are not part of their waking or normal consciousness. She instigated this study after a mystical experience while playing the **violin**: "Profound religious experiences often occur…. It is the wordless meaning of music that provides its power of direction and emotional structure…. Many describe the experience as full of insight; others find a **healing** force; some let the music take them to unexplored provinces of the psyche; while for others it provides a heightened awareness of their ordinary world" (cited in Gardner, pp. 210–211). Bonny claimed that different types of music have different effects according to the listeners and the healing they are requiring. With her colleague Louis Savary, they published their discoveries into the ability of music "to generate greater levels of emotional intensity, depth, and comprehensiveness" in *Music and Your Mind* (Bonny and Savary, pp. 82–83). They also founded a dedicated institute which later became the Association for Music and Imagery situated in Arlington, Virginia.

Bonny, Helen, and Louis Savary (1973). *Music and Your Mind*. New York: Harper & Row.
Gardner, Kay (1990). *Sounding the Inner Landscape*. Rockport: Element.

Borgia, Anthony

Anthony Borgia (1896–1989) was a medium who transcribed the thoughts of a deceased Catholic priest, Monsignor Robert Hugh Benson

(1871–1914), the son of a former Archbishop of Canterbury, Edward White Benson. The spirit allegedly dictated what "life" was like in the world of spirit which he hoped would correct the teaching in his previous Christian existence. One chapter of a book exploring these revelations was devoted to music (Borgia, pp. 61–69). He described music as "a vital element in the world of spirit" with a hall devoted to the subject which was full of every aspect of the art as well as a concert hall for performances. A concert was described consisting of the purest of musical sounds, with harmony as a fundamental law within a musical thought form (Borgia, p. 67).

Borgia, Anthony (1954). *Life in the World Unseen*. London: Odhams Press.

Borley Church

Unusually Borley Church does not have a saint's name as a designation. Harry Price, the famous English psychical investigator called Borley Rectory "the Most Haunted House in England" and his claims in a subsequent book of the same name caused and still cause considerable controversy as to the reliability of his investigation. The rectory, built in 1863 on the site of an earlier rectory, was the scene of numerous poltergeist and apparitional activities until it burned down in 1939 and was later demolished to make way for a small group of new houses. The surviving stable block was one such conversion. There were no musical manifestations of an anomalous kind in the rectory, however, this was not the end of the Borley saga since numerous reports were made stating that some of the manifestations had long occurred in the church opposite and were still prevalent which did indeed include musical manifestations. A massive file of correspondence and articles is housed in the Cambridge University Library, England belonging to the Society for Psychical Research, which provides many details that have been deposited there by numerous authors. For instance, the investigators Paul Tabori and Peter Underwood recorded a young man returning from work who heard singing and **chanting** coming from the church even though it was locked at the time (Tabori and Underwood, p. 160) and they also related the testimony of one Mr. J. May who reported, "I heard soft notes and chords from the organ ... a jumble of atonal chords" (Tabori and Underwood, p. 165). Throughout the text they mention **bells** being heard with no apparent foundation, but these were often the servants' bells within the rectory rather than the bells in the church opposite.

A very detailed account was given by a Mrs. Norah Walrond in the company of the Rector A.C. Henning in October 1947:

As we were walking up the path to the south door I stopped and said, "The organ is playing." My first thought was that there was a service in progress and that therefore we could not go in. Mr. Henning stopped and looked at me. He heard it too.... He darted forward and hurried into the church.... To my amazement the church was empty and silent. We sat down near the organ for a moment and he said "Have you heard the story of the organ playing before?" I assured him I had not.... The whole event was over in half a minute, and it was impossible for anyone to have escaped in the time. We went all over the church. No one could possibly have been there.... From the outside it sounded just like church music, without voices—just an organ playing as it might while the collection is being taken.... Quietly, not loudly, but definitely an organ. When I got home I found from Mr. Price's second book that one other man at least had heard church music there. Also Mr. Henning tells me that others have heard it [cited in Tabori and Underwood, p. 167].

Experiments to produce notes from the organ with trapped air proved fruitless, and although local boys may have been responsible for pranks, it does not explain all the incidents, notably in the latter half of the twentieth century before strict security was imposed on the church building to keep away unwanted sightseers. The investigator Wesley Downes recounted how a couple and their daughter all heard the sound of **Handel**'s "Largo" (from *Xerxes*) playing in the church, but when they reached the porch, the music stopped and when they immediately entered the church it was found to be empty and the organ consul was closed and locked—no one was in sight. In 1985 a "faint form of chanting" (Downes, p. 29) was heard and a solicitor from Norfolk more recently heard music from the organ when nobody was present (*Psychic World*, no further details). The author has visited the church many times over a period of more than thirty years and has even

Borley Church situated opposite the site of Borley Rectory (now demolished) where unaccounted-for organ music has been heard (S. Armitage/Shutterstock. com).

undertaken all-night investigations, but he has not recorded any sounds other than nocturnal animal life and an infrequent motor vehicle. The most comprehensive volume to date (2020) about the history of Borley Rectory and its connected phenomena is *The Borley Rectory Companion* (Adams, Brazil and Underwood, 2003).

Adams, Paul, Eddie Brazil, and Peter Underwood (2003). *The Borley Rectory Companion.* Stroud: The History Press.
Downes, Wesley (1993). *The Ghosts of Borley.* Essex: Wesley's.
Tabori, Paul, and Peter Underwood (1973). *The Ghosts of Borley.* Newton Abbot: David & Charles.

Bosham Bells

Although somewhat steeped in legend rather than facts, the story of the Bosham Bells is nevertheless intriguing. Bosham is a coastal village in West Sussex, England, of some importance since it was mentioned in the Bayeux Tapestry and in the Domesday Book.

Bosham Church was plundered by Danish pirates at an unknown time, who stole the tenor bell. As the ship sailed away, the remaining church **bells** were rung in the church and the tenor bell miraculously joined in thereby destroying the ship. The bell is still said to ring beneath the sea whenever the other bells are rung (Ashliman, 2013–19).

Ashliman, D.L., ed. (2013-2019). *Sunken Bells. Legends of Christiansen Type 7070.* Pitt.edu.

Boudreaux, Ellen

Ellen Boudreaux (1957–) is a blind musical **savant** from the United States who would appear to not only possess an extraordinary musical talent, but also powers of ESP (Treffert, p. 97). In addition to her blindness, she suffered as a child from several other handicaps of both a physical and cognitive nature. However, her musical skills were exhibited from about the age of four and her astonishing keyboard skills have continued ever since. By the age of seven she could transpose orchestral and vocal scores by ear on the **piano** and soon after started improvising in a series of different styles. Her ability to play **Mozart** pieces that she may not have heard before has suggested to some that she may be his **reincarnation** (Treffert, p. 121). As a savant she is unusual in some ways in being female and possessing a sense of rhythm linked to an "uncanny sense of time" which she also displays in guitar playing, which she taught herself as a small child.

Treffert, Darold A. (1989). *Extraordinary People.* London: Bantam Press.

Bozzano, Ernesto

Ernesto Bozzano (1862–1943) was an Italian psychical researcher and prolific writer. After an investigation at Millesimo Castle in the 1920s he became increasingly convinced of the existence of spirit-based phenomena. A particular interest of his were **deathbed** phenomena and particularly those involving music. "In his 1943 book *Musica Trascendentale*, Bozzano studied various musical phenomena, offering forty two cases on music produced by **mediums**; music received telepathically; music heard during hauntings, around deathbeds, and after a death; and phenomena involving music unrelated to death.... He rejected the hallucinatory explanation of hauntings on the grounds that in some cases those who heard music did not know the location was haunted ... he pointed to deathbed cases in which bystanders heard the music, but not the dying person" (Alvarado, 2016). His investigations were taken from the available literature of the 1920s from such publications as the journals of the British and American Societies for Psychical Research as well as Spiritualist publications such as *Light* and they were expanded and reported in **Scott Rogo**'s *NAD* book on transcendental music. The French parapsychologist René Sudre (1880–1968) took issue with many of Bozzano's theoretical interpretations (Alvarado 2013, pp. 147–163).

Alvarado, Carlos S. (2013). "Studying Ernesto Bozzano: Suggestions for Future Historical Studies." *Journal of the Society for Psychical Research* 77.3, no. 912: 147–163.
Alvarado, Carlos S. (2016). "Ernesto Bozzano." *Psi Encyclopedia*. London: The Society for Psychical Research. https://psi-encyclopedia.spr.ac.uk/articles/ernesto-bozzano.

Brahms, Johannes

The German composer Johannes Brahms (1833–1897) was not generally known for his religious fervor or extrovert lifestyle, but he was forthcoming in his views when in conversation with the famous **violin**ist Joseph Joachim in 1896 which was recorded by **Arthur Abell**. Brahms claimed that he had seen things "in a new light" since the death of his friend Clara Schumann (Abell, p. 2). He clarified many of his views about the composing process which went beyond the physical constraints of writing music: "After all, it may be of some interest to posterity to know how the Spirit speaks when the creative urge is upon me" (Abell, p. 2). He went on to explain the details of his communication which involved his internal powers from his soul that would "thrill my whole being" (Abell, p. 5). He was somewhat scathing about science, maintaining,

> the fundamental error of these leading Victorian scientists of today, is that they believe only that which is revealed to the five senses; that which can be

measured, weighed or proved by chemical analysis. Now scientific analysis ignores completely the true relation of the world to mankind; there are many higher, spiritual values such as beauty, love, intuition, harmony, order, inspiration, laws, the wonderful messages of the flowers, and music, which defy scientific analysis; and yet they are no less real than the palpable phenomena to which these scientists attach such importance. In fact, they are much more so, because these higher values are eternal, whereas those gross material things are fleeting and transitory [Abell, p. 34].

Abell's *Talks with Great Composers* provides further details of Brahms' beliefs in paranormal phenomena and his insights into the nature of **inspiration** and the soul or spirit.

The musician Dr. F.H. Wood claimed that Brahms was controlling the medium Tom Tyrell who played the violin and spoke of Brahms' Sextet in B flat. Wood also noted that Tyrell signed himself using what appeared to be Brahms' handwriting (Waring, p. 77).

Abell, Arthur M. (1955). *Talks with Great Composers.* London: Psychic Book Club.
Waring, H. (1949). "Brahms Controlled Medium." *The Two Worlds* 62 (March 11): 77.

Branston Hall

Branston Hall is an eighteenth-century mansion situated a few miles away from the historic English town Lincoln. In 1997 the author was sent a letter relating the experience of the staff there that "the sound of an old, scratched jazz record had been heard when the CD player was empty of any music. Neither do the hotel staff have a jazz recording. The music played for several minutes through the loudspeakers" (private correspondence).

Britten, Emma Hardinge

Emma Hardinge Britten (1823–1899) was an English medium and musician who wrote extensively about her experiences and composed a number of musical works under the pseudonym of Ernest Reinhold. "She trained in Paris for an operatic career but extreme bouts of somnambulism affected her training adversely" and she also played **piano** for Pierre Erard, the founder of the French piano-making firm (Britten, p. 6). She travelled to the United States and maintained very long-lasting contacts there including a friendship with Leah Underhill—the sister of the founders of **Spiritualism** Margaret and Kate Fox. At one séance with Leah she received directions from Spirit to "'go to the piano' where she played martial music" followed by an instruction to "lower the lights" from a discarnate voice whereupon there was the "marching of a heavy body of soldiers, then came repeated explosions as of the firing of musketry, all given in different tones, some like the snapping of a pistol, some like the roar of distant artillery" (Britten 1900, p. 108). In New York she formed a choir, but "at times the piano on which my choir rehearsed to my playing was lifted bodily up in the air, obliging me to request the good invisibles to let us proceed with our practice" (Britten, p. 53). Previously she had heard unknown music in her head, and she put this to good use when she composed a cantata *The Song of the Stars* while in an inspired state which was performed at the Academy Hall, New York, on 24 April 1857 "to press acclaim" (Britten, pp. 57–72). She devoted many pages of her book *Nineteenth Century Miracles* (1884) to both her and other **mediums**' musical experiences (see Britten, pp. 75–76; 143–147; 322; 337–340; 423; 480–481) and similarly in her *History of Modern American Spiritualism* (1869) (see Britten, pp. 57; 90; 143; 178–179; 183–184; 200–203; 289–290; 314; 317–322; 342; 409; 436; 441–442; 463).

Britten, Emma Hardinge (1869). *History of Modern American Spiritualism*. London: Burns.
Britten, Emma Hardinge (1884). *Nineteenth Century Miracles*. Manchester: William Britten.
Britten, Emma Hardinge (1900). *Autobiography of Emma Hardinge Britten*. Ed. Mrs. Margaret Wilkinson. London: John Heywood.

Britton, John

John Britton was a deaf mute who was close to dying from rheumatic fever in Leeds, England, in 1882 when the events surrounding his musical experience were described by his brother-in-law Mr. Septimus Allen, Steward of Haileybury College, Hertfordshire. Both he and his wife claimed to hear music coming from John's room. After John Britton had recovered sufficiently to communicate, he indicated that he had been allowed to "see into Heaven and to hear the most beautiful music" (Allen, p. 181). The skeptical SPR investigator Frank Podmore questioned the Allens about the occurrence and they provided considerable detail of the manifestation even including a plan of the house to illustrate why the music could not have had its origin outside. However, their descriptions of the music varied from "singing—sweet music" to "the full notes of an organ or of an Aeolian **harp**" (Allen, p. 183).

Allen, Septimus (1889). "Collective." *Journal of the Society for Psychical Research* IV (December).

Broadway Bells

A very sparse amount of detail is available for the Broadway **bells**, hidden in Middle Hill in the English county of Worcestershire. They were

allegedly hidden there during the Reformation and can still be heard ringing at night. This even occurred during World War II when such activity
was banned (Hippisley Coxe, p. 94).

Hippisley Coxe, Antony D. (1973). *Haunted Britain*. London: Pan.

Brown, Rosemary

During a period of approximately twenty years Rosemary Isabel
Brown (1916–2001) produced a stream of music allegedly dictated to her
by a variety of dead composers whom she claimed appeared to her both
visually and audibly. Not only was music conveyed to her, but also works
of art, poetry and learned discourses by scientists and philosophers such
as Albert Einstein and Bertrand Russell. The first time Brown saw **Liszt**
she was about seven years old, and she was already "accustomed to seeing the spirits of the so called dead" (Brown, 1971, p. 13). She soon realized
that these visitations and other psychic abilities separated her from other
people, and she mainly kept them to herself to avoid ridicule. Hints of an
interest in such matters can be seen from Brown's own comments about
her mother's psychic tendencies and her grandfather having worked with
Sir William Crookes during his investigations of mediums (Brown, 1974,
p. 48). Brown's mother played the **piano** occasionally and the radio was
sometimes tuned in to easy listening programs. She attended ballet classes
as a child, and she would therefore have come into contact with some of
the lighter classics used for such classes. This possibly prompted a desire
for piano lessons that she received for approximately a year until financial
constraints forced them to cease. In her teens she had two terms of piano
lessons, acquired an upright piano in 1948 and finally a year's further lessons from 1951 to 1952 after the upheavals of World War II. In March 1964
Brown was convalescing after an accident in the school kitchen where she
worked when Liszt appeared to her very vividly one afternoon and took
over her hands as she played the piano to produce music that was not of
her own creation (Brown, 1986, p. 20). During one of these practices, she
was overheard playing a piece that had been given to her by Liszt and she
was accordingly invited to play to the Wimbledon branch of the Churches
Fellowship for Psychical Studies. She soon began to write down these
works at Liszt's dictation and he introduced more dead composers to her.
Chopin was the next to make contact and he was followed by many others such as **Bach, Beethoven, Brahms, Debussy**, Grieg, **Handel** and further well-known composers. She claimed to have written over six hundred
compositions since 1965 mainly for piano, but a notable exception was a

string quartet movement dictated by Brahms and broadcast by the Dartington Quartet in October 1969 (cited in Parrott, p. 27). Brown claimed that Liszt became insistent that the music should be conveyed to a wider audience and Sir George Trevelyan, a member of the Church Fellowship, provided the contact by showing some of her scores to Mary Firth who directed music courses at a college for further education. Firth was impressed with them and in 1968 they started up a fund for her—the Scott Fund. At the time Brown was working in a school kitchen and she gratefully accepted the offer to pursue her compositional activities. However, feeling under increasing pressure because of her funding she resigned it in March 1970. She started receiving piano lessons again to be able to play the composers' music to a higher standard. Responding to claims that she was "suffering" from cryptomnesia she allowed herself to be studied by Professor Tenhaeff, Director of the Institute of **Parapsychology** at Utrecht University, Holland (Parrott, p. 51). She travelled around Europe and in New York to promote her first book *Unfinished Symphonies* which was ghosted by the "agony aunt" Unity Hall and she appeared on *The Johnny Carson Show* (Thomas Brown, p. 6). It may have been her appearance that later prompted Robert Ford to later write the play *The Spiritualist*, first produced in 2013, which was dedicated to her **musical medium**ship. In 1973 further support was given by the pianist **John Lill**, the composer Richard Rodney bennett and other musicians. In 1986 she published her third book *Look Beyond Today* which featured the songs "Look Beyond Today," "Love Is All We Ever Need to Know" and "Just Turn Away" allegedly communicated by **John Lennon**. Bill Barry, an expert on Lennon lyrics, wrote, "John never wrote songs as bad as that" (Barry, 1986).

Musical communications were still very evident with advice allegedly given by Debussy for Richard Rodney Bennett, via Brown, concerning his performance of a Debussy prelude. Bennett felt that this advice had to emanate from some source other than Brown's own knowledge: "We can all imitate Debussy at the piano if we want to, but to create a piece of music— which is coherent as a piece of music—which seems to go very much to the roots of the composer's style by creating it instantly, is much more complicated" (Parrott, p. 50). The music of Viktor Ullmann, who died in Auschwitz, was recounted in some detail. He wrote an unfinished opera in the concentration camp Theresienstadt in Czechoslovakia called *Der Kaiser von Atlantis* with the libretto by a fellow prisoner Peter Kein who was also killed. A copy of the score was conveyed to Kerry Woodward, the Director of the Netherlands Chamber Choir who spent some time with Brown. Without seeing the score, she gave him advice concerning amendments and changes with specific bar references which were conveyed to her from the departed composer. Kerry Woodward made the changes she suggested since he felt they were needed, and the work was performed on the BBC (*Psychic News*, 1979).

A growing number of non-musicians appeared to Brown in the latter part of the twentieth century including poetry from Emily Brontë, Elizabeth Barrett Browning, Rupert Brooke, William Blake, Samuel Taylor Coleridge, John Keats, Edward Lear, Percy Shelley, William Wordsworth and Sir John Betjeman. In addition to music, she received long philosophical explanations of the spirit world from Bertrand Russell; essays for musicians from Sir Donald Tovey; two plays: *Caesar's Revenge* (performed at the **Edinburgh** Fringe Festival in 1978) and *The Heavenly Maze* from George Bernard Shaw; psychology from Jung; paintings from Debussy and others (Brown, 1986). Once more there was controversy concerning the authenticity of her communications. The psychical researcher Renée Haynes (1906–1994) raised the possibility of "secondary personalities" infiltrating Brown's communications, but added, possibly with a degree of irony: "Thus, one may be pretty certain that whatever the source of Mrs. Rosemary Brown's music, so confidently ascribed to various composers in the Beyond, the fact that she knows as 'Liszt' the Control who leads her round the local supermarket, points out the best bananas and adds up her bill for her at the checkout does not mean that Liszt himself is recalled from celestial harmonies to carry out these useful functions" (Haynes, p. 94).

Despite the composer Alan Hovhaness having orchestrated the first part of her Beethoven "Symphony" piano score in 1975, many of her compositions have been described as "lightweight" in content and brief in duration. She responded to the latter criticism in 1971 with pieces of greater length, notably a sonata from Beethoven in C minor consisting of five hundred and twenty-eight bars (cited in Willin, p. 74).

The authenticity of Brown's music has aroused a considerable amount of disagreement. Her original supporters Dr. and Mrs. Firth went on to claim that it was simply an absorption of the styles of the composers, but they later withdrew these remarks. Vernon Harrison (1912–2001), the chairman of the Liszt Society and a member of the Society for Psychical Research, felt her Liszt pieces were "not good enough to carry conviction that they emanate from the sources to which she attributes them … but they are too good to dismiss lightly" (Parrott, p. 13). He was especially fascinated with the Liszt item *Grübelei* which was partly dictated on May 29, 1969, in the presence of a BBC television crew filming "Mrs Brown and the Composers." Other supporters included Hephzibah Menuhin who suggested that the music seemed to come from the composers' early days; Leonard Bernstein who was particularly impressed with her "Fantaisie Impromptu" from Chopin; and Humphrey Searle who praised the "Moment Musical in G minor" from Schubert. Speaking of *Grübelei* he stated: "It is the sort of piece Liszt could well have written, particularly during the last fifteen years of his life" (Parrott, p. 38). Robin Stone and Howard Shelley have played her music, the latter stating her "Schubert contained the composer's 'essence.'" Derek Watson was impressed with her knowledge of Bruckner whom she saw clairvoyantly and Richard Rodney Bennett stated that it was impossible to produce such music fraudulently. Two of Brown's most creditable allies were the famous concert pianist **John Lill** and **Ian Parrott**, professor of music, University College of Wales, who wrote a book about her music. Larry Sitsky of the Canberra School of Music said, "I find that each piece, no matter what its quality, does at least have the stamp of the composer it is supposed to represent ... and it must be said that some pieces are by no means of negligible quality" (cited in *Alpha*, 1979b, p. 23). Other musicians have been more cautious or totally unconvinced as in the case of Denis Matthews. Writing in *The Listener*, June 26, 1969, he described her music as mainly "charming pastiches" with manifestations of style. He claimed that her Beethoven "Largo e maestoso" movement was a vague memory of the "Largo e mesto" from the "D major Sonata op. 10 no. 3" with a misremembered "maestoso" instead of "mesto." Her Bach prelude based on the "C minor" from *The 48* loses its harmonic progression and a Chopin study is a pale shadow of "op. 10 no. 4 in C sharp minor." In short, Denis Matthews suggested that Brown was re-creating compositions using her own conventional skills and not tapping into a psychic source.

Brown admitted to a personal preference for nineteenth-century composers and expressed a desire for Dvorak and **Tchaikovsky** to contact her, but they were not forthcoming. This could be significant in challenging those who would dispute the veracity of Brown's claims as conscious fraud would surely lead her to use those composers she favored. It could be argued that the essence of nineteenth-century music is harmony and despite this many of her dictations rely on melody, e.g., Grieg's *Shepherd Piping* and **Schumann**'s *Longing*. In an attempt to see if she could produce music outside of her own musical tastes, Scott **Rogo**, a musician and psychical investigator, asked for a Monteverdi madrigal, a Machaut choral piece or best of all a dodecaphonic piece by **Schoenberg** or Webern. She claimed that she needed to be on the same wavelength as the composer and could not oblige. Rogo was disappointed with the similarity of the forms of the music (i.e., often ternary) and the over-use of sequences in the melodic line and symmetrical measurement in the barring and phrasing (cited in Willin, pp. 76–77). The conductor and composer André Previn (1929–2019) described some of her music as "third, fourth or fifth rate Liszt." Rosalind Heywood created a psychological profile of her own devising that suggested Brown was driven to the **automatic** production of material beyond her normal capacity by the frustration she felt at her unused artistic mind.

Interestingly she pointed out that Brown's automatism developed after the death of a close member of the family (Heywood, pp. 212–217).

When Brown was asked what she believed the purpose was for her visitations, she replied, "It's not intended just as proof that life continues after death, but to show that there's far more to life now. They [the composers] want to show that there's far more potential in the here and now. They believe that if our consciousness was expanded, then the world would be enriched. Their feeling is that people are too materialistic. If we realized that we are spiritual beings as well, we would derive much more happiness in this world" (*Alpha*, 1979b, p. 24).

Generally speaking, the works are lacking the **inspiration** and feel of the composers named by her. There is too much emphasis on melody at the expense of harmony, and ideas/motives are not developed sufficiently. Opinion is still divided about the authenticity of her music, but from the music currently available it must be concluded that there is very little evidence of original music being dictated to her from the sources she claimed, *but* that nevertheless she tapped into a source of creativity with an origin that is still difficult to understand.

The English housewife Rosemary Brown was the most famous musical medium of the twentieth century (courtesy R. Price-Mohr).

For a selection of literature referring to Rosemary Brown also see Appendix I.

Alpha (1979b). "New Music from Old Masters." Issue 3 (July/August): 22–24.
Barry, Bill (1986). *Psychic News.* 8 March.
Brown, Rosemary (1971c). *Unfinished Symphonies.* London: Souvenir Press.
Brown, Rosemary (1974). *Immortals at My Elbow.* London: Bachman and Turner.

Brown, Rosemary (1986). *Look Beyond Today*. New York: Bantam Press.
Brown, Thomas (2001). "Rosemary Brown Obituary." *The Independent*, November 21, 6.
Haynes, Renée (1982). *The Society for Psychical Research 1882-1982*. London: Macdonald.
Heywood, R. (1971). "Notes on Rosemary Brown." *Journal of the Society for Psychical Research* 46, no. 750 (December): 212-217.
Parrott, Ian (1978). *The Music of Rosemary Brown*. London: Regency Press.
Psychic News (1979). 10 March.
Willin, Melvyn J. (2005). *Music, Witchcraft and the Paranormal*. Ely: Melrose Press.

Burford Priory

Burford Priory in Oxfordshire, England, was built in the sixteenth century on the site of an older Augustinian hospital and it has been used in the interim period as both a religious retreat as well as a private house. It is allegedly haunted by "a little brown monk" (Brooks, p. 135) and the ringing of **bells** at two in the morning, "the time when the medieval monks of Burford were called to worship" (Underwood, p. 43). The sound of unaccounted singing has also been heard close to the monks' burial ground.

Brooks, J.A. (1992). *Ghosts and Witches of the Cotswolds*. Norwich: Jarrold.
Underwood, Peter (1971). *Gazetteer of British Ghosts*. London: Souvenir Press.

Calvados Castle

Calvados Castle, from Normandy in France, was built in 1835 on the ruins of a previous castle. From 1875 for the duration of almost a year, the owners were subjected to increasingly violent poltergeist activity which included **trumpet** calls being heard and an organ playing "which was closed and locked" (Guiley, p. 55). The owners sold the property after **exorcism**s had little effect on the disturbances. The French astronomer and psychical researcher Camille Flammarion (1842-1925) devoted a chapter of his book *Les Maisons Hantées* (1923) to the case.

Flammarion, Camille (1923). *Les Maisons Hantées*. Paris: Ernest Flammarion.
Guiley, Rosemary Ellen (1994). *Encyclopedia of Ghosts and Spirits*. Enfield: Guinness.

Camberwell Palace

The Camberwell Palace of Varieties was a popular theater in Camberwell, **London**, which opened in 1899 and produced increasingly racy shows until its closure in 1956 and demolition soon after. Former "Gaiety Girl" Ruby Miller discussed some strange experiences she had there with the psychical investigator Philip Paul: "I heard an orchestra playing circus music ... but there was no one about" (Paul, p. 94). She later discovered that a lion-tamer had died in her changing room and his act had always been accompanied with circus music. The theater's part-time fireman also recounted that one night he heard single notes being played on a piano in the orchestra pit when the place was deserted. The medium Ena Twigg later held a séance there when she produced some verifiable evidence (Paul, pp. 97–101).

Paul, Philip (1885). *Some Unseen Power*. London: Robert Hale.

Capella, Martianus

Martianus Minneus Felix Capella was a Latin prose writer of the fifth century, who included in his manuscript *De nuptiis Philologiae et Mercurii* a long speech by "Harmonia" where a list of the alleged paranormal attributes of **animals** included "the charming of stags by shepherds' pipes ... the strains of the cithara that attract Hyperborean swans, and the Indian elephants and cobras that can be restrained by music" (cited in Godwin, p. 23).

Godwin, Joscelyn (1987a). *Harmonies of Heaven and Earth*. London: Thames and Hudson.

Carnfield Hall

Carnfield Hall is a fifteenth-century mansion, situated in Derbyshire, England. The psychologist Alan Gauld accompanied by Howard Wilkinson, an electrical engineer, investigated the house in July 1988 and managed to record what sounded like a few bars of harpsichord music when no such instrument was present. The tape recorder used picked up the music, but unfortunately the music faded on the tape after two to three months. Independent witnesses including an accountant also claimed to have heard such music in the house (private correspondence).

Castle Hotel

The original site of the Castle Hotel in Taunton, Somerset, England, dates back to the twelfth century and the notorious "hanging" Judge Jeffreys held his Bloody Assize in the Great Hall of the Castle in 1685. The present hotel does not claim visual manifestations, but instead it has been alleged that the sounds of **violins** can be heard with no known source.

Mead, Robin (1994). *Weekend Haunts*. London: Impact Books.

Channeling

Channeling is a generic term that has become popular in the "New Age" movement to indicate "communication through automatic speech and **automatic writing** with various nonphysical beings, including **angels**, nature spirits, totem or guardian spirits, deities, demons and spirits of the dead; some channelers say they communicate with a Higher Self" (Guiley, p. 61). People who claim to be in contact with musical entities or the spirits of dead composers could also be described accordingly which would include **Rosemary Brown, Leo May, Florizel von Reuter** and many others. During the latter part of the twentieth-century channeling was particularly popular after an entity called "Seth" spoke words of wisdom and divine philosophy through the psychic and poet Jane Roberts (1929–1984) who produced a prolific amount of writing. There are connections in the sensations of channeling with **altered states of consciousness**, trance, **out-of-body experiences** (OOBEs) and the unconscious. A leading source of information about the state is Klimo's *Channeling: Investigations on Receiving Information from Paranormal Sources* (1987).

Guiley, Rosemary Ellen (1994). *Encyclopedia of Ghosts and Spirits*. Enfield: Guinness.
Klimo, Jon (1987). *Channeling: Investigations on Receiving Information from Paranormal Sources*. Los Angeles: Jeremy P. Tarcher.

Chant

"The use of chant captures the essence of modern **magic**.... Chanting changes the flow of oxygen to the brain and can lead to **altered states of consciousness**" (Ennis, p. 17). The mysterious power of chanting can be illustrated in the following story from the research of **Alfred Tomatis**. In the late 1960s he was asked to investigate the depression that was pervading a Benedictine monastery in France. During a visit Tomatis believed that the sickness was caused by the elimination of **Gregorian chanting** from their daily schedule and when it was re-instated the monks returned to their normal healthy vigor (cited in Campbell, pp. 103–104). Other experts who have studied the power of chanting have found that the resonance that chanting causes can stimulate and balance "the energies that generate wholeness—the integration of body, mind and spirit" (D' Angelo, p. 18). It should not be thought that only Gregorian chant encourages these benefits since overtone chanting which is used in Tibetan, Mongolian, Siberian, Buddhist and other cultures can be equally effective: "The great American anthropologist Weston La Barre singled out Tibetan overtone chanting as being one of the most powerful forms of ritual—and indeed **shaman**ic—vocal activity" (cited in Devereux, p. 41). It has been described as "magical voice technique" and as "chanting for psycho-physical trans-formation" (cited in Lee, p. 46). It has even been suggested that the reso-nance achieved in some Wester medieval buildings within the Christian **religion** may have achieved similar impacts (Dewhurst-Maddock, p. 89). Further connections can be found in the chanting of **mantras** as can be found in Zen and other practices (Campbell, 1993). The special-ist in ancient music, early Christian chant and acoustic archaeology, Iegor Reznikoff (1938–) draws attention to the power of chant when directed towards specific parts of the body and he promotes the natural sounds of resonance that were in use before the nineteenth-century equal tempera-ment system was introduced (Reznikoff, p. 17).

Campbell, Don (1993). Interview with Zen Master Seung Sahn conducted by Gary Moore. *Music: Physician for Times to Come.* Wheaton: Quest.
Campbell, Don (1997). *The Mozart Effect.* London: Hodder and Stoughton.
D'Angelo, James (2001). *Healing with the Voice.* London: Thorsons.
Devereux, Paul (2001). *Stone Age Soundtracks.* London: Vega.
Dewhurst-Maddock, Olivea (1993). *The Book of Sound Therapy.* London: Gaia.
Ennis, Giles (2002). "Sacred Breath, Sacred Chant." *Pagan Dawn* 142 (Spring).
Lee, Brian (n.d.). "Overtone Singing." *Caduceus* 39: 45–46.
Reznikoff, Iegor (n.d.). "Therapy of Pure Sound." *Caduceus* 23: 16–18.

Chaplin, Nelsa

Nelsa Chaplin (aka Christabel Portman) was "a highly trained clair-voyant of unusual sensitiveness who, since her earliest days, had been in close telepathic contact with Master Koot Hoomi" (Scott, p. 32). It was gen-erally believed that he was one of the mahatmas that inspired the found-ing of the Theosophical Society by Madame Blavatsky in 1875. Chaplin's musical gifts were, according to the composer **Cyril Scott**, particularly manifested in her **piano** playing when she was taken over by Koot Hoomi and would play **healing** music. She also instructed Scott how he could better serve the **Theosophy** cause through his own music so that "man-kind should be enlightened regarding the esoteric effects of music and its influence upon well-nigh every phase of civilization" (Scott, p. 36). Chap-lin experienced other mystical states undergoing **out-of-body experiences** (OOBEs) to aid her spiritual healing (cited in Summer, p. 27). Since her music was often of an improvisatory style it is not known whether any of it has survived for scrutiny.

Scott, Cyril (1969). *Music: Its Secret Influence Throughout the Ages.* London: Aquarian.
Summer, Lisa (1996). *Music—The New Age Elixir.* New York: Prometheus.

Chladni, Ernst

Ernst Chladni (1756–1827) was a German physicist and musician who discovered in 1787 that if he scattered fine sand onto a metal plate and then vibrated it with a bow for instance, then certain patterns were produced according to the musical harmonics created. The biologist Lyall Watson drew parallels between the patterns displayed and organic forms such as the concentric circles compared to rings in a tree trunk and vanishing spirals in the turrets of shellfish: "These resemblances between archetypal sound-forms and life-forms may not be without their significance" (Tame, pp. 216–217). The **Edinburgh**–based composer Stuart Mitchell believes that the mysteries surrounding the Rosslyn Chapel in Scotland may be uncovered by interpreting the carvings there as representations made by using "Chladni" patterns found in the study of **cymatics** (Allan, p. 42).

Allan, Brian (2006). "Rosslyn's Frozen Music." *Fortean Times* 212 (July): 42.
Tame, David (1984). *The Secret Power of Music*. Wellingborough: Turnstone Press.

Chopin, Frédéric

Frédéric Chopin (1810–1849) was a famous composer from the Romantic period in Western music. He was particularly known for his fine **piano** playing and compositions. He was frequently named by **musical mediums** as a source of their **inspiration** or contact. These included **Georges Aubert, Jesse Shepard, Charles Tweedale** and **Rosemary Brown**. He was also **channeled** by a medium investigated by the author and referred to as "W." Although his examples and Brown's showed some signs of Chopin's style in their composition, experts tended to agree that they were "a pale shadow of Chopin's original works" (private correspondence). Appearances of Chopin after his death have been somewhat rare, although he was said to have actually materialized at a concert of his music in Westminster Hall, **London,** according to the Wesleyan minister the Reverend Dr. Wiseman (Osborn, p. 593).

Chopin's inspiration was described by his lover George Sand as miraculous: "His [act of] creation was spontaneous, miraculous. He found it without seeking, without foreseeing it. It came on his piano, sudden, complete, sublime, or it sang in his head during a walk when he was in haste to let himself hear it by throwing it on to the instrument.... He shut himself into his room for days at a time weeping, walking up and down, breaking his pens, repeating or changing a measure a hundred times, writing it down and scratching it out as often, and starting again the next day with a desparate and exacting perseverance" (cited in Panati, p. 136). Alleged paranormal events centered on the memory of Chopin have been revealed by the pianist Byron Janis (2010) and, according to Lora Jones, he frequently saw ghosts during his life (www.youtube.com/watch?v=f6NRnQ6m3AA).

Janis, Byron (2010). *Chopin and Beyond*. Hoboken: John Wiley and Sons.
Osborn, Edward (1956). "Well-Known Musician Manifests." *The Two Worlds* 63 (March 4): 593.
Panati, Charles (1974). *Supersenses*. London: Jonathan Cape.

Church of the Blessed Virgin Mary

The church of the Blessed Virgin Mary at Oare in Somerset, England was the scene of inexplicable bell ringing which was heard by the brother of the Rev. H.J. Marshall, who on hearing the **bell** ringing went to explore and found the church door shut and "everything in order." He met a fellow clergyman on the way there who was believed to be the ghost of a previous incumbent who frequently greeted new occupants (McEwan, pp. 19–20).

McEwan, Graham J. (1989). *Haunted Churches of England*. London: Robert Hale.

Cicoria, Tony

Anthony Cicoria (1952–) is an American orthopedic surgeon who was struck by lightning in 1994. He slowly recovered from this and returned to his normal life. However, a few weeks later he had a sudden "insatiable desire to listen to **piano** music" (Sacks, p. 5) followed by a craving to play the music himself—notably **Chopin**. He had only received a few lessons as a child and teaching himself piano was very difficult. What happened next was that he started to hear music in his head which he felt the need to play … in his own words, "I was **possessed**" (Sacks, p. 6). Despite being divorced and also suffering in a bad traffic accident, he continued to hear and play music to a fanatical degree which seemed to have stemmed from his **near-death experience** (NDE). The neurologist Oliver Sacks questioned whether Cicoria's lightning strike might have initiated epileptic tendencies in his temporal lobes, but this verdict had too many unaccountable questions within it. His music is available on the CD *Notes from an Accidental Pianist (and Composer)* which includes Cicoria playing his "Fantasia, Op. 1" *The Lightning Sonata*. The music is similar to grand pieces composed during the Romantic nineteenth-century period. What is truly remarkable is how the music came into his head when previously he had not been particularly interested in such music.

Sacks, Oliver (2007). *Musicophilia*. London: Picador.

Cley Hill

Cley Hill, Warminster in Wiltshire, England, is the location of an Iron Age hill fort which may have been used in the past for pagan festivals. It has been reported (Underwood, p. 68) that on various dates during the year strange sights and the sounds of singing are heard with no obvious source. The area has also been cited as a UFO destination which might be connected to a Ministry of Defense barracks close by.

Underwood, Peter (1984). *This Haunted Isle*. London: Harrap.

Cole Mere

Cole Mere is a stretch of water situated in Shropshire, England, and it allegedly contains **sunken bells** that can be heard at various times. Evidently, they were deposited there during the English Civil war by Cromwellian troops during their general destruction of church property (cited in Willin, p. 133).

Willin, Melvyn J. (2005). *Music, Witchcraft and the Paranormal*. Ely: Melrose Press.

Colne Priory

Only a small part of the original Colne Priory in Essex, England, remains, but in the seventeenth-century part of the site was converted into living accommodation. It was said that at 2 a.m. a great **bell** could be heard when no such bell was present. The Cromwellian puritan colonel Richard Harlackenden was skeptical of the story, but it was written that he too witnessed the phenomena (Payne, pp. 99–100).

Payne, Jessie K. (1995). *A Ghost Hunter's Guide to Essex*. Norfolk: Ian Henry.

Coma States

A state of coma is when a person is unconscious and their brain is only operating at its lowest level of activity. Medical research suggests that hearing may still be operational and that music may be of assistance in bringing a patient back into a normal state of existence and it has been recorded that improvised wordless singing seems to be especially beneficial (Aldridge, pp. 345–346). In 1971 a surgeon at the North Middlesex Hospital in **London** used pop music to return two comatose patients to consciousness (cited in Playfair and Hill, p. 236) and Earl Spencer, the father of the late Diana, Princess of Wales, recovered from a coma after his wife played him a recording of "One Fine Day" from **Puccini**'s opera *Madama Butterfly* (Wilson, p. 175). However, a study to "determine whether a comatose patient responded differentially to four types of auditory stimuli—voices of family members and friends, classical music, popular music, and nature sounds" (Jones, pp. 164–171) concluded that responsiveness was greater with family and friends' presence than with the other sounds played.

Aldridge, David (1990). "Where Am I? Music Therapy Applied to Coma Patients." *Journal of the Royal Society of Medicine* 83 (June).
Jones, Rebecca, et al. (1994). "Auditory Stimulation Effect on a Comatose Survivor of Traumatic Brain Injury." *Archives of Physical Medicine and Rehabilitation* 75, no. 2 (February).
Playfair, Guy Lyon, and Scott Hill (1978). *The Cycles of Heaven*. London: Souvenir Press.
Wilson, Ian (1987). *The After Death Experience*. New York: William Morrow.

Combe Manor

Combe Manor in Berkshire, England, was listed in the Domesday Book of 1086 and was rebuilt in 1669. Its history as a priory may have led to the hearing of nuns **chanting** in the premises (Hippisley Coxe, p. 86). It is currently used as a grand wedding venue and there has not been any recent paranormal activity recorded.

Hippisley Coxe, Antony D. (1973). *Haunted Britain*. London: Pan Books.

Confucius

Confucius (551–478 BC) was China's most famous philosopher with wide-ranging thoughts and interests. He believed there to be a "hidden significance to music which made it one of the most important things in life" (Tame, p. 17) and that music was a "tangible force … to be capable of effecting change upon matter itself" (Tame, p. 17). Writing in the *Li Chi* (The Chinese Book of Rites) Confucius stressed that a civilization's harmonious state should be entwined with suitably harmonious music. Believing that "music acts directly on the mind without the medium of thought [he preached] Desire ye to know whether a land is well governed and its people have good morals? Hear its music" (Harrington Edwards, p. 146). No man was equipped to govern unless he could understand music (Hemenway, p. 116).

Harrington Edwards, John (1904). *God and Music*. London: J.M. Dent.
Hemenway, Priya (2008). *The Secret Code*. Lugano: Springwood.
Tame, David (1984). *The Secret Power of Music*. Wellingborough: Turnstone Press.

Cortachy Castle

Situated in the Angus region of Scotland lies the seat of the Earl of Airlie at Cortachy Castle and it is within this family that "music, like the wail of bagpipes and the beating of a **drum**, faint but definite, is said to herald the approach of the death of the head of the Airlie family and the ghostly Airlie drummer has been heard, it is claimed, for generations" (Underwood, p. 14). Lady Airlie informed the investigator Peter Underwood that the drummer had not been heard prior to the death of the last Lord Airlie in 1968. However, it was said that in 1881 the drum had been heard by Lady Dalkeith and Lady Skelmersdale about one hour before the death in America of the current Lord Airlie. From the numerous interpretations of the drumming which are recounted the most official would seem to be that which was conveyed to the author by the Factor of Lord Airlie himself in 1996:

> Legend has it that in the seventeenth century during one of the frequent clashes between the Ogilvy family and Clan Campbell, a Campbell drummer boy was sent to Cortachy under a flag of truce. He was immediately slaughtered by an Ogilvie of the time and hung out of an upper window in his own drum. The legend is that when the death of an Earl of Airlie is imminent, the drum will be heard, There is no record of it having been heard at any other time, but there is some anecdotal evidence that when the present Earl's grandfather was killed at the Battle of Diamond Hill in the South Africa War in 1900, the drum was heard by a member of the family, who was at that time a guest at Achnacarry Castle at Spean Bridge [private correspondence].

Underwood, Peter (1971). *Gazetteer of British Ghosts.* London: Souvenir Press.

Cotehele House

Cotehele House in Cornwall, England, dates from the fourteenth century and visitors have reported hearing "plaintive music" accompanied with a "herbal fragrance" in the oldest part of the house (Underwood, p. 20). In correspondence with the administrator the author was assured that "no such phenomena have ever been recorded here" (private correspondence).

Underwood, Peter (1983). *Ghosts of Cornwall.* Bodmin: Bossiney Books.

Crookall, Robert

Robert Crookall (1890–1981) was an English geologist who wrote numerous books about astral projection and **out-of-body experiences** (OOBEs). Some of his cases involved musical experiences which were reiterated in Scott **Rogo**'s **NAD** volumes. Case no. 123 related the vision of a tunnel and the sound of music being heard as well as perfume being smelled (cited in Rogo, p. 29) and Case no. 158 mentioned "there was also a swelling of beautiful music something like a pipe organ" (cited in Rogo, p. 30). His book *The Study and Practice of Astral Projection* (1960) drew particular attention to the etheric body as a further dimension from the physical body.

Crookall, Robert (1960). *The Study and Practice of Astral Projection*. London: Aquarian.
Rogo, D. Scott (1970). *NAD*. New York: University Books.

Crowley, Aleister

There has been much written about the notorious Edward Alexander Crowley (1875–1947) aka Aleister Crowley or "The Great Beast" and many other names, but it is not generally known that he was quite a fine musician and felt that music had an important role to play in his rituals and in life. There is a recording available of him singing a French song called "Vive la France" accompanying himself on the **piano** (youtube.com/watch?v=fl2_gATgT8s) and the violinist and **magic** assistant **Leila Waddell** (1880–1932) aka the "Scarlet Woman" played in his Rites of Eleusis at Caxton Hall, **London**, in 1910 (King, p. 2084). Crowley believed that "by the spell of his personality and force of his influence he could, where he thought it worthwhile, transform an average talent for any of the arts into veritable **genius**.... Leila Waddell was the example he selected to excel in the art of music" (Cammell, p. 137). Under the pseudonym Francis Bendick he wrote the poem *The Violinist* that suggests an altogether different interpretation of her playing: "Up went her **violin**, and the bow crossed it. It might have been the swords of two skilled fencers, both blind with mortal hate. It might have been the bodies of two skilled lovers, blind with immortal love. She tore life and death asunder on her strings. Up, up soared the phoenix of her song; step by step on music's golden scaling-ladder she stormed the citadel of her Desire. The blood flushed and swelled her face beneath its sweat. Her eyes were injected with blood" (writ-in-water.com/2014/01/01/the-violinist).

During Crowley's time in Zennor in Cornwall, England, he was joined by the English composer Peter Warlock (1894–1930) aka Philip Hesseltine at birth. He changed his name to reflect his interest in the occult and believed that supernatural beings were influencing his compositions. This may have been brought about by Crowley's over-indulgence of alcohol, **drugs** and sexual practices which he encouraged others to participate in (classicfm.com/discover-music/who-was-peter-warlock/).

Cammell, Charles Richard (1962). *Aleister Crowley*. New York: University Books.
King, Francis (1982). "The Wickedest Man in the World." *The Unexplained* 105. London: Orbis.

Crown Hotel

The Crown Hotel in Poole, Dorset, England, was the scene of various poltergeist happenings in the 1960s which included a single note being played on a **piano** when no one was near the instrument, witnessed by Paul Eeles, Malcolm Squire and Eric Dayman in June 1966. In reality this may have been a string either slipping or breaking inside the frame and there has not been any known recent paranormal activity there.

Moss, Peter (1977). *Ghosts Over Britain*. London: BCA.

Culcreuch Castle

Culcreuch Castle, Fintry, Scotland is a thirteenth-century castle that has been converted into a hotel. It has been written that "the wailing of pipes" is often heard in the dining room and in a bedroom known as the "Chinese Bird Room" (Mead, p. 51). The hotel literature mentioned that scientists had investigated the hotel in search of the "phantom piper," therefore in 1997 the author stayed two nights in the "haunted bedroom" with a colleague and did not witness anything other than the clanging of water pipes and the wind howling outside.

Mead, Robin (1994). *Weekend Haunts*. London: Impact Books.

Culzean Castle

Culzean Castle in Ayr, Scotland, was built in the eighteenth century and associated with the Clan Kennedy for many years. General Eisenhower stayed there many times in a luxurious flat presented to him (Underwood, p. 161). Tradition maintains that a phantom piper is heard playing when no such person is present. The administrator of the castle informed the author that no such manifestations had been witnessed in modern times (private correspondence).

Underwood, Peter (1993). *The Ghosthunters Almanac*. Orpington: Eric Dobby.

Cursed Operas

Many people will be aware of the supposed curse attached to Shakespeare's play *Macbeth*, but there are several operas that also have this unfortunate description applied to them. **Halévy**'s opera *Charles VI* was probably the most famous example, but other examples would include Verdi's *La forza del destino* after the baritone Leonard Warren died during a performance in 1960 at the Metropolitan Opera (operavivra.com/blog/opera-superstitions/) and an anonymous opera written about in 1936:

> In the early part of 1921 I began my career as a musician in cinema orchestras, and very soon learned of the baneful consequences which followed the playing of selections from a certain opera. Either the orchestra would be reduced, or a player would die, or the building be burnt to the ground. [He listed various other problems that he encountered when the music had been played.] I became interested in Spiritualism [and] I decided to ask the control what she thought of the superstition … [she replied] "it is purely the power of your thought—your own thought and belief and the thoughts of others." There was nothing in the playing of the music that could bring about such results, but as yet we realize little of what can be accomplished by mind as manifest in thought [Sadler, p. 424].

The first Metropolitan Opera production of the opera *The Makropulos Affair* by Leoš Janáček (1854–1928) had its opening night in January 1996, but it ended prematurely when the tenor Richard Versalle died on stage from a heart attack. Despite this the opera has not acquired a cursed status as yet.

Sadler, R. (1936). "The Fateful Opera." *Prediction* 9 (October).

Cymatics

"Cymatics" from the Greek for "wave" is the term used by Hans Jenny to describe "the power of sound to shape otherwise disorganized substances. Through Jenny's apparatus it is possible literally to *see* [sic] what one is hearing" (Tame, p. 217). The shapes encountered are very similar in some cases to those that appear in nature, as has been seen in the **Chladni** plates. Jenny makes his views clear about the significance of the designs in his influential book *Cymatics: A Study of Wave Phenomena & Vibration* (2001) and more recently Alexander Lauterwasser used the music of **Beethoven**, **Stockhausen**, the group *Kymatik* and overtone singing, to produce photographs of striking wave patterns reproduced in his book *Water Sound Images* (2007). It has been suggested that crop circles might originate from cymatic activity as the sound waves interacted with the physical crops, at least when not produced fraudulently. Many of the shapes are similar in design to those which Jenny discovered (Silva, pp. 15–16).

Jenny, Hans (2001). *Cymatics: A Study of Wave Phenomena & Vibration*. Macromedia Press.
Lauterwasser, Alexander (2007). *Water Sound Images*. Macromedia Press.
Silva, Freddy (2005). "Crop Circles … Created by Sound?" *Fate* (February): 12–21.
Tame, David (1984). *The Secret Power of Music*. Wellingborough: Turnstone Press.

Dagg Poltergeist

The Dagg family witnessed substantial poltergeist activity in 1889 on their farm in Clarendon, Quebec, Canada. Numerous townspeople also signed witness statements confirming the events that lasted for three months. The disturbing incidents centered upon an eleven-year-old adopted girl called Dinah McLean who attracted spontaneous fires, objects being thrown around and a mouth organ playing on its own. A deep gruff male voice, often using obscenities similar to the **Enfield poltergeist**, was heard when she was present (Wilson, pp. 97–101). The story was originally published by the *Ottawa Free Press* on November 25, 1889.

Wilson, Colin (1981). *Poltergeist! A Study in Destructive Haunting.* London: New English Library.

Dalberg, Friz

Johann Friedrich Hugo Freiherr von Dalberg (1760–1812) was a composer and churchman who was also supportive of the music theory of **Pythagoras** (Godwin, p. 177). He claimed to have experienced the **magic** of the "music of spirits" when the "Genius of Harmony hovered around my bed and whispered to me secrets of the higher mysteries of spiritual music…. It was a **dream**, but the remembrance of it still looms forth as though through a mist. The earthly veil fell from my eyes, I left the Earth behind, and was suddenly floating in the measureless spaces of the universe … and what magic filled my ears! The spheres turned with the most magnificent song" (cited in Godwin, p. 178). He also expounded on the inner states of "soul music."

Godwin, Joscelyn (1987b). *Music, Mysticism and Magic.* London: Arkana.

Dance

The subject of dance with its accompanying music is too vast to do justice to in this work. However, mention must be made of the range of music that is traditionally associated with dance in activities that occur beyond its normal practice of social enjoyment and lean towards its sacredness or mystical connotations. Gerald Gardner (1884–1964) the founder of so-called "Gardnerian **Witchcraft**" wrote about "Old Stone Age" hunters and drew attention to what he believed was their early dance and music practices:

Their chief form of worship was probably the dance, a group dance performed with fanatic fervours in a circle, for by the circles they made in the depths of the caves they evidently had the concept that a circle magically constructed conserves power. They probably had crude drums, and there is a cave painting in France of a man dressed in a bull's hide with horns, dancing and twanging the string of a small bow. It is probable that by a number of people twanging bow-strings they could produce a harp-like effect. It was probably a symbolic dance performed with wild abandon till they reached a state of ecstasy. To primitive people a dance is a prayer, by which they attain atonement with the gods [Gardner, p. 47].

The music of the "whirling" **dervishes** allows the dancers to achieve their spectacular hypnotic movements in what is undoubtedly an **altered state of consciousness**. The music associated with **voodoo** and **witchcraft** rites encourages trance-like states. **Shamans** from different cultures use music as an aid to their contact with spirits and Christian groups such as the Shakers and Holy Rollers were similarly motivated during spiritual revelations. Indeed, **religion**s of every manner would appear to place an importance on it in their rituals and supernatural attributes (Reik, pp. 295–297). **Tarantism** was responsible for the evolvement of the Tarantella dance which allegedly cured or was at least therapeutic in its treatment. The **drum** has long been associated with both supernatural practices as well as the perfect instrument to dance to because of its rhythmic pulse and often loud volume. Generally speaking, percussive instruments are the most common accompaniment and in the hands of skilled performers they can induce euphoric states that can take some people into realms that are beyond their normal existence ... an encounter with the gods? (Wosien, 1974).

Gardner, Gerald B. (1982). *Meaning of Witchcraft*. New York: Magickal Childe.
Reik, Theodor (1958). *Ritual*. New York: International Universities Press.
Wosien, Maria-Gabriele (1974). *Sacred Dance*. London: Thames and Hudson.

D'Aranyi, Jelly

Jelly Aranyi de Hunyadvár (1893–1966) was a Hungarian violinist and the great-niece of the famous violinist Joseph Joachim. She settled down in **London** and was quite famous in her own day as both a soloist and ensemble violinist. According to the Swedish diplomat Erik Palmstierna (1877–1959) d'Aranyi received contact from the spirit world concerning her performance of **Bach**'s "Sonata in E minor" which contradicted the edition she was using. She studied an original version of the sonata lent to her by a colleague at the Royal College of Music where she discovered that the advice that she had been given by the "spirit" was correct (Palmstierna, pp. 347–350). In 1933 she was contacted by the spirit of **Robert Schumann** via a ouija board. She was told to find and play a posthumous work for **violin** and **piano** which neither she nor her fellow musicians in London had any knowledge of. She returned to questioning the spirit of Schumann as to its whereabouts and made contact with the spirit of Joachim who indicated where the music was to be found—the Hochschule für Musik in Weimar. Palmstierna set about tracking the music down on a visit to Berlin and eventually found a hitherto unknown violin concerto in the archives belonging to the *Preussische*

Jelly d'Aranyi was contacted by the deceased composer Robert Schumann as to the existence of his lost violin concerto (Wikimedia Commons).

Staatsbibliothek. Further complications arose since Schumann's daughter had forbidden its publication and there were some contradictions, from the spirit, as to the key of the work. After further arduous negotiations and help from the spirit world, various scores were discovered, and she performed the work at its London premiere at the Queen's Hall on February 16, 1938. Considerable weight to the origin of her discovery was given by the music authority Professor Sir Donald Tovey who stated in *The Times* that "I assert my positive conviction that the spirit of Schumann is inspiring Jelly d'Aranyi's production of Schumann's posthumous violin concerto" (cited in *Psychic News*, p. 3). Jessica Duchen has written a novel about d'Aranyi which combines fact and fiction about her involvement with the concerto (Duchen, 2016).

Duchen, Jessica (2016). *Ghost Variations*. London: Unbound Digital.
Palmstierna, Erik (1937). *Horizons of Immortality*. London: Constable.
Psychic News (1969). "'Curious' Messages from 'Dead' Composers Puzzle Journalist." April 5.

Davenport, Ira and William

The brothers Ira Erastus Davenport (1839–1911) and William Henry Davenport (1841–1877), usually known as the "Davenports," were American magicians in the late nineteenth century specializing in illusions which typically took place inside a spirit cabinet. They toured the USA as well as England with seemingly spiritualistic phenomena involving the playing of musical instruments and their flight through the air while the brothers were tied-up in a wooden box: "As soon as the light was extinguished, a tambourine and guitar sailed across the room while a **violin** gently thrummed of its own accord" (Melechi, p. 208). There were contradictions concerning their claims of spiritual presences and most magicians believed them to fake their phenomena. A number of companies including Sylvestre's in Chicago and Gamage's and Hamley Brothers in **London**, produced catalogues of trick instruments and other devices that were for sale (Sylvestre, 1901) which included a trick guitar which played by itself and contained false panels for the concealment of props. Sometimes the staged performances were reported in detail: "The musical instruments were placed near them on a table, and the sitters joined hands. The moment the light was extinguished, the instruments while playing, flew about the room, circling

Ira and William Davenport were the brothers who entertained audiences far and wide with their musical exploits allegedly from the spirit world (Flickr/ Wikimedia Commons).

near the ceiling and floor and close to the sitters, who were touched by them and felt the strong currents of wind they made, for they moved with great velocity.... After a minute or so the light was turned up, when the mediums were found bound as before, and the musical instruments on the sitters' knees" (Campbell Holms, p. 331). The scientist Michael H. Coleman drew attention to the brothers' encouragement of a belief in their psychic powers in some circles and also quoted witnesses' disparaging comments about the music heard in their performances (Coleman, pp. 186–187).

Campbell Holms, Archibald (1925). *The Facts of Psychic Science and Philosophy*. London: Kegan Paul.
Coleman, Michael H. (1997). "Correspondence." *Journal of the Society for Psychical Research* 62, no. 849: 186–187.
Melechi, Antonio (2009). *Servants of the Supernatural*. London: Arrow Books.
Sylvestre, Ralph E. (1901). *Gambols with the Ghosts*. Spiritualistic Effects Catalogue.

Deathbed Music

A differentiation will be made here between deathbed music, when the percipient actually dies, and **near-death experiences** (NDEs), when the person close to death survives. Sometimes the music is only heard by the dying person and sometimes it is heard by all or some of the people gathered together. The music varies, but it is usually restful and concordant … possibly "angelic." Incidences have been reported in a number of different sources and these have also been repeated in other literature. Some cases have already been mentioned (see **Barrett**) which will therefore not be repeated here. A selection will be given and the reader is directed to the sources below for further examples.

The German writer Johan Wolfgang von Goethe (1749–1832) was on his deathbed when several people, including his daughter-in-law Ottilie, his copyist and a manservant, all claimed to have heard mysterious music which "resounded from above, as if they came from a higher world, sweet and prolonged chords of music which weakened little by little until they faded away" (cited in Rogo, p. 64). The music continued at irregular intervals until his death around midnight and no one ever discovered its origin. It was not mentioned whether Goethe also heard the music which was described as if it came from a **piano**, a choral **chant**, an organ or a concertina. In the case of Louis XVII, the dying child claimed to hear beautiful music, but the guard in attendance heard nothing (*Light*, 1921, April 30). Further cases were reported in James Hyslop's "Visions of the Dying" (Hyslop, 1918) which included **angels** singing and beautiful music being heard by the patient, but not those people in attendance. In a case described in *Light*, a Spiritualist publication, the patient heard "heavenly music" but not everyone present heard it (*Light*, 1921, 14 May) whereas everyone present heard what Scott **Rogo** called "transcendental music" in a case submitted by Professor Arthur Lowell in the same magazine (cited by Rogo, p. 74).

The Society for Psychical Research's monumental collection *Phantasms of the Living* (1886) contains many examples of deathbed music being perceived. An example which was given further clarity by the participants was:

> In 1870 I lost a dearly loved daughter, 21 years old; she died at noonday, of aneurism. At night, my only other daughter was with me, when all at once we both assumed a listening attitude, and we both heard the sweetest of spiritual music, although it seemed so remote, my ears were hurt listening so intently. Till some hours after, my dear girl and I were afraid to inquire of each other had we heard it, for fear we were deluded, but we found both had been so privileged and blessed.... Mr. Yates perfectly well remembers how myself and the daughter who is now living were affected by hearing music that night, such as mortals never sang.... I can speak with certainty respecting the beautiful music my dear mother and I heard on the 26th November 1870. I shall never forget it; we were both afraid to speak, it was so exquisite.... The two windows in the room were shut tight and fastened; and as near as I can remember, it must have been between 2 and 3 in the morning. The music lasted several minutes [*Phantasms of the Living*, p. 891].

Cases from the archives of the Society for Psychical Research are still investigated to this day and this was also true of another occurrence from the 1870s. A lady referred to as Mrs. Z. stated on her deathbed that she could hear heavenly music, which she believed was welcoming her to heaven, but she also recounted that she heard a specific voice singing which she recognized as Julia X. Colonel Z (Mrs. Z.'s husband) later checked with Julia X.'s husband who confirmed that she had not only died at the time Mrs. Z. had heard her voice, but also that she had been singing continuously until her actual death (Myers, p. 339). A Miss Emily Horne gave an account of hearing "the most divine music" which lasted for about two minutes. It was also heard by her two-year-old brother who was with her at the time. When they went to the room where a **piano** was kept nobody was there and she later discovered that an aunt had died in Natal at exactly the same time as the music was heard ... to the minute (Myers, p. 388).

Barrett, William (1926). *Death-Bed Visions*. London: Methuen.
Gurney, Edmund, Frederic W.H. Myers, and Frank Podmore (1886). *Phantasms of the Living*. London: Trübner.
Hyslop, James H. (1918). "Visions of the Dying." *Journal of the American Society for Psychical Research* XII, no. 10.
Light (1921, April 30). XLI, no. 2103.
Light. (1921, May 14). "Music Heard at Deathbeds."
Myers, Frederic W.H. (1903). *Human Personality and Its Survival of Bodily Death*. Vols. I and II. London: Longmans.
Rogo, D. Scott (1972). *NAD*. Vol. 2. New York: University Books.

Debussy, Claude

Claude Debussy (1862–1918) was a French composer who was influential in the creation of impressionist music. He was a chosen composer by **Rosemary Brown**, the **musical medium**, and one piece dictated to her (*Le Paon*) was scrutinized in the Music Department of the University of Sheffield where it was agreed by Professor Eric Clarke and the author that it was, at best, a pastiche of Debussy's work and did not sound authentic (private documents). He was however seriously involved with the occult according to the composer and Theosophist **Cyril Scott** who wrote that Debussy "introduced ancient Atlantean music into the modern age" and different claims suggested he was a "Grand Master" of the mysterious esoteric society the "Priory of Sion" (cited in Lachman, pp. 132–137).

Lachman, Gary (2002). "Concerto for Magic and Mysticism: Esotericism and Western Music." *Quest* 90, no. 4 (July–August): 132–137.

Denny Abbey

The ruins of Denny Abbey, near Cambridge, England, have long been thought to be the location for the mysterious **chanting** of plainsong (Harries, p. 69). The author met with a custodian of the property and was told that she and previous wardens had heard distant chanting which may or may not have been music travelling from surrounding areas. She also claimed that visitors had occasionally asked her where the music was coming from when they had heard it themselves. She was keen to explain how it could not have originated elsewhere (private correspondence).

Harries, John (1974). *The Ghost Hunter's Road Book*. London: Rupert Crew.

Dervishes

The Mevlevi order of whirling dervishes founded by Jalalu'didin **Rumi** (1207–1273) are followers of a **Sufi** spiritual path which is immersed in music, **dance** and ecstasy. "They are the ones … who make themselves as a medium of resonance of the music they hear. Therefore music touches them differently from any other person; music touches the depth of their being. Thus moved by music, they manifest different conditions … termed by Sufis *hal*" (Khan, p. 57). There is a belief that music is the "finest of arts [which] helps the soul to rise above differences" (Khan, p. 62) "for music helps to free the physical effort from conscious thought, since both mind and will must be suspended if ecstasy is to be attained" (Trimingham, p. 200). Through the teaching of **Hazrat Inayat Khan** (1882–1927) the mystical traditions of Sufi music and the power that it gives its practitioners has been made available in the West: "It is not ordinary music, this dervish music, it is music you drink with your whole body, your whole being, and you live this music" (Friedlander, p. 127). The power of the music with its associated trance state allows the dervishes to inflict "severe injuries upon themselves without pain or bleeding, then heal the wounds within seconds, leaving scarcely a scar" (Chambers, p. 45).

Sometimes the dervishes' music and dance performance is not the whirling that is expected, as was described by a reporter during an annual festival in Fez in Morocco:

> After about two hours, the older man, who had been constantly chanting the name of Allah, rose to his feet with two of the others. They took off their turbans and let down their incredibly long hair. Standing in a line holding on to each other, slowly they began to move their heads back and forth, gradually increasing the speed until they had joined the rhythm of the drums ... they were leaping and bending, twirling and chanting, eyes rolling and totally unaware of the audience ... spinning off on their own. The state of their ecstasy was electrifying. The old Sufi master guided his companions into states of contact with Allah through drums and chants ... where we lose all sense of this reality and "leave"

The **Whirling Dervishes dancing in an entranced altered state of consciousness in Konya on December 16, 2016, at the Mevlana Culture Center** (recai cabuk/ Shutterstock.com).

... I started to shake and tremble, my breathing quickened and I felt my heart bursting.... [Bamford, pp. 13–15].

Bamford, Deasy (2001). "Fez Festival of Sacred Music." *Kindred Spirit* 54 (Spring).
Chambers, John (1995). "Secrets of Self-Healing Dervishes." *Fate* July: 45–48.
Friedlander, Shems (1992). *Music by Nezih Uzel in The Whirling Dervishes.* New York: State University of New York Press.
Khan, Hazrat Inayat (1991). *The Mysticism of Sound and Music.* Boston: Shambhala.
Trimingham, J. Spencer (1973). *The Sufi Orders in Islam.* London: Oxford University Press.

Devil

Although the Devil is often thought of in terms of the personification of evil within a religious belief, this has not stopped him from exhibiting a contradiction of the spiritual, elevating experience that music can provide. "The Christian Fathers tried to stamp out of music all traces of its pagan influence and to give music a spiritually curative virtue" (Alvin, p. 13). "Diabolus in musica" (the triton) was generally condemned from at least the Middle Ages not only for its dissonant sound but also because it separated the two perfect intervals of the fourth and fifth which were used in organum (Reese, 1941). The Devil invented lewd songs and was joined by other members of his gatherings in their performance of "villainous musicke" playing a wide range of instruments—the pipes, tambourine, a "Jewes trump" and even "a horse's skull which he plays as a zither" (cited in Willin, pp. 44–45). The mesmerizing effect of the music on the assembled company was undoubtedly profound especially within the belief system of notably the sixteenth and seventeenth centuries. Fears about **witchcraft** and demonic activity were rife at the time. Robert Burns (1759–1796) sums up such activity in his fictional work *Alloway's Auld Haunted Kirk*: "At Winnock bunken in the East then sat Old Nick, in shape of beast; a towzie tyke, black, grim and large. To gie them music was his charge" (cited in Alvin, p. 14).

Alvin, Juliette (1975). *Music Therapy.* London: Hutchinson.
Reese, Gustave (1941). *Music in the Middle Ages.* London: J.M. Dent & Sons.
Willin, Melvyn J. (2004). *Music in Pagan and Witchcraft Ritual and Culture.* PhD Thesis. University of Bristol.

Devil's Trill Sonata

The Italian composer Giuseppe Tartini (1692–1770) allegedly wrote the "**Violin** Sonata in G minor" which is more commonly known as the *Devil's Trill Sonata*, after he had dreamed that the **Devil** had appeared at the end of his bed playing the trill that appears in the last movement of the sonata. The date of its composition in 1713 has been disputed by music scholars who suggest the more likely date of the 1740s (Holman, 1992). Tartini's account of the circumstances that led to its composition appears in J.G. de Lalande's *Voyage d'un françois en Italie* (Paris, 1769):

> One night I dreamt that I had made a bargain with the Devil for my soul. Every-thing went at my command—my novel servant anticipated every one of my wishes. Then the idea struck me to hand him my fiddle and to see what he could do with it. But how great was my astonishment when I heard him play with con-summate skill a sonata of such exquisite beauty as surpassed the boldest flight of my imagination. I felt enraptured, transported, enchanted; my breath was taken away; and I awoke. Seizing my violin I tried to retain the sounds that I had heard. But it was in vain. The piece I then composed, the Devil's Sonata, although the best I ever wrote, how far below the one I heard in my dream! [cited in Holman, 1992].

As to the veracity of the story Carl van Vechten wrote that "it was thought-ful of the devil to write this sonata in the style of the eighteenth century" (van Vechten, p. 556) presumably hinting that he did not believe the Devil had actually invaded Tartini's **dream**.

Holman, Peter (1992). "Notes on Sonata in G minor *Il trillo del Diavolo*." https://www.hyperion-records.co.uk/tw.asp?w=W9581.
Vechten, Carl van (1919). "On the Relative Difficulties of Depicting Heaven and Hell in Music." *The Musical Quarterly* 5, no. 4 (October): 553–560.

Dickmountlaw Farm

Dickmountlaw Farm lies quite close to the Scottish town Arbroath. It has been recorded that the sound of bagpipes can be heard from under-ground which people believe to be one Tam Tyre with his dog who were seeking shelter in a cave but were never seen again. It has been claimed that his pipes can also be heard from underneath the hearthstone at the farm (Hippisley Coxe, p. 178).

Hippisley Coxe, Antony D. (1973). *Haunted Britain*. London: Pan Books.

Didgeridoo

The didgeridoo is a wind instrument traditionally about one and a half meters long made from a hollowed-out tree—often eucalyptus—and it is strongly associated with the Aborigine population of Australia. It is played by blowing into one end and using circular breathing to maintain a continuous sound. It is said that "Music is spirit, spirit is music.... I knew that in playing and singing the old people did experience what they considered another dimension to reality" (Turner, pp. 35–50).

A firsthand experiment concerning the didgeridoo and a player (Jan) from Holland was undertaken by the author in 1996. Jan asked to be regressed since he believed he may have been an Aborigine in a previous life. During his regression he picked up and played his instrument and the session was recorded. He played without a break for about seventeen minutes and then was brought back to his normal waking existence. He realized he had been playing because his lips "tingled" but he could not remember anything else from the session. When listening back to the tape he was amazed at the sound he was making since, he claimed, that he was not physically able to play the didgeridoo in the way in which he was playing in his **altered state of consciousness** (personal notes/correspondence).

Turner, David H. (2000). "From Here into Eternity: Power and Transcendence in Australian Aboriginal Music." *Indigenous Religious Musics.* Ed. Ralls-MacLeod and Harvey. Aldershot: Ashgate.

Ditchfield, David

David Ditchfield was dragged under a moving train in February 2006 for some distance during which time he had a **near-death experience** (NDE). His injuries were substantial and life threatening. After a long period of recovery, the messages he believed he received from either his subconscious or "spirit" convinced him to initially undertake a painting of the visions and then express them with music. He had no experience of classical music, but he felt the music should be of an orchestral nature with a solo singer and finally he received the **inspiration** to compose the work which received its first performance in St. Ives, Cambridgeshire, England, in 2008. Ditchfield told the author, "An outside source guided me since I'm not classically trained" (private notes from interview May 8, 2009).

The music *The Divine Light* is available through *www.davidditchfield. co.uk.*

Dockacre House

Dockacre House in Launceston, Cornwall, England, has a reputation for **flute** music to be heard whenever a death is about to happen in the house (Underwood, p. 36). An actual flute housed there has been blocked up and turned into a walking stick. The author contacted one Mrs.

Buckridge who had owned the house for many years, and she replied that although she believed the house to be haunted, she did not believe in the music story (private correspondence).

Underwood, Peter (1983). *Ghosts of Cornwall*. Bodmin: Bossiney Books.

Drake's Drum

Sir Francis Drake (c. 1540–1596) was a notable character in British history, famous for sailing around the world and helping to defeat the Spanish Armada in 1588. Reportedly, on HMS *Royal Oak*, a victory **drum** roll was heard when the Imperial German Navy surrendered in 1918. The ship was then searched but neither a drum nor a drummer was found on board and eventually the phenomenon was put down to the legendary drum (*Folklore, Myths and Legends of Britain*, p. 161).

Folklore, Myths and Legends of Britain (1973). London: Reader's Digest Association.

Dreams

Dreams would seem to be an ideal way to make contact with the inner realms of the mind to allow unconscious revelations to materialize in which capacity they have been mentioned in several other sections of this publication. One such example concerns a daughter of Sir George Mackenzie who dreamed that while she was at a party, she heard a beautiful and quite complicated piece of music which she sought to write down on awakening. Because of her frail state this was not allowed, but some ten days later she experienced the same dream again during which she actually saw the musical notation and played it in the dream (Crowe, p. 37). A less well-known account where music has been forthcoming was described by Rahel Varnhagen (1771–1833) who spoke of one particular dream where the harmony was so overwhelming that she "wept, prayed, and cried out again and again: 'Have I not said that Music is God?'" (Godwin, p. 206). The psychical researcher Richard Hodgson (1855–1905) recounted a dream he had when he was eighteen or nineteen years old. The music he heard had such an effect on him that he "began to learn the **violin**" and practiced regularly for four years (Myers, p. 369). The composer Jonathan Harvey (1939–2012) wrote to the author about relying on dreams or meditation for ideas (private correspondence). In the world of pop music dreams have been the vehicle of **inspiration** for such musicians as Paul McCartney with "Yesterday," Jimi Hendrix with "Purple Haze" and Billy Joel with "The River of Dreams" (Cormier, 2016). The country singer Johnny Cash (1932–2003) recorded his dreams and after a vivid dream about a musical arrangement which was different to anything he had ever envisaged before (use of Mariachi **trumpets**) he issued what turned out to be a massive hit song "Ring of Fire." Further dreams and songs followed (Chaffin, pp. 54–55).

A formal study on music in dreams was conducted by Valeria Uga which found that "nearly half of the recalled music was non-standard, suggesting that original music can be created in dreams" (Uga, p. 351). The British cellist Steven Isserlis claimed that the composer **John Tavener** appeared to him in a dream after his death and conveyed information about a piece that was unknown to him at the time, which proved to be correct with further investigation (*Psychic News*, p. 7).

Chaffin, Kym (2008). "The Dream Life of Johnny Cash." *Fortean Times* 233 (March): 54–55.
Psychic News (2017). "Composer Sir John Tavener." July.
Crowe, Catherine (2000). *The Night Side of Nature*. Ware: Wordsworth Editions.
Godwin, Joscelyn (1987b). *Music, Mysticism and Magic*. London: Arkana.
Myers, Frederic W.H. (1903). *Human Personality and its Survival of Bodily Death*. Volumes I & II. London: Longmans.
Cormier, Roger (2016). https://www.mentalfloss.com/article/66007/15-songs-came-dreams.
Uga, Valeria, et al. (2006). "Music in Dreams." *Consciousness and Cognition* 15, no. 2 (June): 351–357.

Drugs

Discussing drugs within the realm of music and the paranormal poses many problems. The author and researcher Paul Devereux writes that the use of different drugs in the Americas generates different types of musical experience in rituals. For instance, ayahuasca involves singing, chanting and whistling, whereas the peyote cactus has horns, drumming and even the guitar attached to it (cited in Devereux, p. 38). The controversial writing of Carlos Castaneda (1925–1998) described a peyote "button" fueled experience when "I was able to detect a definite melody. It was a composite of high-pitched sounds, like human voices, accompanied by a deep bass drum" (Castaneda, p. 98). Undoubtedly people taking drugs or alcohol in sufficient quantities may well believe that they are perceiving music in new and possibly exciting ways, but in reality, this may not be so … or is it? For instance, the composer **Hector Berlioz** admitted to taking opium and the program attached to his *Symphonie Fantastique* does not hide this if one is to read autobiographical characteristics into it. However, does this mean again, for instance, that **Beethoven** would not have been able to write his masterpieces without consuming large quantities of wine? Is the human brain so burdened with technology, being methodical and analytical that it requires the stimulus of drugs or alcohol to activate the artistic and creative aspects that it contains? Similar to discussions about so-called left and right brain traits the answers are not straight-forward. An evasive answer to this question is perhaps that some people in some circumstances can access these **altered states of consciousness,** whereas others cannot respond in a similar way. Or putting it another way, different people, taking different drugs, have different experiences according to their bodies, minds and arguably their souls.

Castaneda, Carlos (1968). *The Teachings of Don Juan: A Yaqui Way of Knowledge.* London: Penguin.
Devereux, Paul (2001). *Stone Age Soundtracks.* London: Vega.

Drummer of Tedworth

Probably the most famous instance of inexplicable drumming was the phenomenon known as the "Drummer of Tedworth" (or Tidworth) which was described in a document first recorded by the Rev. Joseph Glanvill, a chaplain to King Charles II and a Fellow of the Royal Society, in 1666 known as *Saducismus Triumphatus: Full and Plain Evidence Concerning Witches and Apparitions* (Glanvill, 1681). He wrote that a beggar named William Drury annoyed the townsfolk of Ludgarshall near Tedworth in Wiltshire, England by constantly banging his **drum** and harassing the people. He was duly arrested and put in jail by the magistrate John Mompesson and his drum was confiscated and taken to the magistrate's house in Tedworth:

> Immediately poltergeist events broke out including the drum playing by itself.... Mompesson took the precaution of burning the drum, but the sounds of drumming continued to be heard including military tattoos and specifically the jig *Roundheads and Cuckolds go dig, go dig* ... the manifestations at Mompesson's house continued and the case became celebrated enough for a Royal Commission to be sent to investigate it, whereupon the disturbances ceased, only to return after the commissioners' departure. It appealed to the populace's imagination sufficiently for a broadside ballad to be published about it (Price, pp. 391–393). In 1716 Joseph Addison wrote a comedy about it called *The Drummer or the Haunted House* and in more recent times Edith Sitwell wrote a poem—*The Drum* [cited in Willin, pp. 144–145].

The fate of Drury was not known other than having been set free from jail, he re-offended and was sentenced to be transported, but he escaped before the punishment could be realized and he was not seen again.

Glanvill, Joseph (1681). *Saducismus Triumphatus: Full and Plain Evidence Concerning Witches and Apparitions.* London: Thomas Newcomb.
Willin, Melvyn J. (1999). *Paramusicology: An investigation of Music and Paranormal Phenomena.* PhD thesis. Music Department. University of Sheffield.

The Drummer of Tedworth. An early example of poltergeist activity involving drumming (Wikimedia Commons).

Drums

Drums play a prominent role in different aspects of anomalous music experience throughout the world both past and present.

Drum defines an instrument in which thin, strong material, usually animal skin, is stretched tightly across a frame to produce a percussive and resonating sound when struck either with hands or sticks. Drums are made of whatever materials are available and suitable.... Modern technology now provides us with fiberglass shells and plastic skins or even a little computer that can sound like different drums.

In the ten thousand years of its history the drum has spread all around the planet and evolved into many different shapes and sizes, like the up-to eighteen feet tall log drums of the New Hebrides and South Pacific, made of a hollowed tree trunk. The barrel shaped *dadaikos* of Japan can be so big that one could park a Ford Fiesta inside it. On the other hand there are small drums like the Tibetan *damaru*, often made of the upper halves of a male and female skull [Christen, p. 33].

There are many examples of them being heard when no such music should have been possible—notably at **Cortachy Castle**, **Herstmonceux Castle**, the Golden Hill Fort on the Isle of Wight, various **battlefields** and probably most famous of all the **Drummer of Tedworth**. However, their importance is amplified when they are said to possess fundamental paranormal qualities, such as has been claimed for **Drake's Drum** and for the royal sacred drum of the ancient kings of Buganda (a part of Uganda): "When it was first made and whenever it was given a new skin, the blood of the ox whose hide was used, was poured over it.... When the drum was beaten it was believed that the life and strength of this blood flowed into the king, renewing his power and authority" ("Drum," p. 725). Although the drum is used in **voodoo**, **witchcraft** and similar ceremonies, its importance is particularly stressed in the **shaman** ceremonies where it can even be used to travel on to supernatural realms: "It is used primarily, as a means of altering the consciousness of the shaman, to allow him or her to enter a trance state in which he or she can travel out of this world" (Matthews, p. 117). Between 1985 and 2010 *Shaman's Drum: A Journal of Experiential Shamanism* was published by the Cross-Cultural Shamanism Network in order to disseminate knowledge about the subject. In Lapland the drum was not only used for inducing trance, but also as a tool for divination. The Ashanti in Ghana use their drums for practical **dance** purposes as well as for enhancing a ritual to awaken the spirits. In short, they are "an effective bridge to the supernatural" ("Drum," p. 726). A survey that the author sent to practicing wiccans in 2004 asking about musical preferences in rituals received considerable support for drums and drumming: "generally a rapid, rather hypnotic drum beat [is chosen] ... which can be accompanied by dancing as well, helps one achieve a light trance state that can induce what Jung would call active imagining, visionary experiences etc ... rhythmic drumming and **chanting** can induce trance states in which spirits are seen and communicated with" (Willin, p. 131).

Christen, Thomas (n.d.). "The Drum—Heartbeat of Ancient and Modern Times." *Caduceus* 23: 32–35.
"Drum." (1970). *Man, Myth and Magic*. Drum. London: Purnell.
Matthews, John (1991). *The Celtic Shaman*. Shaftesbury: Element Books.
Willin, Melvyn J. (2004). *Music in Pagan and Witchcraft Ritual and Culture*. PhD thesis. History Dept. University of Bristol.

Duntrune Castle

Duntrune Castle is situated in Argyl, Scotland, and was the setting for a gristly tale concerning a piper who played to warn the Clan MacDonald of an attack by the Clan Campbell. He was caught by the enemy and his hands were cut off which was verified to some extent when a skeleton was unearthed there with all the fingers missing (Underwood, p. 164). Despite this his ghost was said to have continued playing there. The author received a letter from the owner of the castle who knew of the legend but had not experienced the music himself. He did mention that an **exorcism** had taken place there in about 1870 to dispel evil presences (private correspondence).

Underwood, Peter (1993). *The Ghosthunters Almanac*. Orpington: Eric Dobby.

Dunwich

Dunwich is now a small village on the coast in Suffolk, England. In the fourteenth century much of the much larger town was swept out to sea by a series of violent storms. Despite stories of "the sunken church **bells** ring to warn of impending storms" (Bord, p. 79), the curator of the local museum informed the author that he believed the tides might occasionally move any bells that may be below the sea resulting in the clapper striking the bell and causing a sound to be heard. He also commented that other churches along the coast might give the illusion of the sounds coming from below the sea.

Bord, Janet, and Colin (1990). *Atlas of Magical Britain*. London: Sidgwick & Jackson.

Dupuis, Jean

The strange story of the concert pianist Jean Dupuis (pseudonym) is told by William Seabrook in his book *Witchcraft: Its Power in the World Today* (1940). In chapter four, "Ten-cent-store Doll in France," it relates Seabrook's investigation with a French journalist Orlet (pseudonym) of a cursed doll that was used to dumbfound the growing career of Dupuis. After a disastrous performance when his fingers refused to work properly, they discovered a hidden doll dressed in evening clothes with its hands crushed in a carpenter's vice. This was the last straw in a number of occurrences that had plagued the pianist after he had started dabbling in esoteric matters. Unfortunately, Seabrook does not convey to his readership the outcome of these events or what happened to the doll.

Seabrook, William (1940). *Witchcraft: Its Power in the World Today*. New York: Harcourt Brace.

Eddy Brothers

The brothers William (1832–1932) [?] and Horatio (1842–1922) [?] Eddy were from Vermont and they claimed to have had psychic abilities from an early age. Inside a spirit cabinet William would claim that the spirits were playing a selection of musical instruments, notably the tambourine and the guitar, whereas Horatio was usually in sight. In 1874 Colonel Henry Olcott (1832–1907), a founding father of the Theosophical Society, investigated the brothers and was very impressed with them (Olcott, 1875). However, the psychical investigator Hereward Carrington (1880–1958) was highly critical and revealed how they managed their tricks in his book *The Physical Phenomena of Spiritualism* (Carrington, pp. 193–195). Sir Arthur Conan Doyle (1959–1930) wrote about the brothers in his two-volume books *The History of Spiritualism* (Conan Doyle, 1926) praising their **medium**ship.

Carrington, Hereward (1907). *The Physical Phenomena of Spiritualism*. Boston: Herbert B. Turner.
Conan Doyle, Arthur (1926). *The History of Spiritualism*. London: Cassell.
Olcott, Colonel Henry S. (1875). *People from the Other World*. Hartford: American Publishing Company.

Edinburgh

The capital of Scotland has numerous examples of anomalous music which includes the faint sounds of bagpipes sounding from a tunnel under Edinburgh Castle and after the Plague struck the city in 1645 much of what was Mary Kings Close was blocked off with new buildings being built in 1750 after a disastrous fire. A few years later **drums** were heard in the area playing what was thought to be an English march rhythm, but there was no English army near at the time. Just over one mile away from the castle is Charlotte Square where the faint sound of a **piano** has been heard when no such music was being played (Matthews, pp. 2–9).

Matthews, Rupert (1993). *Haunted Edinburgh*. Andover: Pitkin.

Elgar, Edward

It has not been possible to find any paranormal connections between the life's experiences or writings of Sir Edward William Elgar (1857–1934) and his fine **near-death experience** work *The Dream of Gerontius*. However, he did collaborate with the occultist Algernon Blackwood who wrote the novel *A Prisoner in Fairyland* which was subsequently turned into a play *The Starlight Express* with incidental music by Elgar. He regarded "himself as the medium—the all but unconscious medium by which they [his works] have come into being" (cited in Inglis, p. 64). It has also been recorded that Elgar's ghost can be seen at Fittleworth, where he spent his last days with his wife, and many local residents believe that his spirit still inhabits the area (Cuin, 2012). Furthermore, he was claimed to be in post-death contact with a musical **medium** investigated by the author (private correspondence).

Cuin, A.L. (2012). www.british-paranormal.co.uk › the-ghost-of-elgar-fittl.
Inglis, Brian (1987). *The Unknown Guest—The Mystery of Intuition*. London: Chatto &Windus.

Elm Vicarage

There is very little evidence for the **bell** that is meant to toll at this vicarage near Wisbech, Cambridgeshire, England. Allegedly a monk called Brother Ignatius failed to sound the warning bell to warn of an impending flood and many monks were subsequently drowned. The investigator Peter Underwood "found no records to establish this plausible story although there were many pointers to the present vicarage having been built on the site of an ancient monastery" (Underwood, pp. 67–73). He did manage to interview reliable witnesses who had indeed heard the ringing and there were other phenomena discovered of a non-musical nature.

Underwood, Peter (1996). *Guide to Ghosts & Haunted Places*. London: Piatkus.

Enfield Poltergeist

Between 1977 and 1978 extreme poltergeist activity was recorded at a council house in the **London** borough of Enfield. The manifestations seemed to be particularly attracted to a young girl, Janet, and to a lesser extent her sister Margaret. Detailed books about the phenomena have been written by psychical researchers including Playfair (2011) and Willin (2019). The entity that seemingly possessed Janet occasionally asked for music to be played—it had a preference for "jazz" and was also happy to sing childish songs using the harsh, gruff voice of the spirit of the old man that was having power over her. These recordings of much of the activity witnessed are in the archives of the Society for Psychical Research and are under the custodianship of the author.

Playfair, Guy Lyon (2011). *This House Is Haunted*. White Crow.
Willin, Melvyn J. (2019). *The Enfield Poltergeist Tapes*. White Crow.

Enticknap, Clifford

Clifford Enticknap (1950–2019) believed he was a **channel** for the music of **Handel**. He insisted that he had a long history of contact with Handel, having been developed on Atlantis where Handel was a great teacher called Joseph Arkos and "that prior to this he was on the planet Jupiter with some other 'great' composers" (cited in Willin, pp. 69–70). Enticknap also believed that he had been a female pupil of Handel in the eighteenth century which was confirmed to him by a medium. He wrote a very long—over four hours—oratorio called *Beyond the Veil* part of which was recorded by the London Symphony Orchestra with the Ambrosian Chorus and Leslie Fyson as the baritone soloist (*Spirits from the Past*, BBC 12 August 1980) which he financed himself. The music consists of a pastiche of Handel's style and the words are often very incongruous in their rhyme and meter: "One critic [Nancy Banks-Smith writing in *The Guardian*, August 13, 1980] compared them with the unfortunate poetry of William McGonagall, [displaying a] total lack of talent" (Picknett, p. 281).

Picknett, Lynn (1989). *Out of This World*. London: Macdonald & Co.
Willin, Melvyn J. (2005). *Music, Witchcraft and the Paranormal*. Ely: Melrose Press.

Entrainment

Possibly only on the borders of paranormality is the concept of musical entrainment, whereby independent rhythmic processes react together in seemingly mysterious ways. This is manifested in the coordination that can be witnessed between groups of musicians or dancers when they function together as a whole, but without an obvious attempt to do so.

The study of this phenomena has been researched at length by Martin Clayton, professor of music at Durham University, England (Clayton, 2012).

Clayton, Martin (2012). "What Is Entrainment? Definition and Applications in Musical Research." *Empirical Musicology Review* 7, no. 1–2.

Epilepsy

Musicogenic epilepsy is a rare form of complex reflex epilepsy with seizures induced by listening to music, although playing, thinking or dreaming of music have all been noted as triggers provoked by different musical stimuli in different people. Oliver Sacks devotes a chapter of his book *Musicophilia* to the subject (Sacks, pp. 23–29). Some report seizures according to the genres of music such as jazz, classical, choral or popular music. For others the trigger may be a particular type of instrument or a composer: "usually a complex piece of instrumental music in which many instruments are involved such as a dance band or a full orchestra" (Devereux, p. 60). Seizures are said to have been triggered by church **bells**, hymns or even the French national anthem (https://www.epilepsysociety.org.uk). Although it cannot be described as paranormal as such, its rarity and relative lack of understanding places it in the anomalous category. It would seem to be the opposite of the **Mozart Effect** when positive outcomes result from listening to music. "This rare phenomenon convincingly demonstrates that music has a direct effect upon the brain" (Storr, p. 35).

Devereux, Paul (2001). *Stone Age Soundtracks*. London: Vega.
Sacks, Oliver (2007). *Musicophilia*. London: Picador.
Storr, Anthony (1992). *Music & the Mind*. London: HarperCollins.

Ewloe Castle

Ewloe Castle is situated in Flintshire, Wales, and dates back to the thirteenth century. Its location, approached through woods via footpaths, lends itself to an eerie atmosphere. There are various phenomena attached to it including "ghostly singing" (Bord, p. 83). The paranormal investigator Tracy Monger claims to have heard "old-time music" during one investigation there with no obvious sound source discovered (tracymonger.wordpress.com).

Bord, Janet, and Colin (1992). *Modern Mysteries of the World*. London: BCA.

Exorcism

Many **religion**s use exorcism to drive out spirits or demons according to whichever religion is being advocated. In the West Christianity has often been shown to use the rites of exorcism when appropriate and after much investigation, but music has not been a feature of such ceremonies. However, in African and **voodoo** rites music and **dance** have been far more significant and arguably necessary. The ngoma healers in Tanzania use music when releasing patients from a spirit's spell: "The spirits like the music, so they may make themselves manifest.... Once the healer has established the type of spirit before him, in the person, he begins the corresponding type of music" (Janzen, p. 59). An example of an exorcism using music has been described from an eye-witness account [edited for conciseness]:

> In the hut, right in the centre, sits the patient.... The master of the proceedings, the *gobela*, holds in his hands his tambourine.... Several persons are gathered there, some with their tambourines, some with great zinc drums, others with calabashes filled with small objects, which are shaken and make a noise like rattles.... There is a frightful din which lasts through the night ... until the performers in this fantastic concert are overcome by fatigue. But this is only the orchestra, the accompaniment to which must be added, and it is of the greatest importance, singing, the human voice, the chorus of exorcists.... The melodies of these exorcists' incantations are of a particularly urgent, incisive, and penetrating character [cited in Oesterreich, pp. 140–141].

In voodoo, music and trance are a vital part of such ceremonies, which can be misunderstood by Western scientists who have been influenced by past exorcisms born of the demon mania of the Middle Ages. The concept of voodoo trance and exorcism are not fully understood: "C.G. Jung summarizes by saying that western science is still miles from interpreting and understanding these phenomena" (Chesi, p. 275).

Chesi, Gert (1980). *Voodoo: Africa's Secret Power*. Wörgl: Perlinger Verlag.
Janzen, John M. (2000). "Music in African Ngoma Healing." *Music Healing in Cultural Contexts*. Ed. Penelope Gouk. Aldershot: Ashgate.
Oesterreich, Traugott Konstantin (1930). *Possession: Demoniacal and Other*. London: Kegan Paul.

Fairy Music

It could be argued that fairy music is so entrenched in the world of folklore that it has no place in the current volume, but nevertheless there are many people who believe in the existence of these elementals and claim to have witnessed their music. Examples can be found from Loch Nell Castle and the Island of Skye (Hippisley Coxe, pp. 165–166); Glen Helen in the Isle of Man (cited in Godwin, p. 46) and many others. The parapsychologist Dr. Serena Roney Dougal felt the subject important enough to devote a whole chapter of her book *Where Science and Magic Meet* to the substance and significance of fairies, which includes several music examples, and the medieval historian Karen Ralls-MacLeod wrote about the enchanting music of the fairy **harp** being referred to by St. Patrick as having a suspicious "twang of the fairy spell" (Ralls-MaCleod, p. vi).

A converse explanation to the authenticity of fairy music was sent to

the author by Alastair McIntosh who related: "I frequently delight in playing my penny whistle in remote locations outside and often muse as to the
extent to which distant walkers will take it as evidence that the faeries are
still alive and well" (private correspondence).

Godwin, Joscelyn (1987a). *Harmonies of Heaven and Earth*. London: Thames and Hudson.
Hippisley Coxe, Antony D. (1973). *Haunted Britain*. London: Pan Books.
Ralls-MacLeod, Karen (2000). *Music and the Celtic Otherworld*. Edinburgh: Polygon.
Roney-Dougal, Serena (1991). *Where Science and Magic Meet*. Shaftesbury: Element.

Farinelli

Farinelli (1705–1782) was the stage name of Carlo Maria Michelan-
gelo Nicola Broschi, a famous Italian castrato singer with a phenomenal
vocal range. In 1737 during a visit to the court of Philip V of Spain he was
invited by the Queen to sing to Philip to try and relieve him of his melancholic condition which was having an adverse effect on the kingdom. Philip
was overcome by his singing and made a complete recovery—such was
the power of Farinelli's voice. The music historian Charles Burney (1726–
1814) related that Farinelli sang to the King the same songs every night for
ten years until Philip's death (Burney, p. 505). Two of these were "Pallido
il sole" and "Per questo dolce amplesso" by the composer Johann Adolph
Hasse (1699–1783).

Burney, Charles (1789). *A General History of Music, from the Earliest Ages to the Present
Period*. London.

Fludd, Robert

Robert Fludd (1574–1637) was an English medical doctor who wrote
several treatises devoted to music stressing harmony as being a means to
understanding the universe. He drew attention to the mysterious power of
music: "For music moves a body by setting in motion the airy nature, and
by purified air arouses the spirit and the airy bond of soul and body. And
music, by its virtue renders evil spirits more kindly.... There is therefore
no doubt that music can have the miraculous power of moving not only
common people but even the very princes" (Godwin, p. 146). His life and
studies coincided in many ways with that of **Johannes Kepler** (1571–1630)
notably in their study of and sometimes disagreement about the **music of
the spheres** (Aveni, pp. 91–97).

Aveni, Anthony (1996). *Behind the Crystal Ball*. London: Boxtree Limited.
Godwin, Joscelyn (1987b). *Music, Mysticism and Magic*. London: Arkana.

Flute

The flute in its various types seems to be a popular instrument for connections with paranormality and legends and there can be confusion when the word "pipe" is used in the same context. The Greek goddess Athene was believed to have invented the instrument, but beyond mythology it has been associated with the voices of spirits in a sacred scenario (Hays, pp. 435–453). The unknown source of flute music has been heard in country lanes around Liphook in Hampshire, England and a case was posted on the internet in 2020 which described in some detail an unnerving experience hearing flute music during the night, once again with no known source (lacunadaze www. reddit.com). "Piped" music has been heard in various other UK locations during the day when it has been thought to have had a calming effect (Smith, p. 53). It is often the chosen instrument when a suitable player is available, for neo-pagan rituals to communicate with nature spirits, which possibly links with a belief in Pan's mythological playing of the syrinx or panpipes (Willin, pp. 37–38). The traditional Japanese bamboo flute, the shakuhachi, also has musical superpowers attached to it. An early pioneer of Buddhism called Kakua enlightened the emperor with his playing of a melody (Berendt, p. 177). In Melanesia the sound of a bamboo flute is said to be the voice of the spirit in which the men of the tribe "feel a mystical identification" (Cranstone, p. 1799).

Berendt, J. (1987). *Nada Brahma: The World Is Sound*. London: East West.
Cranstone, Bryan A.L. (1970). "Melanesia." *Man, Myth and Magic*. Vol. 4. London: Purnell.
Hays, Terence E. (1986). "Sacred Flutes, Fertility, and Growth in the Papua New Guinea Highlands." *Anthropos* 81: 435–453.
Smith, Stuart (2001). "Pan Pipes?" *Fortean Times* 145 (April): 53.
Willin, Melvyn J. (2004). *Music in Pagan and Witchcraft Ritual and Culture*. PhD thesis. History Dept. University of Bristol.

Forrabury

Forrabury in Cornwall, England is the scene of another **sunken bells** report alleging that they sank into the sea during a storm and can be heard again whenever a storm is brewing. The investigator Peter Underwood claimed to have talked to people who also witnessed "phantom boats with phantom crews" in the same location (Underwood, p. 26).

Underwood, Peter (1983). *Ghosts of Cornwall*. Bodmin: Bossiney Books.

Fountains Abbey

Fountains Abbey in Yorkshire, England was founded in the twelfth century and functioned as a Cistercian establishment until the Dissolution of the Monasteries by Henry VIII in 1539. Its history of **chanting** being heard in the Chapel of Nine Altars is often mentioned in the literature (Hippisley Coxe, p. 136). The author received a letter from Mr. M. Newman, the Regional Archaeologist for the Yorkshire region, who informed him that "**Gregorian chant** is played through a public address system [which] is sometimes overlooked by some visitors" (private correspondence).

Hippisley Coxe, Antony D. (1973). *Haunted Britain*. London: Pan Books.

Fox, Virgil

Virgil Keel Fox (1912–1980) was a child **prodigy** and a flamboyant popular American organist who made many recordings. He believed that he saw an apparition of **Franz Liszt** and then received telepathic instructions from him concerning the performance and interpretation of an old organ score by Liszt that he was practicing on the organ at Saint Stephen's Cathedral in Vienna (cited in Klimo, p. 163).

Klimo, Jon (1987). *Channeling: Investigations on Receiving Information from Paranormal Sources*. Los Angeles: Jeremy P. Tarcher.

Friml, Rudolf

Charles Rudolf Friml (1879–1872) was a Czech composer and pianist who spent most of his professional career in the United States. He explained that when he worked at the **piano**, he let the spirit guide him and he didn't actually compose himself. He often started his concerts with improvisations, and he felt he was a tool that was being used to convey a musical message (Klimo, 1987). The psychologist Susan Blackmore wrote that he used a ouija board to "regularly" contact **Chopin** and other composers (Blackmore, p. 109).

Blackmore, Susan, and Adam Hart-Davis (1995). *Test Your Psychic Powers*. London: Thorsons.
Klimo, Jon (1987). *Channeling: Investigations on Receiving Information from Paranormal Sources*. Los Angeles: Jeremy P. Tarcher.

Fyvie Castle

Fyvie Castle is situated near Aberdeen in Scotland and was originally built in the thirteenth century. It is unusual in so far as the musical phenomenon attached to it is said to be the ghost of one Andrew Lammie who has been heard playing a **trumpet** there (Underwood, pp. 173–174). The story was preserved in a ballad collected by Francis James Child in the nineteenth century (Child, 1904).

Child, Francis James (1904). *English and Scottish Popular Ballads.* Ed. Helen Child Sargent and George Lyman Kittredge. Boston: Houghton Mifflin.
Underwood, Peter (1993). *The Ghosthunters Almanac.* Orpington: Eric Dobby.

Galli-Marie, Célestine

Célestine Galli-Marie (1837–1905) was a French operatic mezzo-soprano who premiered Pergolesi's *La serva padrona.* During the thirty-third performance in 1875 of the Bizet opera *Carmen* at the Opéra Comique in Paris, she became inexplicably anxious and in the third act, after Carmen foresees her own death in the "Card Trio," she collapsed backstage. She believed that something dire had happened and she learned the next day that Bizet had died that very night (Martin, 2011).

Martin, Gale (2011). https://operatoonity.com/2011/05/30/opera-and-premonition.

Ganzfeld

"Ganzfeld" is the German word for "complete field," and it is a type of experiment that is used in **parapsychology** experiments to seek evidence for extra sensory perception (ESP). Subjects are placed in a comfortable seated position with headphones playing white noise and a dim red light shining through protected eyes. Meanwhile a sender at a different location attempts to send to the receiver telepathically an image or, in the author's studies, a piece of music that has been randomly selected. There have been hundreds of different experiments with varying degrees of success (Honorton, 1977), but the music-based ganzfeld series of experiments was unique at the time of its first publication. In some trials a few individuals did seem to possess telepathic capabilities that allowed them to convey the essence of pieces of music between them. One such example involved the receiver feeling he was being "sent" music that was "serious … heavy orchestral … solemn … people standing together … revolution … powerful … crowds" (Willin, p. 41). The sender was attempting to send telepathically the "March to the Scaffold" from **Berlioz**'s *Symphonie Fantastique.* In another trial the receiver tapped out a rhythm which was very similar indeed to the rhythm that was being listened to by the sender (Willin, p. 44). The American parapsychologist Kathy Dalton conducted experiments using undergraduates

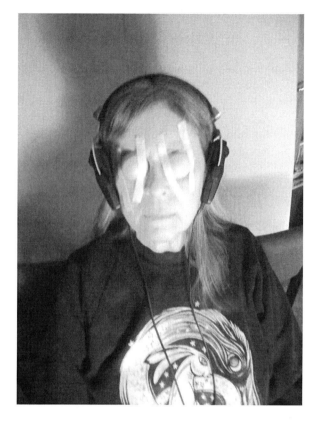

**Ganzfeld Experiment whereby telepathy is used in an altered state of conscious-
ness to "send" music to a distant participant (author's photograph).**

from the Juilliard School who obtained particularly high scores in her
ganzfeld studies (Dalton, 1997). It would seem from *some* of the results
that a few people have the capability to communicate with each other in a
non-physical way and that music can enhance this facility.

Dalton, Kathy (1997). "Exploring the Links: Creativity and Psi in the Ganzfeld." *Proceedings of
    Presented Papers: The Parapsychological Association 40th Annual Convention.*
Honorton, Charles (1977). "Psi and Internal Attention States." *Handbook of Parapsychology.*
    Ed. B.B. Wolman. New York: Van Nostrand.
Willin, Melvyn J. (1999). *Paramusicology: An Investigation of Music and Paranormal Phenom-
    ena.* PhD thesis. Music Department. University of Sheffield.

Genius

"Genius" is a word with multiple interpretations and definitions
according to different people, places and historical times. The musicologist

Wilfred Mellers (1914–2008) summed up its usage: "it is in the nature of a slippery subject that one cannot expect to know what one is talking about" (Mellers, p. 167). It possesses many of the attributes of **magic** within its scope, which, for the purpose of this entry, will only be explored from musical examples. **Mozart**'s precocity is often cited in the realm of the genius and **Beethoven**'s compositions seemed to combine the "laws of Nature and of the human psyche" (Mellers, p. 169) in ways which indicated an outstanding ability. Other forms of musical genius became close to madness as might be the case with **Schumann**; hypersensitivity in **Chopin** and performing prowess in **Liszt**'s character. **Wagner**'s prolific capability places him in this privileged company, but personal preferences inevitably arise. How can **Bach, Handel, Berlioz** or Schubert be excluded, and, within the realm of performers, the alleged feats of musical **savants** should surely also be included. Erich Wolfgang Korngold (1897–1957) was a composer noted for his film scores and as a child **prodigy** when he was known as the "little Mozart" (cited in Price-Heywood, p. 60). From within the pop and jazz culture many more names could probably be added all of whom are displaying talents which are beyond what might be called normal ability.

Mellers, Wilfrid (1989). "What Is Musical Genius?" *Genius. The history of an idea.* Ed. Penelope Murray. Oxford: Basil Blackwell.
Price-Heywood, W.P. (1913). "Musical Prodigies and Automatism." *Journal of the Society for Psychical Research* 16 (April).

Gershwin, George

George Gershwin (1898–1937) was an American pianist and composer who wrote the opera *Porgy and Bess* and the ever-popular *Rhapsody in Blue*. He claimed that he heard and even saw on paper the complete construction of the *Rhapsody in Blue* when he was on a train journey (Klimo, 314). **Rosemary Brown** and another **musical medium** investigated by the author both claimed that Gershwin was in touch with them from the spirit world, but it has not been possible to find any musical examples to compare with the music he wrote when he was alive.

Klimo, Jon (1987). *Channeling: Investigations on Receiving Information from Paranormal Sources.* Los Angeles: Jeremy P. Tarcher.

Ghosts

Ghosts is a composition by the Scottish composer Gordon McPherson (1965–) which came to fruition in a somewhat strange way. He received an award from the National Lottery fund through the Creative Scotland awards "for research that will lead to an orchestral suite on the paranormal" (Wojtas, 2003). He hoped to visit various haunted locations and to collect electronic voice phenomena which he would combine into an orchestral and electronic score. The work was finally performed as part of the *Plug Festival* in Glasgow in May 2007 and consisted of three works based on alleged paranormal experiences: a manifestation of **Chopin**; the Winchester Mystery House in the United States; and the electronic voice phenomena discovered in the "Spiricom" project (www.heraldscotland.com/news/12776802.plug-festival-mcphersons-ghosts-rsamd-glasgow/).

Wojtas, Olga (2003). "A Haunting Work Inspired by the Spirit of Chopin and Other Ghosts." *Times Higher Education Supplement* (July 26).

Gight Castle

The ruins of Gight Castle are to be found close to **Fyvie** in Scotland. The castle was built in the fifteenth or sixteenth century and passed through many owners before becoming derelict. There is a tradition that a piper can be heard playing there when no such person is present, but this has not been verified.

Folklore, Myths and Legends of Britain (1973). London: Reader's Digest Association.

"Gloomy Sunday"

The song "Gloomy Sunday" has attracted a number of myths to it so one must be cautious in providing any indisputable facts about it. It was possibly written by the Hungarian composer Rezső Seress and published in 1933 with lyrics either by him or László Jávor. Various English translations of the very depressing words were made, and the song was heard in Britain and the United States. It was allegedly associated with numerous suicides, and it has been written that "suicide is a motif found in many songs, and some research has suggested that the words of such songs may themselves contribute to suicidal feelings. Music is used in therapeutic settings because of its power to create positive emotions; the corollary must be that music also has the ability to arouse negative ones" (Kimberley, p. 37). It has been recorded by such diverse artists as Billie Holiday, Ray Charles, Elvis Costello, Marianne Faithfull and John Williams in an instrumental arrangement for the film *Schindler's List*. An orchestral version was recorded by the Boston Chamber Orchestra for the film score of

The Tenants Downstairs (multiple sources). Jávor's translated version of the lyrics include gloom-laden statements about tears, sorrow, forever sad and death.

Kimberley, Christopher (2008). "Gloomy Sunday." *Fortean Times* 236: 36–37.

Gnawa

Gnawa music is played by a Moroccan brotherhood of initiates who "consider music as essential to the revelation of the universe ... songs, instrumental music and **dances** are signs and symbols of a whole web of knowledge and ideas, and dictate a series of mystical techniques" (Shiloah, p.71). Listening to music played on the gumbri—a long-necked three-stringed lute—allows the "souls to be caught in a lake of allusions" (Shiloah, p. 71). The music is used in **healing** and **exorcism** rites.

Shiloah, Amnon (2000). "Jewish and Muslim Traditions of Music Therapy." *Music as Medicine.* Ed. Peregrine Horden. Aldershot: Ashgate.

Grant, Joan

Joan Marshall Grant Kelsey (1907–1989) was an English author and firm believer in **reincarnation** who became famous through her historical novel the *Winged Pharaoh* (1937) which was judged to be an accurate historical account of ancient Egyptian history and practices despite her having no previous knowledge of it. On one occasion a professor of engineering at Cambridge University (C.G. Lamb) and a friend of Joan's grandmother (Jennie) told Joan that Jennie could have been a great pianist. Joan claimed that she had given her lessons in a previous existence, and she played a piece which had a profound effect upon him: "Only one copy of that music ever existed.... I happen to know that the manuscript of that music, together with several other manuscripts of similar value, was burned two years before you were born" (Stemman, p. 129).

Stemman, Roy (1989). "The strange history of Joan Grant." *Out of This World.* London: Macdonald.

Great Leighs

The village of Great Leighs in Essex, England attracted the attention of the famous investigator Harry Price in 1944 when he was informed that the church **bells** had tolled inexplicably; the bell ropes had played reversed chimes; the church clock was malfunctioning, and a host of agriculturally based incidents had occurred that had baffled the farmers and locals. There was other disruption that strongly hinted of poltergeist activity. Price visited the area on October 11, 1944, having been contacted by *The Sunday Pictorial* the week before. After learning of the removal of a large stone that had allegedly been placed over the burial site of the witch of Scrapfaggot Green, Price advised the replacing of the stone to its original position, whereupon the phenomena ceased.

Price, Harry (1993). *Poltergeist*. London: Bracken.

Gregorian Chant

Gregorian **chant** was named after Pope Gregory I (c. 540–604 CE) who allegedly received the music from the Holy Spirit, symbolized by a dove sitting on his shoulder and communicating with him. In reality he and others probably brought together a vast amount of plainsong chant over a period of many centuries which was disseminated throughout the Christian

Gregorian Chant notation with illumination from an original source housed in the Convent of St Claire in Carmona, Spain (Joaquin Ossorio Castillo/ Shutterstock.com).

Church (Le Mée, pp. 48–50). Many claims have been made for its power over the human psyche and its ability to prolong the sense of space and time. Its reverberation, notably in massive Gothic cathedrals, can promote **altered states of consciousness** from the listeners. Furthermore, there are claims of its actual ability to heal as in the example of the **Tomatis** investigation of the Benedictine monks' depression and as a specific physiological health aid in "slowing down the rate of breathing and thereby slowing down the heart. It follows that a reduction of blood pressure occurs during the chanting" (Weeks, p. 48).

Le Mée, Katharine (1994). *Chant.* London: Rider.
Weeks, Bradford S. (1993). "The Physician, the Ear and Sacred Music." *Music: Physician for Times to Come.* Ed. Don Campbell. Wheaton: Quest Books.

Gurney, Edmund

Edmund Gurney (1847–1888) was an English academic who studied at Cambridge University and was the joint founder of the Society for Psychical Research with Henry Sidgwick and Frederic W.H. Myers in 1882. After studying classics and medicine he studied music before turning to psychical research. His *The Power of Sound* (1880) was an important work on the aesthetics of music and although not containing examples of paranormality it undoubtedly affected his later investigations and research into the subject.

Edmund Gurney was a founding member of the Society for Psychical Research and a musician (courtesy Mary Evans Picture Library).

Gurney, Edmund (1880). *The Power of Sound.* London: Smith, Elder.

Hálek, Václav

Hálek Václav (1937–2014) was a Czech composer who had the undoubtedly paranormal capability of being able to hear music emanating from mushrooms! He believed it was a spiritual experience as he tuned into them, hearing each mushroom's individual music. Some of his works include *Mushrooms for 'cello* and works for **piano**, clarinet, **trumpet**, etc. He has given interviews about his gift (youtube.com/watch?v=pEEgCQ-J0Gck) and believes "all of us have a special gift; it's just a matter of finding out what it is" (*Fortean Times*, p.10).

Fortean Times (2004). "Mushroom Melodies." 190 (December): 10.

Halévy, Fromental

Jacques-François-Fromental-Élie Halévy (1799–1862) was a French composer who wrote the opera *Charles VI* in 1843. It attracted the reputation of being cursed after one tenor aria "God punish him and strike him low" was immediately followed by the death of a stagehand; a member of the public; and a member of the orchestra on successive nights. The opera was withdrawn only to be revived by Napoleon III in 1858, but when he narrowly escaped death on the night before the planned performance, it was taken off the repertoire (Brookesmith, p. 85).

Brookesmith, Peter, ed. (1984). *Incredible Phenomena*. London: Orbis.

Hallucinations

The word "hallucinations" or specifically "musical hallucinations" could be used to describe many of the phenomena that are described in this book. The music psychologist Diana Deutsch provides an informative and concise derivation of the word and its associations: "The term *hallucination* is derived from the Latin word *alucinari* or *hallucinari*, meaning 'to wander in the mind,' 'to talk idly,' or 'to rave.' The word was used imprecisely for centuries to refer to illusions, delusions, and related experiences. It was not until the work of the French psychiatrist Jean-Etienne Dominique Esquirol in the early nineteenth century that the word came to signify a definite sensation when no external object capable of arousing that sensation was present" (Deutsch, p. 137). Indeed, a major work published by the Society for Psychical Research in 1894 devoted to paranormal phenomena was entitled a *Census of Hallucination*. However, the modern implication of illusion in witnessing sights and sounds which are not actually present does not apply to that work, but more an exploration of the phenomena to discover what sources the manifestations might come from. The word is used in this respect throughout and should not necessarily imply that the phenomena heard did not have a tangible presence even though many definitions would oppose this interpretation (Smith, p. 153; *Science Daily*, 2000).

The neurologists Jules Baillarger (1846) and Wilhelm Griesinger (1867) published information about the hallucinatory experience, but much of the interest in the subject was concealed as people were worried about being branded insane. Other researchers claim to have confirmed the region of the brain and condition that causes this rare and bizarre disorder (American Academy of Neurology, 2000). Professor Anthony Gordon, the Chair in Anaesthesia and Critical Care at Imperial College, **London** concluded that musical hallucinations "arise in people with hypersensitive or diseased ears, irrespective of whether they occur in fever, delirium, mental illness, hyperventilation, hangover, drug-taking, before or after sleep, during sensory isolation, in mystics etc." (Gordon, pp. 11–22). Music psychologists provide their own interpretations of the phenomena, but research would suggest that listening to popular music might decrease the auditory hallucinations in schizophrenics, as was suggested in a study by Gallagher et al. (Gallagher, pp. 67–75). **Dreams** and hypnagogic states would also seem to be conducive to musical hallucinations.

Many examples of phantom music can be found in a number of key sources. Notably Scott **Rogo**'s **NAD** books (1970; 1972); ***Phantasms of the Living*** (1886); and *Musicophilia* (2007) by Oliver Sacks. The latter devotes a complete chapter to such phenomena and describes cases from a personal viewpoint involving the perception of such diverse music as tunes from *The Sound of Music*, "Michael, Row Your Boat Ashore," "O Come All Ye Faithful" and "Frère Jacques" (Sacks, pp. 49–86). On other occasions the descriptions of the music heard can be very vague, as in the case of Mary Jobson when numerous people heard "beautiful music" during a period of sixteen weeks (Crowe, p. 319) and the case of two women walking near a lake in Ireland in the last century when they heard very loud music that terrified them to such an extent that they ran out of the fields they were in to escape it. They also claimed that despite there being no wind, the trees bent under its force (Meddop, 179–180). An example of phantom singing was recounted from Paris when a woman heard "beautiful **chanting**" in the church "La Madeleine," but no one else present could hear it. She remembered the tune sufficiently to write it down and publish it (O' Sullivan-Beare, p. 235). Solo chanting was heard by two ladies when they were alone on Glastonbury Tor as well as "the sound of a thin shrill voice responding to the tones of the priest" (*Two Worlds*, p. 215). When they descended passers by denied hearing any such sounds, but it was noted that the date of the occurrence was May 30—the traditional date of the death of the legendary King Arthur. Mr. Eric Williamson from Devon, England heard a brass band playing in 1916, when no one else present could hear it (MacKenzie, pp. 83–84).

Sir Ernest Bennett recounted several rectory or churchyard haunt-ings, which he referred to as poltergeist phenomena, including musical manifestations being heard. Case no. 10 from 1889 described an unspeci-fied churchyard in Scotland where a genuine witness, referred to as "J. L. B.," heard music coming from the churchyard from an unknown source on more than one occasion. He later discovered that it had also been heard by "Sir Y. Z." and "Lady Z." "In the last case the music resembled that of a choir, unaccompanied by instruments. In my case there was nothing resembling vocal music" (Price, pp. 311–312).

The composer **Schumann** was especially prone to such musical hallu-cinations which varied from being "angelic" to "demonic" (cited in Sacks, p. 51) and the Russian pianist Sviatoslav Richter (1915–1997) constantly heard a violent recurring musical phrase which was based on the dimin-ished seventh chord (Monsaingeon, 2001). The music of the American composer Charles Ives (1874–1954) has been said to be hallucinatory in nature, but, as far as it is known, he did not admit to such experiences him-self. There are many examples of such activity in the lives of saints, mystics and other people with deeply held religious convictions. Many **near-death experiences** involving musical phenomena have also been designated as hallucinatory which is also true of the many accounts of such phenom-ena to be found in haunted churches, castles and stately homes etc. (Wil-lin, pp. 146–188).

The public continues to recount examples up to the present time: "five of us heard a female singing, which was a new activity in an area being renovated. At the end of the night, we were outside about to leave and we all heard old style music, sounded like it was coming from the roof. We checked everywhere and the music was not coming from else-where. The museum was empty at the time" (private correspondence). Another example was reported by a gentleman in 2003 who wrote that he kept hearing "country and western music and 60s pop music" which he would normally listen to. His wife could not hear the music and he had no idea where it was coming from (private correspondence, September 2020). A lady suffering from tinnitus wrote of her relief at hearing "orchestral music" for a few weeks which was so loud that she initially thought it was coming from the street outside, it gradually died away in time leaving her with the unpleasant tinnitus condition (Murkoff, p. 26). Other examples have included "hearing the *Harry Lime* theme music"; organ music; and singing all occurring when nobody was obviously producing the music themselves.

Perhaps one has to decide for oneself whether musical hallucina-tions are simply conjured up from the internal workings of the mind or brain or whether they have an external source which might be natural, like nearby music being played, or paranormal whereupon there is no such source.

American Academy of Neurology (2000). "Rare Hallucinations Make Music in the Mind." *Science Daily*, 9 August. www.sciencedaily.com/releases/2000/08/000809065249.

Crowe, Catherine (2000). *The Night Side of Nature*. Ware: Wordsworth Editions.

Deutsch, Diana (2019). *Musical Illusions and Phantom Words: How Music and Speech Unlock Mysteries of the Brain*. New York: Oxford University Press.

Gallagher, A.G., T.G. Dinan, and L.J.V. Baker (1994). "The Effects of Varying Auditory Input on Schizophrenic Hallucinations: A Replication." *British Journal of Medical Psychology* 67: 67–75.

Gordon, Anthony G. (1997). "Do Musical Hallucinations Always Arise from the Ear?" *Medical Hypotheses* 49, no. 1: pp. 11–22.

MacKenzie, Andrew (1987). *The Seen and the Unseen*. London: Weidenfeld and Nicolson.

Meddop, John (1922). "Correspondence." *Occult Review* XXXVI, no. 1 (July): 179–180.

Monsaingeon, Bruno (2001). *Sviatoslav Richter: Notebooks and Conversations*. Trans. S. Spencer. Princeton: Princeton University Press.

Murkoff, Mrs. B. (1994). "Beautiful Music, but from Where?" *Enigmas* (November–December).

O'Sullivan-Beare (1921). "Psychic Music." *Occult Review* XXXIII, no. 1 (January): 235.

Price, Harry (1993). *Poltergeist*. London: Bracken Books.

Sacks, Oliver (2007). *Musicophilia*. London: Picador.

Smith, J. David (1992). "The Auditory Hallucinations of Schizophrenia." *Auditory Imagery*. Ed. Daniel Reisberg. Mahwah: Lawrence Erlbaum.

"The Two Worlds." (1928). *Marvellous Music Mystery* 41 (April 6): 215.

Willin, Melvyn J. (1999). *Paramusicology: An Investigation of Music and Paranormal Phenomena*. PhD thesis. Music Department. University of Sheffield.

Halpern, Steven

Steven Halpern (1947–) is an American New-Age mind-body-spirit composer and musician. His preferred instrument is the electric **piano,** and his prolific output strives to provide **healing** which is frequently linked to the chakras. His breakthrough came about with his album *Spectrum Suite* in 1976 and his "Music for Mindfulness. Inner Peace Music" concept continues to flourish with many soundtracks available to purchase. Some of his claims to bring "relief to the stress and strain of our 20th Century lifestyle" (publicity flyer) have been strongly opposed by experienced music therapists such as Lisa Summer: "This 'Halpern Effect' as Halpern modestly labels it, is in actuality nothing more than pressing the vibrato button on his Fender Rhodes and turning a control that determines the extent of the vibrato to near maximum … nor was he the first nor will he be the last to make use of this much-overused, trite sound effect. His claim that the vibrato in his pieces is produced by elaborate preparations or mysterious unknown forces is simply bomphilogy. Perhaps Halpern discovered the 'Halpern Effect' in his laboratory … or lavatory" (Summer, pp. 182–183).

Summer, Lisa (1996). *Music—The New Age Elixir*. New York: Prometheus Books.

Hampton Court Palace

Hampton Court Palace is situated in a **London** borough, and it was built for Cardinal Wolsey around 1515 who rose to power in the reign of Henry VIII. It has been claimed that the palace is haunted by numerous ghosts and specifically "the sound of **piano** playing from empty rooms" is said to be heard (Underwood, p. 124). The Deputy Curator, Works of Art informed the author that he did not know of any musical phenomena in the Palace (private correspondence).

Underwood, Peter (1984). *This Haunted Isle*. London: Harrap Limited.

Handel, George Frideric

George Frideric Handel (1685–1759) was a German composer who spent a considerable amount of time in England where he became famous for his oratorios, operas and orchestral works. He was also an accomplished organist. His best-known oratorio *Messiah* was composed in about three weeks during which he believed that he was dictated the music from God rather than creating it himself (cited in Tame, p. 16). Handel allegedly contacted both **Rosemary Brown** and **Clifford Enticknap** from the spirit world and provided them with new musical works.

Tame, David (1994). *Beethoven and the Spiritual Path*. Wheaton: Quest Books.

Harmful Music

If, as is generally believed, music has therapeutic properties which can help cure illnesses and enhance **healing**, then it is possible that it can also do harm in equally mysterious ways. The power of music to overwhelm self-control and leave the listener open to the sinister designs of the hypnotizing musician has proved highly influential in culture, literature and politics in a number of very different contexts (Kennaway, 271). The Duchess, in *The Duchess of Malfi* (1614) by John Webster, is tortured by "musical madmen" one of whom sings "O let us howle some heavy note" (Eubanks Winkler, p. 114) whereby they "infect their courtly auditors." There are examples of music inducing epileptic seizures (cited in Sacks, pp. 18–22) and actual fear in musicogenic **epilepsy** (Sacks, pp. 23–29). Melancholic music such as "**Gloomy Sunday**" can arouse suicidal thoughts and martial music has long been used to rouse warriors to battle. Roberto Assagioli identifies music that "arouses the instincts and appeals to the lower passions" as likely to produce

"injurious effects," as is music that is melancholy and depressing (Assagioli, 2010). When rhythm and volume combine with **dance** a frenzy can be
achieved which might be harmful to physical or mental health to an abnormal degree and, when not fully understood, to possibly a paranormal extent.
Sonic warfare with its uses and abuses of infrasound does not have specific
musical criteria, but nevertheless shares some of its attributes concerning
volume, timbre, pitch and rhythm (Sargeant and Sutton, pp. 30–33).

Assagioli, Roberto (2010). "Music as a Cause of Disease and as a Healing Agent." Chapter
    7, Center for Awakening's Psychosynthesis Program. Psychosynthesis Wisconsin. 29
    December.
Eubanks Winkler, Amanda (2006). *O let us howle some heavy note*. Bloomington: Indiana
    University Press.
Kennaway, James (2012). "Musical Hypnosis: Sound and Selfhood from Mesmerism to Brain-
    washing." *Social History of Medicine* 25, no. 2 (May): 271–289.
Sacks, Oliver (2007). *Musicophilia*. London: Picador.
Sargeant, Jack, and David Sutton (2001). "Sonic Warfare." *Fortean Times* 153 (December):
    30–33.

Harp

There are many folk legends attached to the harp and its music has
been popular as a source of musical **hallucination** in numerous locations including the castles at **Inveraray** and **Culcreuch** in Scotland and
as an instrument with **magical** powers in *High Magic's Aid* (Gardner, 117).
Since before the Renaissance period the harp or lyre has been identified
as a chosen instrument for **angels** to be seen playing in church decoration. The reasons for this are unknown other than the **Bible** mentions
the harp, albeit not in connection with angels, but the belief in the "Harmony of the Spheres" with its resonant sounds may have been prompted
by the resonance that abounds in harp music. It is highly unlikely that the
lyre of the Greek god Apollo or the dwarf-like Egyptian god Bes, found
its way into church decoration. The harp has been used extensively in
the field of music-thanatology which is a part of palliative care for the
dying. It is a musical/clinical practice that unites music and medicine
via the harp and voice. A music-thanatologist provides music that is tai-
lored to each specific physical, mental and emotional situation and can
help to ease symptoms of pain and anguish (www.mtai.org) (chaliceof-
repose.org). The work of Therese Schroeder-Sheker (1950–) was par-
amount in the inauguration of this **therapy** (Schroeder-Sheker, 1991,
pp. 7–8) and claimed that St. Patrick's Hospital in Missoula, Montana,
"is the only hospital in the world with twenty-seven harps and resident
singing-harpists—in-training" (Schroeder-Sheker b, p. 25). (Also see
Schroeder-Shecker c, pp. 21–26).

Gardner, Gerald Brosseau (1999). *High Magic's Aid*. Thame: I-H-O Books & Pentacle.
Schroeder-Sheker, Therese (a) (1991). "The Luminous Wound." *Caduceus* 14 (Summer): pp. 7–8.
Schroeder-Sheker, Therese (b) (n.d.). "Music for the Dying." *Caduceus* 23: 24–27.
Schroeder-Sheker, Therese (c) (n.d.). "Anointing the Dying with Sound." *Caduceus* 40: 21–26.

Harpham

Harpham is a small village in Yorkshire, England which is the home to the "Drummer Boy's Well." The legend concerns a drummer boy called Tom Hewson who was allegedly either murdered there or accidently killed by a member of the St. Quintin family to obtain the land from William the Conqueror. Since that time the sound of a **drum** has been heard coming from the well whenever the head of St. Quintin family is about to die (Hippisley Coxe, p. 135).

Hippisley Coxe, Antony D. (1973). *Haunted Britain*. London: Pan Books.

Harriet G.

Harriet G., whose real name is not known, was a musical **savant** who was described in 1970 as "a forty year old, single, Italian woman who had been known as 'mentally retarded' all her life" (Viscott, p. 495). At an early age she achieved a remarkable level of musical ability by the age of four being able to play a range of orchestral instruments and possessing perfect pitch, despite not being able to talk until she was nine or having personal hygiene capability. She could read music and had a "prodigious memory" for music and other non-musical numerical feats (Treffert, p. 22–23). What makes her case beyond the normal, even for a musical savant, was the fact that "having attended every concert of the Boston Symphony Saturday evening series for well over two decades. She knows the name, age, address, family structure, indiscretions, marital problems, and personal musical history of every member of the entire orchestra. She rhapsodizes over conductors and can trace their musical genealogy back a hundred years" (Treffert, p. 23). Her practical musical skills were phenomenal being able to play the **piano** in the style of different composers, transpose pieces, improvise with variations, add ornamentation characteristic to the composers concerned and most amazing of all improvise in the style of two different composers simultaneously ... one with the left hand and the other with the right hand (Treffert, pp. 23–24).

Treffert, Darold (1986/2006). *Extraordinary People: Understanding Savant Syndrome*. Rev.d ed. Lincoln: Universe.
Viscott, David, S. (1970). "A Musical Idiot Savant." *Psychiatry* 33/4: 494–515.

Hastings Castle

Hastings Castle was built a few miles from where the famous Battle of Hastings took place in 1066. There are numerous ghosts associated with it, but the musical example consists of organ music that has frequently been heard there (Underwood, p. 91). The author has visited the site on several occasions and not witnessed anything himself. Battle Abbey was built very close to the actual site and a nocturnal investigation by a Mr. Vane-Pennell and his sister was rewarded with the sound of a man's voice singing part of the "Gloria in excelsis" and the appearance of an unknown "cowled monk" (O' Donnell, p. 140).

O'Donnell, Elliott (1939). *Haunted Churches*. London: Quality Press.
Underwood, Peter (1971). *Gazetteer of British Ghosts*. London: Souvenir Press.

Healing

"Music is the greatest power I have ever experienced. I doubt if anything else equals its power to act upon the human organism" (Tame, p. 158). The examples of the power of music to heal in currently little known and possibly paranormal ways is vast and several books have been devoted to the subject in their own right (Horden, 2000). A complete edition of the magazine *Caduceus* (no. 23, n.d.) is devoted to the subject and draws attention to such diverse aspects as music for the dying; music at the **deathbed**; music **therapy**; and "resonances of the cosmos." Although some aspects of therapy are seemingly anomalous the examples mentioned here will be more direct and arguably spectacular in their impact. The belief system of the patient must play a role in the treatment when witch doctors and **shamans** use **magic drums** to play over the patient.

Faith healing is one aspect that seems to provide many examples of varying veracity and durability in the success of the cure, but often with only a limited musical input. The animal magnetism practiced by Franz Anton **Mesmer** (1734–1815) used his own music and that of **Mozart** as an accompaniment to his treatments. However, the direct influence of music upon the body has been researched as far back as the ancient Greeks and probably before then. Indeed, the word *music* itself is derived from the Greek *mousike* covering a wider range of subjects than the word implies today. It should not be forgotten that the god Apollo was the god of music and medicine, and his son Asclepius is the traditional patron of medicine to this day. **Martianus Capella** provided some precise information as to how to cure various ailments: "The ancients were able to cure fever and wounds by **incantation**. Asclepiades healed with the **trumpet** patients who were stone death, and Theophrastus used the flute with mentally disturbed patients. Is anyone aware that gout in the hip is removed by the sweet tones of the aulos?" (Godwin, pp. 41–42). Many of the Greek discoveries were then followed up by the Arab nations in the following times. "Some physicians in antiquity thought that the peculiar sound vibrations produced by the **flute** could affect man's body, independently from the emotions.... Suitable music, especially played on the zither, was recommended during meals to help the digestion" (Alvin, p. 41).

The Christian belief system was suspicious of the direct healing suggested, unless a spiritual and Christian viewpoint was present, and illnesses such as **tarantism**, with a possible musical cure, bordered on pagan practices to be condemned. Nevertheless, bands of musicians were employed throughout Italy and Germany to try and quell the violent disease. From the Renaissance onwards more medical practitioners became interested in the healing powers of music (Alvin, p. 45) and increasingly there was research into the purely physiological effect of music. In *Medicina Musica* one reads that singing "influences the motion of the heart, the circulation of the blood, the digestion, the lungs and breathing" (Browne, p. 12). In more recent times J. Dogiel (cited in Campbell, p. 3) published studies describing experiments where music affected blood circulation in 1830 and Antoine Joseph "Hector" Chomet wrote the treatise *The Influence of Music on Health and Life* in 1846 which was presented to the Paris Academy of Sciences. Rodolph Radau quoted Baptista Porta (1540–1615) in 1872 "according to whom a flute of hellebore cured dropsy; a flute of poplar wood sciatica; while a pipe of cinnamon wood was a sovereign remedy for fits of fainting" (cited in Diserens, p. 79). [Diserens' book includes a particularly useful bibliography of articles and papers devoted to the subject up to the 1920s.]

After the conclusion of the two World Wars the research into music and medicine was given a considerable boost by the first publication in English with a range of contributors devoted to the subject namely *Music and Medicine* (Schullian and Schoen, 1948). Moving further into the twentieth century one has to tread carefully with some of the claims that have been made for miraculous cures often using New Age music as the source of treatment: "To my surprise I found music healers making extraordinary claims such as the ability to cure cancer with 'subsonic frequencies' ... or to end obesity with music that utilized 'Pythagorian intonation' ... New Age music healers have created amongst themselves a philosophy which lacks clarity and logic" (Summer, back cover). However, it might be upheld that generally speaking New Age practitioners use music to promote positive well-being, inspired by the natural sounds of nature such as the songs of whales or the sea (Drury and Tillett, p. 149).

The author Barbara Hero has used the ratios of **Pythagoras** to process his knowledge into actual music "to bring the individual into harmony with the universal energies" (Hero, p. 15). Singing has even been classed as "one of the most intimate forms of alchemy that we can ever experience" (Gilchrist, p. 14) and it has been suggested that **Baroque** music may have also been inspired by it (Singer, p.69). However, the results that have come about through use of the **Mozart Effect** and in particular Mozart's **piano** sonata K448, have been studied by academia and have been somewhat positive (Browne, 2001). Don Campbell (1946–2012) first drew attention to the effect which had originally been explored by **Alfred Tomatis**. He listed the ways in which music with certain characteristics, which could often be found in **Mozart**'s music, might be used for the assistance of physical ailments:

> To slow down and equalize brain waves.
> To improve respiration.
> To improve the heartbeat, pulse rate and blood pressure.
> To reduce muscle tension and improve body movement and
>   coordination.
> To affect body temperature.
> To increase endorphin levels.
> To regulate stress-related hormones.
> To boost the immune system.
> [Campbell, pp. 65–85].

Joint research was undertaken between American and English medical institutions which raised "the tantalizing possibility that music and emotional self-management may have significant health benefits in a variety of clinical situations in which there is immune-suppression and autonomic imbalance" (McCraty et al., pp. 167–175). Neither should one ignore the huge amount of research that has also been undertaken into the healing effects of music on the minds of patients suffering mental problems details of which were illustrated as early as 1904 (Harrington Edwards, pp. 165–191). This broader treatment of music and healing was encompassed in a symposium on "Music, Healing and Culture: Towards a Comparative Perspective" held in **London** in August 1997 which led to a book devoted to the subject (Gouk, 2000). There have also been claims that music has been efficacious in restoring consciousness in **coma** patients. Serious research in the twenty-first century has found that the use of music during operations has lessened or, in some cases, replaced the need for anesthetic (Conrad, pp. 1980–1981) and at the very least it has eased post-operative trauma (Hole, pp. 1659–1671). The surgeon Ralph Spintge has conducted invasive and very painful operations without anesthetic on patients who have seemingly felt no pain, which have been filmed as evidence (Robertson, 1996). He has also written about the field as a whole and as a joint editor, commissioned other experts' comments (Spintge and Droh, 1985). With these advances in the understanding of the musico-medical phenomena it is likely that what, in the past, would have been firmly in the realm of the paranormal, will be understood further and advanced into a more normal reality.

For examples of further clinical trials see:

Alvin, Juliette (1975). *Music Therapy*. London: Hutchinson.
Browne, Anthony (2001). "Mozart sonata offers hope to epileptics." *Observer*, 1 March.
Browne, Richard (1729). *Medicina Musica*. Nottingham: John Crooke.
Campbell, Don (1993). *Music: Physician for Times to Come*. Wheaton: Quest Books.
Campbell, Don (1997). *The Mozart Effect*. London: Hodder & Stoughton.
Chomet, Hector (1875). *The Influence of Music on Health and Life*. New York. G.P. Putnam's Sons.
Conrad, Claudius (2010). "The Art of Medicine Music for Healing: From Magic to Medicine." *The Lancet* 376 (11 December): 1980–1981.
Cotoia, Antonella, et al. (2018). "Effects of Tibetan Music on Neuroendocrine and Autonomic Functions in Patients Waiting for Surgery: A Randomized, Controlled Study." *Anesthesiology Research and Practice* 2018, Article ID 9683780, 8 pages. https://doi.org/10.1155/2018/9683780.
Diserens, Charles M. (1926). *The Influence of Music on Behavior*. Princeton: Princeton University Press.
Drury, Nevill, and Gregory Tillett (1997). *The Occult: A Sourcebook of Esoteric Wisdom*. New York: Saraband.
Gilchrist, Cherry (n.d.). "The Alchemy of Voice." *Caduceus* 19: 14–15.
Godwin, Joscelyn (1987b). *Music, Mysticism and Magic*. London: Arkana.
Gouk, Penelope (2000). *Musical Healing in Cultural Contexts*. Aldershot: Ashgate.
Harrington Edwards, John (1904). *God and Music*. London: J.M. Dent.
Hero, Barbara (n.d.). "Healing with Sound." *Caduceus* 23: 12–15.
Hole, Jenny, Martin Hirsch, Elizabeth Ball, and Catherine Meads (2015). "Music as an Aid for Postoperative Recovery in Adults: A Systematic Review and Meta-Analysis." *The Lancet* 386 (24 October): 1659–1671.
Horden, Peregrine, ed. (2000). *Music as Medicine*. Aldershot: Ashgate.
McCraty, Rollin, Mike Atkinson, Glen Rein, and Alan D. Watkins (1996). "Music Enhances the Effect of Positive Emotional States on Salivary IgA." *Stress Medicine* 12: 167–175.
Mitchell, L.A., and R.A.R. Macdonald. (2006)."An Experimental Investigation of the Effects of Preferred and Relaxing Music Listening on Pain Perception." *Journal of Music Therapy* 43, no. 4: 295–316.
Robertson, Paul (1996). *Music and the Mind*. Three-part series for Channel 4 (UK). May.
Schullian, Dorothy M., and Max Schoen (1948). *Music and Medicine*. New York: Henry Schuman.
Singer, André, and Lynette (1995). *Divine Magic*. London: Boxtree.
Spintge, Ralph, and Roland Droh (1985). *Music in Medicine*. Basel: Roche.
Summer, Lisa (1996). *Music—The New Age Elixir*. New York: Prometheus Books.
Tame, David (1984). *The Secret Power of Music*. Wellingborough: Turnstone Press.

Herstmonceux Castle

Herstmonceux Castle, in East Sussex, England, was built in the fifteenth century and has a drumming legend attached to it involving a giant man beating a **drum** through "The Drummer's Hall" (Underwood, p. 94). The author received a letter from the Operations Director of the castle denying any known reports of musical phenomena there (private correspondence).

Underwood, Peter (1971). *Gazetteer of British Ghosts*. London: Souvenir Press.

Hoax

Intentional hoax is always a factor that must be taken into account whether reports of paranormal activity involve music or otherwise. There are several reasons why people might want to deceive investigators. These include skeptical motives—wanting to dupe people to show their naivety; purely for mischievous reasons—"a bit of fun"; possible financial reward, for instance, the author was offered money to confirm an alleged haunting which he refused; loneliness—wanting the company of investigators; seeking fame—being named in newspapers or other media outlets. The tenth letter of Sir Walter Scott relates one such example where an officer of the hussars offered to stay in the haunted room of a Hungarian castle after a celebratory evening there:

> He had not slept an hour when he was awakened by a solemn strain of music.... Three ladies, fantastically dressed in green, were seen in the lower end of the apartment, singing a solemn requiem ... at length he tired.... The major began to grow angry ... he said "I must consider this as a trick for the purpose of terrifying me, and as I regard it as an impertinence, I shall take a rough mode of stopping it." With that he began to handle his pistols ... "I will but wait five minutes." The ladies sang on ... he fired both pistols against the musical damsels—but the ladies sang on! The trick put upon him may be shortly described by the fact that the female choristers were placed in an adjoining room, and that be only fired at their reflection thrown forward into that in which he slept by the effect of a concave mirror [Scott, pp. 225–226].

Modern-day safeguards usually involve setting traps by means of audio-visual equipment as well as being highly observant of the whereabouts of people when the phenomena is claimed to occur. To give one example ... the investigator Peter Underwood was informed by several investigators that they had witnessed "paranormal music" from a house in England and he decided to investigate. He visited the house and met its single occupant, a male widower. Underwood heard the music himself but discovered that a hidden remote system had been set up in the house which the owner was activating whenever he wanted to. He had enjoyed the company of visitors and the fun in the process (Underwood, p. 10).

Scott, Sir Walter (2001). *Letters on Demonology and Witchcraft*. Ware: Wordsworth.
Underwood, Peter (1996). *Guide to Ghosts & Haunted Places*. London: Piatkus.

Home, Daniel Dunglas

Daniel Dunglas Home (1833–1886) was a Scottish medium who moved at an early age to America. During his eventual travels around Europe and America his fame escalated since he produced a wealth of different paranormal phenomena usually in lighted conditions. He did not charge for these **séances**, but he received gifts wherever he went. The phenomena he produced included: raps, objects moving including a **piano** and table with people sat on it, changes in items' weight in his presence, light effects, sounds and music as well as the playing of an accordion and other instruments with only one hand touching them, handling hot coals without ill effects, bodily elongation and **levitation**. The accordion was not the chromatic keyboard type of instrument that one is accustomed to seeing today, but rather a fairly small concertina-like instrument with a limited range of notes. He was researched by Lord Adare and the physicist Sir William Crookes, among others, both of whom witnessed remarkable musical feats and the former saw him levitate out of a window. Crookes was particularly impressed with him and devoted a large collection of writings about his investigations (Medhurst, 1972). Music was often heard in Home's company that had no known source:

> [The accordion] was held suspended in the cage by one of Home's hands extended over and resting upon the upper wire of the cage. This was under the table, but in such a position that the company could witness all the proceedings; Professor Crookes' assistant being permitted even to go under the table and give an accurate report of what was going on. In this position there was first the regular accordion movements and sounds with the instrument suspended from Home's hand; then it was taken out and put in the hand of the next sitter, still continuing to play; and finally, after being returned to the cage it was clearly seen by the company generally, moving about with no one touching it [Britten, p. 147].

Further musical manifestations were reported consisting of songs being played on the accordion without Home's hand touching it including "The Last Rose of Summer" and "Home Sweet Home" (Britten, pp. 143–144). In a New York conference the distinguished Judge Edmunds witnessed a guitar playing by itself in a well-lighted room:

> The guitar, at a distance of five or six feet from the party, was played upon exquisitely, and for several minutes, by some power other than that of anyone bodily present. The instrument was partly in shadow and the hand that swept the strings could not be seen, but the music was surpassingly beautiful. It was of a character entirely new to those who listened, and was sweeter, softer, and more harmonious than anything I have ever heard. Portions of it were filled with a certain soft melody that seemed to be the echo of other music far away, and

for the exquisite sweetness of which there are no words…. They could see him [Home] clearly and he had not been involved, so far as they could tell, in the mysterious playing [Edmunds, pp. 46–47].

Possibly the most dramatic performance of music being played on the accordion was recounted by William Crookes's wife Ellen on March 9, 1893:

The accordion was immediately taken from his [Home's] hand by a cloudy appearance, which soon seemed to condense into a distinct human form, clothed in a filmy drapery, standing near to Mr. Home between the two rooms. The accordion began to play (I do not remember whether on this occasion there was any recognized melody), and the figure advanced towards me till it almost touched me, playing continuously. It was semi-transparent, and I could see the sitters through it all the time … as it was giving me the accordion I could not help screaming. The figure immediately seemed to sink into the floor to the waist, leaving only the head and shoulders visible, still playing the accordion, which was then about a foot off the floor. Mr. Home and my husband came to me at once…. [cited in Medhurst, pp. 219–220].

There was the possibility that he used trick instruments since they were available at the time and the skeptic James Randi suggested Home could have played a small harmonica concealed under his moustache (Randi, p. 159). The author has tried this without any success at all, but it has been suggested that a suitable instrument may have been invented prior to Home's demonstrations (Coleman, p. 187). Stage conjurors have pointed out that the accordion could have been attached to "a loop of catgut, by which means Home could turn the accordion round. There was also on the market a self-playing accordion" (Pearsall, p. 88). It has also been stated that Home used powers of suggestion to influence his sitters (Brandon, pp. 268–269), but this implies that literally hundreds of people over several years were all subject to this deception without realizing it. The controversy concerning Home has continued unabated and despite a few claims of fraud which have not been validated, he remains one of the most important mediums in the realm of music and its paranormal demonstrations (Lamont, 2005).

Brandon, Ruth (1984). *The Spiritualists*. London: Weidenfeld and Nicolson.
Britten Emma Hardinge (1884). *Nineteenth Century Miracles*. Manchester: William Britten.
Coleman, Michael H. (1997). "Correspondence." *Journal of the Society for Psychical Research* 62, no. 849: 186–187.
Edmunds, I.G. (1978). *The Man Who Talked with Ghosts*. Nashville: Thomas Nelson.
Lamont, P. (2005). *The First Psychic: The Peculiar Mystery of a Notorious Victorian Wizard*. London: Little, Brown.
Medhurst, R.G. (1972). *Crookes and the Spirit World*. London: Souvenir Press.
Pearsall, Ronald (1973). *The Table-Rappers*. London: BCA.
Randi, James (1995). *The Supernatural A-Z*. London: Headline.

Daniel Dunglas Home was the most famous medium of the nineteenth century and he was never discovered cheating despite his miraculous feats both musical and otherwise (courtesy Mary Evans Picture Library).

Accordion allegedly used in D.D. Home's séance which is housed in the library of the Society for Psychical Research in London (author's photograph).

Hope House

Hope House is an early nineteenth-century impressive private house situated in Little Burstead, a small village in Essex, England. Near to the time of Christmas in 1951 a Mr. B. Murray heard a **piano** playing without anyone touching it there and he also reported a **bell** sounding unaccountably (Payne, p. 38).

Payne, Jessie K. (1995). *A Ghost Hunter's Guide to Essex*. Norfolk: Ian Henry.

Houdini, Harry

There is not an obvious connection between Harry Houdini (1874–1926) (born Erik Weisz) and paranormal music. Indeed, he devoted most of his working life to proving the lack of basis for paranormality within **Spiritualism** and was well aware of the numerous trick instruments that were available at various outlets at the time. Ten years after his death a "final" séance was held publically by the medium Dr. Edward Saint and Houdini's widow "Bess" which failed to conjure up his spirit. In 2015 the composer Jay Capperauld wrote *Houdini's Death Defying Spectacular* for chamber orchestra & multimedia which includes a recording of the actual final séance (jay-capperauld.com/).

Husk, Cecil

Cecil Husk (1847–1920) was an English professional singer and a member of the famous Carl Rosa Opera Company. He started to lose his sight and turned to mediumship believing himself to be psychic. Husk manifested materializations as well as causing a zither to play by itself in **séances** and produced an "astonishing volume" when singing both bass and tenor through his control's voice called "Uncle" (Fodor, pp. 177–178). During one séance he not only manifested **Liszt** through his **piano** playing but also Napoleon III (Betteley, p. 438).

Betteley, W. Ravenscroft (1888). "Remarkable Materialization and Musical Phenomena." *The Medium and Daybreak* (July 13): 438.
Fodor, Nandor (1934). *Encyclopedia of Psychic Science*. London: Arthurs Press.

Hyde Farm

Hyde Farm is situated in the village of Great Wigborough, Essex, England, and is believed to be haunted by a ghost referred to as "Prudence" about whom nothing is known other than she may have been killed in the garden there. The occupiers in the latter part of the twentieth century heard the sound of a **piano** being played in an empty room in the house and they have also witnessed poltergeist activity (Payne, pp. 45–46).

Payne, Jessie K. (1995). *A Ghost Hunter's Guide to Essex*. Norfolk: Ian Henry.

Incantation

The word is derived from the Latin *cantare* "to sing" and although an incantation is not sung in the accepted use of the term, neither can it be said to be simply spoken. The purpose of an incantation is to effect change outside of normal methods and it is therefore an example of **magic** and a "principle whereby music creates flow and changes of consciousness" (Webster, p. 113). It uses words as "weapons of power" which varies from a mantra the words of which can be more repetitive (Cavendish, pp. 1418–1420). The ethnomusicologist Gilbert Rouget (1916–2017) drew a distinction between trance music and incantation, but nevertheless drew favorable attention to Jules Combarieu's (1859–1916) *La musique et la magie* (1910) which linked magic with incantation (Rouget, p. 240). In Malaya the *pawang* (**shaman**) **chants** a "special song" to the accompaniment of a **violin** to induce the appearance of his spirit "control." The musicians increase the pace of his incantation until he is **possessed** by the spirit whereupon the music stops instantly (Bracelin, p. 82).

The occultist **Aleister Crowley** used incantations in his rituals, some of which have been recorded, to summon up entities which reveal a curious droning voice, but with melodic and rhythmic fluctuations (www.youtube.com/watch?v=SfY34oBXbZw). Shamanic incantations, often from Scandinavian and northern sources have persisted into modern times (Edgar, pp. 406–410) and the Australian Aborigines' traditions provide strong links between such musical sounds and the gods (Drury, p. 55).

Bracelin, Jack L. (1999). *Gerald Gardner: Witch*. Thame: I-H-O Books.
Cavendish, Richard (1970). "Incantation." *Man, Myth and Magic*. Vol. 4. London: Purnell.
Drury, Nevill (1996). *Shamanism*. Shaftesbury: Element Books.
Edgar, Marjorie (1936). "Finnish Charms and Folk Songs in Minnesota." *Minnesota History* 17, no. 4: 406–410.
Rouget, Gilbert (1985). *Music and Trance: A Theory of the Relations Between Music and Possession*. Chicago: University of Chicago Press.
Webster, Sam (2001). *Modern Pagans*. San Francisco: Re/Search Publications.

Indridason, Indridi

Indridi Indridason (1883–1912) was a remarkable Icelandic medium who displayed a variety of paranormal demonstrations during his **séances** in Reykjavík. He believed that the famous mezzo-soprano Maria Felicia Malibran (1808–1836) spoke and sang through him and it was agreed by those present that the singing was of a highly trained quality and far beyond that possessed by the medium or anyone else present. On one occasion Indridason produced multiple voices singing a **Chopin** piece that was being played on a harmonium at the time. The Norwegian composer Edvard Grieg (1843–1907) appeared several times soon after his death and **automatic writing** produced Grieg's signature which was found to be correct (Haraldsson, 2018).

Haraldsson, E. (2018). "Indridi Indridason." *Psi Encyclopedia*. London: The Society for Psychical Research.

Inspiration

The origin of the word "inspiration" comes from the Latin "to breathe into" (Merriam-Webster Dictionary) but since the medieval period it has evolved via theological interpretations into its current usage. A host of creative artists have used the word with an unearthly emphasis to describe its characteristics. George Eliot felt she was "possessed"; George Sand spoke of "*the other*"; Wordsworth spoke of "trance-like states"; Thackeray said, "It seems as if an occult Power was moving the pen; and Kipling even referred to his personal 'Daemon'" (Tyrrell, p. 32). **Arthur Abell**'s interviews with composers made considerable use of the word in the discussions about the source of their compositions. **Brahms** speaking of inspiration felt he was "appropriating that same spirit to which Jesus so often referred" (Abell, pp. 13–14) and **Richard Strauss** felt "when in inspired moods" his visions found him "tapping the source of Infinite and Eternal energy.... **Religion** calls it God" (Abell, p. 86). Joscelyn Godwin defines "three main levels of musical and artistic inspiration" (Godwin, p. 85) which he describes as the "avataric" level; the "spiritus" which is an element of "Memory"; and "self-expression" (Godwin, pp. 85–87). When a divine source is ascribed to such moments, be they from a believed religious source or any other external origin they are firmly in the paranormal category. The concert pianist **John Lill**, in conversation with the author, spoke of his mind intermingling with **Beethoven**'s during a performance of his music: "a complete thrill when you're feeling inspired" (Willin, p. 67). He strongly believes his source of inspiration is binding with the energy of departed composers and notably Beethoven.

The author and musicologist Rosamond Harding (1898–1982) devoted a detailed book to the nature of inspiration with one chapter specifically devoted to music (Harding, 1967) where she spoke of **Debussy**'s belief that "one should never hurry to write but leave everything to that many-sided play of thoughts—those mysterious workings of the mind which we too often disturb" (Harding, p. 71). She also wrote about **Wagner**'s reliance upon dreams and she quoted imagery from a host of other composers. Sir Michael Tippett (1905–1998) believed he was "operating in an entirely different way in a different field" when he was composing (cited in Dobinson, p. 29) and Jean Sibelius (1865–1957) felt that composition came "from a higher sphere." He was particularly interested in extra sensory perception, **dreams** and **premonitions** (Dobinson, p. 29).

Abell, Arthur M. (1955). *Talks with Great Composers*. London: Psychic Book Club.
Dobinson, George (1997). "Composers and the Paranormal." *Light* 117, no. 3 (Winter): 28–30.
Godwin, Joscelyn (1987a). *Harmonies of Heaven and Earth*. London: Thames and Hudson.
Harding, Rosamond E.M. (1967). *An Anatomy of Inspiration*. London: Frank Cass.
https://www.merriam-webster.com/words-at-play/the-origins-of-inspire.
Tyrrell, G.N.M. (1954). *The Personality of Man*. Melbourne: Penguin.
Willin, Melvyn J. (2005). *Music, Witchcraft and the Paranormal*. Ely: Melrose.

Inveraray Castle

Inveraray Castle in Strathclyde, Scotland, is the seat of the Dukes of Argyll, the head of Clan Campbell. It was built in the eighteenth century more as a mansion than an actual castle. Several sources mention a number of hauntings including a harper who is heard playing by visitors occasionally (Underwood, pp. 181–182). He was allegedly hanged there sometime in the past and his playing is said to herald a death in the Campbell family. The Duke of Argyll contacted the author and denied knowledge of any "ghostly **harp** music" being heard there (private correspondence).

Underwood, Peter (1993). *The Ghosthunters Almanac*. Orpington: Eric Dobby.

Jacob, Zouave

Auguste-Henri Jacob (1828–1916), aka Le Zouave, was a famous French healer in Paris during the late nineteenth and early twentieth century. His career started in the army as a trombonist and brass player in the band of the Zouave regiment of the Imperial Guard. He became known to the public when he undertook numerous **healing**s through the effect of his "fluid." It has not been possible to ascertain whether he used his musical skills during the course of his many healings (Britten, pp. 66–69).

Britten, Emma Hardinge (1884). *Nineteenth Century Miracles*. Manchester: William Britten.

Jumièges Abbey

Jumièges Abbey situated in Normandy, France, was built in the seventh century and was used as a Benedictine monastery and abbey until its destruction during the French Revolution. Its impressive ruins were visited by a family on July 6, 1913, when it was reported:

> I suddenly became aware of the sound of a large number of men's voices which seemed to come from the open space on our left where the few scattered stones marked the site where the monastic choir had been. The singing was very soft … and then the music left my attention as I heard my father exclaim: "Why, there are monks singing." … I determined to pretend I had heard nothing, until I learned from my companions if their experience had been the same as my own. I found this was the case, and we agreed that the voices were chanting "Vespers" … —a psalm in Latin. We tried to think of possible natural explanations, but the present parish church was a kilometer and a half from there—so the caretaker told us—besides which, if the sound had come from there, we should have heard it for longer than a few seconds…. [Anne, pp. 119–120].

The account was corroborated in writing by the other members of the family and further enquiries verified the lack of normal possible musical sources. The fact that they heard the music initially without reference to each other makes less feasible the collective **hallucination** theory which is usually proposed after one person's experience is then claimed to have been witnessed by others—usually visual.

Anne, Ernestine (1915). The *Journal of the Society for Psychical Research* 17 (December).

The ruins of Jumièges Abbey in France where unknown chanting was heard by a family visiting there in 1913 (makasana photo/Shutterstock.com).

Jurieu, Pastor Pierre

Pastor Pierre Jurieu (1637–1713) was a French theologian and writer. He wrote a series of letters in 1689 (Jurieu, pp. 156–160) which described the hearing of music from invisible sources during the persecution of the Huguenots in France in the seventeenth century. He referred to "the sound of **trumpets** ... and the singing of psalms, a composition of many voices, and a number of musical instruments were heard day and night at many places.... The scale of the phenomena was too vast to be attributed to **hallucination**" (cited in Fodor, 258).

Fodor, Nandor (1934). *Encyclopedia of Psychic Science.* London: Arthurs Press.
Jurieu, Pierre (1689). "The Seventh Pastoral Letter. Concerning Songs, and Voices, which were heard in several places in the Air." *The Pastoral Letters....* London: T. Fabian and J. Hindmarsh.

Kampmann, Reima

Reima Kampmann (1943–1992) was a Finnish psychiatrist who became known for his work into hypnotic regression. One case has proved to be controversial because of different interpretations of the contradictory information available. It concerned his regression of a teenage or older girl known as "Dorothy" who believed herself to have lived before in medieval England where she learned to sing the song "Sumer is icumen in." In a second session where she was told to go back to an earlier time in her present childhood, she remembered seeing the song in a history of music book (Sigdell, 1995?). The case of **reincarnation** or not would depend on whether she had indeed seen the song before and remembered it under hypnotism or whether this was an example of a genuine regression back to a previous life (Kampman, pp. 215–227).

Sigdell, Jan Erik (1995?). "Biased evaluations of regression experiences." www.christliche-reinkarnation.com/PDF/Biasedev.pdf.
Kampmann, Reima (1976). "An Experimental Study." *International Journal of Clinical and Experimental Hypnosis* 24, no. 3 (July): 215–227.

Kepler, Johannes

Johannes Kepler (1571–1630) was a German astrologer, astronomer and mathematician who was also fascinated by the idea of world harmony which consisted of musical laws of harmony which "differs markedly from that of the natural sciences which is characterized above all by causal thinking, a quantitative perception of the world, and a functionalistic procedure with mathematics at its core" (Godwin, p. 125). The concept of harmony governing the laws of the universe may not involve physical music as such, but it certainly promotes a different perspective on the "interpretation of the world" (Godwin, p. 127) or, as the composer Paul Hindemith (1895–1963) maintained, "the time may return when musical rules will be an essential part of the code of the physical sciences…. Harmonic, melodic and rhythmic laws would transform the world's woes and falsehood into an ideal habitat for human beings" (*Caduceus*, p. 3).

Godwin, Joscelyn (1989). "Kepler's World Harmony and Its Significance for Today." *Cosmic Music*. Rochester: Inner Traditions.
Hindemith, Paul (n.d.). *Caduceus* 23: 3.

Khan, Hazrat Inayat

Hazrat Inayat Khan (1882–1927) was an Indian teacher, philosopher and musician who was in many ways responsible for bringing Sufism to a greater Western understanding. His most famous book *The Mysticism of Sound and Music* (1991) provides insights into many aspects of the esoteric and mystical effects of music and the mind. Chapters include "Esoteric Music," "**The Music of the Spheres**," "The Mysticism of Sound," "The Manifestation of Sound on the Physical Sphere," "The Psychological Influence of Music," "The Healing Power of Music" and "Spiritual Attainment by the Aid of Music." They comment on aspects of music which lay outside of its normal understanding. These attributes include the ancient Chinese belief that the universe was created by music and that **chant**ing can lead to mystical communication "additionally believed to send out cosmic vibration" (Drury and Tillett, pp. 148–149).

Drury, Nevill, and Gregory Tillett (1997). *The Occult: A Sourcebook of Esoteric Wisdom*. New York: Saraband.
Khan, Hazrat Inayat (1991). *The Mysticism of Sound and Music*. Boston: Shambhala.

Koons, Jonathan

Jonathan Koons (1811–1893) was a farmer living in a remote area of Athens, Ohio, in the United States in the mid-nineteenth century. He became interested in **Spiritualism** when he was told in a séance that he and his eight children had mediumistic talents. He subsequently built a log cabin next to his house in which to hold spiritual meetings and he filled it with **drums**, triangles, tambourines, a guitar, banjo, **fiddle** and other musical instruments. When the room was in darkness these instruments would allegedly be played by the spirits. The attendant spirits would also sing as if they were "a full choir of voices ... most exquisitely" (cited in Fodor, pp. 192–193). There were other manifestations which were partially illuminated by a phosphorous light (Podmore, pp. 246–247).

> A reveille was then beaten by the spirits on the tenor and bass drums with tremendous power and almost distracting effect. Mr. Koons then took up one of two violins that were lying on the table before us, and drew his bow across it. Immediately the other was sounded, and presently the full band of all the instruments, of which there must have been quite a dozen, joined in keeping admirable time, tune and concert. After the instrumental performance, Mr. Koons asked for a vocal accompaniment from the spirits, which they at once complied with, and I think if anything can give an idea of heaven upon earth, it must be the delightful music made by that angelic choir [Curnow, p. 65].

Not surprisingly their neighbors did not approve of the noisy activity, and they were eventually forced to leave the area and it is not known what happened to them afterwards.

Curnow, Leslie (1925). *The Physical Phenomena of Spiritualism*. London: Two Worlds.
Fodor, Nandor (1934). *Encyclopedia of Psychic Science*. London: Arthurs Press.
Podmore, Frank (1902). *Modern Spiritualism*. Vol. I. London: Methuen.

Legend

This work for **piano** and orchestra was written by the English composer John Nicholson Ireland (1879–1962) in 1933. The background to its composition was curious since it was directly related to a paranormal experience. During a stay near his weekend cottage at Harrow Hill he stopped for a picnic at a regular spot close to where "a small prehistoric hill-fort and a Neolithic flint mine" were to be found and also close to a ruined church with a connection to a bygone lepers' colony (cited in Dobinson, p. 338). He was irritated that a group of children were there dancing quite close to him, but they did not make any sound and were dressed strangely. He briefly looked away, but when he looked again, they had vanished. He contacted the author Arthur Machen who replied, "So you've seen them too!" As Dobinson notes, "*Legend* reflects the movements of the children and the atmosphere of the path he had taken to that place. It was dedicated to Machen" (p. 338).

Dobinson, George (1998). "The Case for Retrocognition." The *Journal of the Society for Psychical Research* 62 (April).

Leith Hall

Leith Hall, situated in the Grampians, Scotland, was built in the seventeenth century, added to in the eighteenth and was the home for many years of the Leith family. There have been various alleged musical anomalies associated with the house including pipe music, drumming and a **chant**ed mass (Underwood, p. 188) which seem to have taken place in the 1960s and 1970s. Nothing has been reported recently other than unsubstantiated rumors.

Underwood, Peter (1993). *The Ghosthunters Almanac*. Orpington: Eric Dobby.

Lemke, Leslie

Leslie Lemke (1952–) was born in Milwaukee and adopted by Joe and May Lemke when he was six months old. He is a musical **savant** who was described by the psychiatrist Darold A. Treffert as "the most remarkable savant I have ever met, or read about, or studied" (Treffert, p. 104). Lemke is blind, is cognitively handicapped, and has cerebral palsy, but he has managed to play and sing in English, German and Greek and he has a wide repertoire of classical music. He has given concerts and appeared on television shows on numerous occasions since beginning his concert career in 1974. He amazes his audiences with such feats as this: "After a single hearing of a 45-minute opera tape he can transpose the music to the **piano** and also sing the score back in the foreign language in which he heard it" (Treffert, p. 109). The word "miracle" is often applied to his performances.

Treffert, Darold A. (1989). *Extraordinary People*. London: Bantam Press.

Lennon, John

It is perhaps not surprising that the famous ex-Beatle John Winston Ono Lennon (1940–1980) would attract legends of music from beyond the grave and there have been several examples. **Rosemary Brown** claimed music and contact from him; the medium Joe Power has related messages; the Indian guru Deepankar Virat has received messages in Hindi from him (www.imdb.com/title/tt6719934/); a retired printer from Wales, Mike Powell, claims to have received hundreds of tunes from him (*Metro*, p. 29) and the author investigated one such claimant, who produced a suitably Lennon-like song, but he did admit to having been obsessed with his music for a long time (private investigation).

Metro. (2011). "Lennon 'sends me his songs.'" May 31: 29.

Fourteenth-century Levens Hall mansion house in Cumbria is the site of a family curse and haunting where unaccountable harpsichord music has been heard playing (Kevin Eaves/Shutterstock.com).

Levens Hall

Levens Hall, Cumbria, England, is a manor house built on an original site in the fourteenth century. There has been a tradition of a family curse and hauntings for many years, but in an earlier part of the twentieth century a visiting priest was aware of harpsichord music being played continuously during his visit with the player "wreathed in light" (Brooks, p. 167). He was told that a power cut had not made this possible and that the owner of the house, Oliver Robin Bagot, was away on business. The priest even recognized the tune being played—a "Grand"—which was one that was played by Bagot. No explanation was ever forthcoming.

Brooks, J.A. (1990). *Britain's Haunted Heritage*. Norwich: Jarrold.

Levitation

The levitation of objects, specifically stones, through the application of music, may seem unlikely. It is well-known in legend that the walls of Thebes were raised by the power of Amphion, son of Zeus, playing the lyre but it has been investigated outside of mythology and Edgar Cayce (1877–1945) believed the Great Pyramid was built using levitation techniques helped by song and **chant** (cited in Godwin, p. 12). The **Bible** contains the story of Joshua and the walls of Jericho for its destruction, but a far more recent account has been researched concerning the alleged levitation of giant blocks of stone in Tibet by two Swedish scientists Henry Kjellson (1891–1962) and a Dr. Jarl (cited in Playfair and Hill, pp. 137–140). The account stated that in 1939 the two researchers witnessed a number of **drums** and **trumpet**s that were used to raise the stones some two hundred and fifty yards into the air on to a platform. It was further claimed that two films were made of this event which were confiscated by the "English Scientific Society. The work of Bruce Cathie in *Acoustic Levitation of Stones* provides the details" (becomingborealis.com/acoustic-levitation-of-stones). The sound healer Jill Mattson suggests that sound was used to build "cities and monuments" in ancient Mexico, Bolivia, Peru and Egypt. Chaldean priests lifted large stones at Baalbeck with chanting and at Tiahuanaco in Bolivia ancient builders used trumpets as building tools (academia.edu). Commander Ralph Stanbury wrote that "in *The Secret Doctrine* (Vol. 2, Adyar Edition) [by Helena Blavatsky] one John Worrell Keely (1837–1898), in the 1890s, was able to play a certain note on the **violin** which would drive a motor at high speed or lift a model into the air" (Stanbury, p. 9). Keely's subsequent commercial motor engineering ventures were seriously disputed. Another scientific solution to the enigma of levitation has been suggested by the so-called "Hutchison effect" devised by the Canadian John Hutchison (1945–) which he discovered when experimenting with the ideas of Nikola Tesla (1856–1943) (www.hutchisoneffect.com).

academia.edu/39190246/Sounds_and_Ancient_Methods_of_Levitation_Moving_Large_
    Objects_with_ Sound_Energy?email_work_card=reading-history.
Godwin, Joscelyn (1987a). *Harmonies of Heaven and Earth*. London: Thames and Hudson.
Playfair, Guy Lyon, and Scott Hill (1978). *Cycles of Heaven*. London: Souvenir Press.
Stanbury, Ralph (1999). "Some Thoughts on Levitation." *Light* 119, no. 1 (Summer): 8–10.

Lill, John

John Richard Lill (1944–) is an English concert pianist who is acclaimed as an expert on the interpretation of **Beethoven**'s music in particular. He has generally been impressed by **Rosemary Brown**'s compositions and also spoken of his own spiritual beliefs. During a lengthy interview with the author he expanded on these matters and about "paranormality" within music generally. He believed he was "helped" to win the Moscow **Tchaikovsky** Competition when a figure appeared to him who proved to be Beethoven: "Our two minds intermingle, but normally it's just a tremendous sensation which goes beyond any drug … you are nearly always aware of being in safe hands and the more you go into dangerous territory, the more help there is" (Willin, pp. 67–68). He explained that his words and views "came to him from the spiritual dimension…. You can be a **channel** through which this force works without limit" (Willin, p. 68). Lill also spoke about receiving from Beethoven part of a tenth symphony which was dictated to him, and he mentioned his own positive beliefs in **reincarnation**. He stressed "because something is rare it doesn't mean that it doesn't exist," but he feared that "simplistic journalists and the sensation-seeking popular press will twist his words and brand him as either a nutter or some quaint loony falling around in a state of trance" (Gillard, 1980). He believes that "he has concrete evidence of contact from dead composers which he either sees or hears and when he has received information he has subsequently checked it out in encyclopedias and found it to be true" (Lill, 1977).

Gillard, David (1980). "Con spirito." *Spirits from the Past*. BBC I (August).
Willin, Melvyn J. (2005). *Music, Witchcraft and the Paranormal*. Ely: Melrose.
Lill, John. (1977). in conversation with Leslie Smith. *All in the Mind*. BBC I Radio 4 (June 29).
[A transcript of the John Lill interview can be seen in Willin, Melvyn J. (1999). *Paramusicology: An Investigation of Music and Paranormal Phenomena*. PhD thesis. Music Department. University of Sheffield.]

Lina

Lina was the name given to a medium discovered by Albert de Rochas d' Aiglun (1837–1914), a French Lieutenant-Colonel at the end of the nineteenth century. "Once hypnotized, she showed an extreme degree of response to music, to the point at which any musical vibration would evoke expressive and interpretative movements" (cited in Godwin, p. 158). Her reactions to receiving mild electric shocks from a *polyphone* caused reactions that corresponded to the actual rhythms of the music being played unheard by her (Rochas, 1900).

Godwin, Joscelyn (1995). *Music and the Occult*. New York: University of Rochester Press.
Rochas, Albert de (1900). *Les sentiments, la musique et le geste*. Grenoble: Falque & Perrin.

Lincoln, Abraham

Abraham Lincoln (1809–1865) was the President of the USA until his assassination in 1865. He not only had an interest in **Spiritualism** because of his wife's involvement, but he also attended several **séances** himself and his alleged premonitory dream of his own death is often written about (Guiley, p. 200). However, what is less well-known was his attendance at a séance on February 5, 1863, with Colonel Simon F. Kase and others when the famous American medium Mrs. Belle Miller became entranced while playing the **piano** (a three-corner grand) which levitated and beat time on the floor with the music. Lincoln suggested that some of the men in attendance should climb up on the piano to weigh it down, to see if the **levitation** would stop, but despite this it allegedly continued to rise up and down (cited in Stemman, p. 23). A full description of this event was published by Nettie Colburn Maynard (Maynard, 1917).

Guiley, Rosemary Ellen (1994). *The Guinness Encyclopedia of Ghosts and Spirits*. Middlesex: Guinness.
Maynard, Nettie Colburn (1917). *Was Abraham Lincoln a Spiritualist?* Chicago: Progressive Thinker.
Stemman, R. (1975). *Spirits and Spirit Worlds*. London: Aldus Books.

Liszt, Franz

It is remarkable how many times the name of Franz Liszt (1811–1886) is mentioned in the accounts of anomalous music. He was named as a composer who made contact from the spirit world by **Georges Aubert**, **Jesse Shepard**, **Virgil Fox**, the Finnish musical medium Margit Selin, "Count Ravencastle" and most famous of all **Rosemary Brown**. Experts in his music, namely Vernon Harrison and **Ian Parrott**, were both particularly impressed with the Liszt-Brown connection.

One incidence in Liszt's life may have been **premonitionary** since he brooded on **Wagner**'s funeral music in *Parsifal* writing his own example of funereal music in 1882 (*La Lugubre Gondola*). Wagner died the following year in Venice (Parrott, p. 31). Ian Parrott believed that Liszt could have been a composer who wanted to continue composing after his death.

Franz Liszt was a well-known pianist and composer in the nineteenth century who was often chosen by musical mediums as their source of inspiration or paranormal contact (Everett Collection/Shutterstock.com).

Parrott, Ian (1978). *The Music of Rosemary Brown*. London: Regency Press.

London

London arguably contains more examples of alleged paranormal music manifestations than any other town or city in the UK, which one might expect bearing in mind the size of its population and the wealth of history attached to it. Some of these places have already been mentioned in the main body of the text when it was thought they deserved special discussion and many more have been omitted when their legitimacy was open to more questions than usual. For instance, The King's Arms, Peckham Rye has a tradition of an old-time singsong being heard, but this may stem from its popularity or pranks being staged: "Neighbors say they heard rousing choruses of wartime songs from the cellar late at night, reminiscent of the community singing customers used to do to take their minds off the bombing while sheltering in the King's Arms" (Hallam, p. 191). Frustratingly, the hymn singing that has been reported in Lawrence Street in North London has not been given a specific location other than being reported by a Mrs. Rea Thirlby with a similar absence of date (Hallam, pp. 149–150). Bell ringing was claimed to have occurred at 50 Berkeley Square in the 1870s, the location of other alleged hauntings (Underwood, 1971, p. 128) but one of the owners informed the author that "he had not heard of any musical phenomena, though, [he added flippantly] 'a certain tuneless humming sometimes emanates from various offices at dull moments'" (private correspondence). One of the landmarks of history in England, the Tower of London, has many stories of hauntings and poltergeist attached to it, but there would seem to be only one brief mention of music, or specifically **chant**ing, that was described by "an American guest staying at the Queen's House" in 1978 (Underwood, 1984, p. 230). A policeman on night duty outside Westminster Abbey heard music from inside the abbey and believed he saw a procession of "black-clad figures, walking in twos," even though the building was locked and closed (O'Donnell, pp. 14–15). Despite considerable evidence of a ghostly procession of monks being witnessed at St. Dunstan's Church in East Acton (Hallam, pp. 155–158) they would seem to be silent, since there are almost no reports of anomalous music being heard there.

Hallam, Jack (1975). *Ghosts of London*. London: Wolfe.
O'Donnell, Elliott (1939). *Haunted Churches*. London: Quality Press.
Underwood, Peter (1971). *Gazetteer of British Ghosts*. London: Souvenir Press.
Underwood, Peter (1984). *This Haunted Isle*. London: Harrap Limited.

Magic

What is magic? For the purpose of this entry the *Oxford English Dictionary* suffices: "The power of apparently influencing events by using mysterious or supernatural forces." The word's origin is thought to be from the Greek *megus* or *magein* meaning either "great" as in science or from the philosophy of Zoroaster respectively (Guiley, p. 212). This is in contrast to its other definition involving tricks for entertainment purposes. It is possible that when humans first created music, they still believed that it had a paranormal origin: "in all known civilizations music has been believed to have a divine origin. It exists, like emotions, in some nonphysical realm. Music is everywhere to be heard, but it can't be touched" (Hemenway, p. 119). It has been considered not as a creation of man, but as the work of a "supernatural being" (Combarieu, p. 113). Furthermore, Jules Combarieu (1859–1916) believed that "the efficacy of musical magic is one of the most important facts in the history of civilization… [and] that music introduces us to 'an intelligible world of ideas' [and] unveils the essence of things" (Diserens, p. 54). Music and magic's position within alchemy was described in 1618 in the Rosicrucian Hermeticist Michael Maier's *Atalanta fugiens*, where alchemical engravings and texts were "designed to be set to music in the form of a fugue for three voices, the musical score actually being printed with the text. One suspects that these fugues were composed specifically to be sung in the laboratory, each at the relevant stage of the process of transmutation" (cited in Baigent and Leigh, p. 200).

The composers **Cyril Scott** and **Alexander Scriabin** both seemed to amalgamate music and magic together as did the occultist **Aleister Crowley** in ways which had possibly not been so prevalent since Renaissance times when music was implicated "most profoundly in the theory and operation of magic" (Tomlinson, p. xiii). One only has to look to the works of Marsilio Ficino (1433–1499) such as *De vita coelitus comparanda* (1489) for evidence of this.

It would seem that "music gives access to regions in the subconscious that can be reached in no other way" (Drinker, p. xv) other than by magic and that this is not limited to great philosophical thinkers since "the primitive musician believes that by directing the force of rhythm and sound upon a thing, a person, or a situation, he can make it conform to his will" (Drinker, p. 4). The Omaha Native Americans believe that certain songs can affect other people's actions when directed towards them and the magical power of songs are also used by the Australian Aborigines (Haddon, pp. 42–60), in addition to their use of the bull-roarer which "always represents the voice of a spirit" (Reik, p. 285). The bull-roarer's use is not limited to Australia, but is also used as the voice of Lefin, a red-haired spirit dwarf of the Tambaran in Papua New Guinea (cited in Devereux, p. 43). The shamanic song "is often endowed with magical power [and] claims, in certain cases at least, to transform the world" (Rouget, p. 131).

In some cultures, these beliefs have not changed into the twenty first century. During a conversation the author had with the high priestess of a contemporary wiccan coven, she stated: "Music is psychologically important to our wellbeing. It also connects to the psyche and triggers raised levels of consciousness. Music is integral to magick [sic] because it weaves spells on the soul. The use of music is both complex and vital" (private conversation, 2005). Even within the highly scientific world of **parapsychology**, music and magic has been linked with the energy that is raised from what has been called "natural magic, peasant magic, pagan magic, the magic of the Earth and which brings the Earth alive ... coming from **inspiration**" (Roney-Dougal, p. 191). The English musician, occultist and founder of the cult band Coil, John Balance (1962–2004) was a practitioner of magick [sic] and explored it in his musical compositions which he linked to **shaman**ic practices. Drug-taking and **dreams** were also used as part of this paranormal musical experience (Pilkington, pp. 22–24). The legendary Jimi Hendrix believed that music was magic "a supernatural power ... a magical science [where] rhythm could become hypnotic—putting the hearer in a trance-like condition" (Dannemann, p. 112).

Baigent, Michael, and Richard Leigh (1998). *The Elixir and the Stone*. London: Penguin Books.
Combarieu, Jules (1909). *La musique et la magie*. Paris: A. Picard et fils.
Dannemann, Monika (1995). *The Inner World of Jimi Hendrix*. New York: St. Martin's Press.
Devereux, Paul (2001). *Stone Age Soundtracks*. London: Vega.
Diserens, Charles M. (1926). *The Influence of Music on Behavior*. Princeton: Princeton University Press.
Drinker, Sophie (1995). *Music & Women*. New York: Feminist Press, City University.
Guiley, Rosemary Ellen (1999). *The Encyclopedia of Witches and Witchcraft*. New York: Checkmark Books.
Haddon, Alfred Cort (1910). *Magic and Fetishism*. London: Constable.
Hemenway, Priya (2008). *The Secret Code*. Lugano: Springwood.
Pilkington, Mark (2001). "Sounds of Blakeness." *Fortean Times* 142 (January): 22–24.
Reik, Theodor (1958). *Ritual*. New York: International Universities Press.
Roney-Dougal, Serena (1991). *Where Science & Magic Meet*. Shaftesbury: Element.
Rouget, Gilbert (1985). *Music and Trance. A Theory of the Relations Between Music and Possession*. Chicago: University of Chicago Press.
Tomlinson, Gary. (1993). *Music in Renaissance Magic*. Chicago: University of Chicago.

Manchester

An empty office in Peter Street, Manchester, England, was the location reported in the *Manchester Evening News* on 24 October 1968 for the sound of woodwind being heard, as well as two years earlier, which had no explanation as to its sound source. It was described as "thin piping tunes" (Michell & Rickard, p. 83).

Michell, John, and Robert J.M. Rickard (1983). *Phenomena*. London: BCA.

Manners, Peter Guy

Peter Guy Manners (1935–2009) was an English osteopath who used "an electrical **cymatic** device which sends sound through applicators into the body at predetermined areas of contact" (Gardner, p. 126). His private clinic was held at Bretforton Hall in Worcestershire, England, where he claimed to treat many people successfully. His methods and results have been thoroughly scrutinized and heavily criticized (Summer, pp. 183–186) and the author was similarly bewildered by his use of actual music during his **healing** sessions during a visit some years ago.

Gardner, Kay (1990). *Sounding the Inner Landscape*. Rockport: Element.
Summer, Lisa (1996). *Music—The New Age Elixir*. New York: Prometheus Books.

Manning, Matthew

The English psychic healer Matthew Manning (1955–) was allegedly the focus of poltergeist activity in the 1960s which was investigated by A.R.G. Owen (1919–2003) and others finding what they believed to be positive evidence (Fletcher, p. 104). In his vocation as a healer Manning stresses the use of music "as a crucial ingredient of my work" (Manning, p. 163) which he believes enhances their receptivity to energies.

Fletcher, Ian. (1975). *The Journal of the Society for Psychical Research* 48 (June).
Manning, Matthew (2007). *Your Mind Can Heal Your Body*. London: Piatkus.

Mantras

A mantra is a sacred sound which is sung repeatedly to access the subconscious and allow the innermost depths of the mind to be realized. It does not necessarily have a specific musical content, but nevertheless involves melodies and rhythms which are indicative of music. Mantras are often repeated in the journey to achieve *Nada Brahma*, the concept that the world is sound. Sometimes overtone singing is manifest during the **chant**ing which sounds particularly impressive—even paranormal—when executed by the Mongolian Tuvan people of Siberia (Berendt, p. 28). Different cultures refer to mantras by different names and with diverse attributes. The Chinese and Japanese may refer to them as "koans" and the Sufis as "wazifah." The latter have "a highly developed sense of sound and music" (Berendt, p. 33) which aids them on their journey to enlightenment whereas Tantric practices which also use mantras often explore sexual practices.

Berendt, J. (1987). *Nada Brahma: The World Is Sound*. London: East West.

Martian Music

The psychical researcher Harry Price provided a humorous chapter in his book *Confessions of a Ghost-Hunter* (1936) devoted to the claims of mediums who believed they were in contact with certain higher beings living on the planet Mars. One of these provided **channel**ed music which he made recordings of on a wax cylinder. It consisted of a "crooning love song," which he described as "certainly unearthly ... and rather like a solo by a crowing cock" (Price, p. 128). His other Martian contacts did not provide any music.

Price, Harry (1936). *Confessions of a Ghost-Hunter*. London: Putnam.

May, Leonard (Leo)

In 1993 the author was contacted by the Society for Psychical Research and asked to investigate a man who believed he was **channeling** the spirit of the famous tenor Enrico Caruso (1873–1921). His name was Leo May (1942–2017?) and he lived near Cambridge, England. The author visited him several times and was immediately impressed with his very fine operatic tenor voice, which he claimed was guided by the spirit of Caruso even though he had only had a few singing lessons in the past and had not studied Italian. During a long investigation the author could not find signs of fraudulent activity on his part, and neither was financial gain an element of his claims. May appeared on several television programs where his singing was acclaimed, and he released a few compact discs of his favorite songs and arias. After the death of his wife in 1997 he stopped singing for a time. After a brief return to performance he died of cancer (Willin, pp. 117–121). The audio-visual library of the Society for Psychical Research contains recordings of him singing made by the author as well as private recordings.

Willin, Melvyn J. (1999). *Paramusicology: An Investigation of Music and Paranormal Phenomena*. PhD thesis. Music Department. University of Sheffield.

Mediums and Music/Musical Mediums

Psychic and spiritualist mediums have been attracted to music in different ways throughout the centuries and up to and including the present time. Concerning what was called "supernormal" music in the past, mediums have generally believed that "harmonious sounds are essential or helpful, while inharmonious sounds are retarding" (Leaf, p. 651). Music has manifested itself in them in both a variety of ways and importance. Some have composed music given to them by dead composers or performed under the direction of dead performers, whereas others have produced music from allegedly psychic sources or have caused instruments to play by themselves without their physical contact. Verification has similarly varied from the statements of a few unqualified people to the authentication of trained musicians and the conditions for the performances have ranged from loosely investigated—if at all—to tightly controlled and well-researched.

[The following table allows this diversity to be seen at a glance and highlighted entries receive greater details in the general text. The identities of some of the mediums have been concealed to protect their identity].

Name	Dates When Known	Country of Origin	Type/s of Phenomena	Investigator/ Information
"A"	flourished late 20th/early 21st century	UK	Music from John **Lennon**	author
Georges Aubert	flourished turn of 20th century	France	**Piano** playing—dead composers	Institut Génèral Psychologique
Emma Hardinge Britten	1823–1899	UK	Piano playing from spirits	Spiritualist and own writing
Rosemary Brown	1916–2001	UK	Music from dead composers	Musicians and own writing
Nelsa Chaplin	?–1927	UK	Piano playing from spirits	Cyril Scott's publications
Ira & William Davenport	1839–1911 1841–1877	U.S.	Spirits playing instruments	Spiritualist and skeptic writing
The Eddy Brothers	flourished late 19th/early 20th century	U.S.	Spirits playing instruments	Spiritualist and skeptic writing
Clifford Enticknap	1950–2019	UK	Music from **Handel**	self-promotion
"G"	flourished late 20th/early 21st century	UK	Music from Novello	author
"H"	flourished late 20th/early 21st century	UK	Music from **Tchaikovsky**	author

Name	Dates When Known	Country of Origin	Type/s of Phenomena	Investigator/ Information
Daniel Dunglas Home	1833–1886	UK	Multiple phenomena	William Crookes
Indridi Indridason	1883–1912	Iceland	Voices from spirit	Spiritualist and skeptic writing
Jonathan Koons	1811–1893	U.S.	Voices/spirits playing	Spiritualist and skeptic writing
"M"	flourished late 20th/early 21st century	UK	Music from Arnold Bax	author
Leo May	1942–2017 [?]	UK	Voice from Caruso	author
Florizel von Reuter	1890–1985	U.S.	**Violin** playing—**Paganini**	Own publications
Jesse Shepard	1848–1927	UK	Piano & singing dead composers	Spiritualist and own writing
"T"	flourished late 20th/early 21st century	UK	Music from **Beethoven**	author
Charles Tweedale	?–1944	UK	Contact from Stradivarius	Own publications
"W"	flourished late 20th/early 21st century	UK	Music from **Chopin**	author

It cannot be expressed too many times how varied were the characteristics, personalities and musical education of the musical mediums. Taking just the examples that the author investigated and interviewed personally one sees a whole range of differences in their attributes. For instance, "H" had no musical training of any description; "T" had some basic piano and theoretical knowledge, whereas "M" possessed a Licentiate in organ playing from Trinity College of Music, **London** and "A" was already an accomplished guitarist and singer. "W" was a piano teacher with an obsession with the music of Chopin. Under scrutiny from experts in the field the music of "H" was thought to be 'awful' and the Chopin works from "W" were not thought to be authentic. There were mixed responses to the music of "T" and "G," but the Bax composition by "M" was praised and **Leo May**'s "Caruso" was also impressive. The personalities of the people interviewed were similarly diverse. May and "A" were firmly in the extravert category, whereas "T" was quiet and introverted. Mostly they believed that the sources of their **inspiration** were from the "spirit realms," but "T" was not so sure believing that some sort of unknown "energy" might be responsible (Willin, pp. 46–95). The author was also contacted by a man referring to himself as "Count Ravencastle." He claimed that the composer **Liszt** was taking over his hands as he played the piano. Interestingly, he had contacted two members of the Society for Psychical Research some twenty years earlier with claims of precognition and the ability to **channel** various composers (Carr and Korner, pp. 5–6). The author visited him, with a colleague, at his house in Oxford—somewhat bizarrely he lived in his sizeable and carpeted garage—and he played the piano therein. The music consisted of fast and grandiose scales and arpeggios and bore little resemblance to the music of Liszt. In another case it was not possible to discover any detailed information about the American astrologer, trance medium and pianist/ composer Maxine Bell (1916–1997) of Los Angeles, other than she allegedly "had her Beethoven symphony performed locally in 1945" and was preparing a "**Brahms** piano concerto and a Tchaikovsky ballet" (cited in Freedland, p. 215).

An altogether different case concerned the conductor and composer Dennis Gray Stoll (1912–1987) who believed that the spirit of Sir Thomas Beecham (1879–1961) directed him towards the composition of ancient Egyptian music, which he (Stoll) had composed in a previous life. Stoll undertook several works which were performed from this inspiration (Carr, 1978) and in 1969 formed his own ensemble—the Nefer Ensemble—to accompany a group of Ancient Egyptian Temple Dancers that he had founded (www.starwisdomteaching.com/about/dennis-stoll/).

Mediums who were not known as musical mediums as such, but who nevertheless produced music in their **séances** included Catherine Mettler, the teenage daughter of a Hartford, Connecticut, doctor who it is claimed was "daily influenced by spirits whom all skilled musicians recognize by their graphic and peculiar style to be those whom they claim; namely, **Mozart**, Beethoven, Weber, and others, who each perform with marked and unmistakable individuality. Sometimes the compositions are wholly original and improvised upon given subjects. Sometimes they are recognized chef d'oeuvres of celebrated masters, of whom the medium has scarcely ever even heard" (Britten, p. 203). Miss Maud MacCarthy claimed to have received divine instruction on the **violin** from a luminous being when she was a child, and later she received singing lessons from an "**angel** teacher" who inspired her to study Indian music where "she learned to sing scales of twenty-four microtones to the octave in ten minutes" (McCarthy, p. 228). Mrs. Belle Miller caused a piano to leap in the air, even when men were sat upon it, as she played inspired music on it (Maynard, p. 33). On another occasion a piano sounded chords with no one touching it and also "[it] was raised at least four inches, and then slowly let down" (Crowell, p. 165). Harry Price wrote about the "Strange Case of Madame X" (Price, 131–139) which included among many dramatic alleged mediumistic activities, the ability to play the piano well beyond her normal capability. The famous medium Mina Crandon (1888–1941)—better known as "Margery"—was thoroughly investigated by numerous psychic investigators including William McDougal, W. Franklin Prince, Hereward Carrington and J. Malcolm Bird. The latter heard the sound of a bell in one of her séances as well as "notes as if a piano were being struck, some sort of harmonica" (Rogo, p. 104). The playing of musical instruments when conditions suggested that it was not possible, for instance, the hands of the mediums were tied or being held, occurred during the séances of other celebrated mediums such as **Stella C.** and Annie Eva Fay (Medhurst and Barrington, pp. 1781–1793). Despite being securely tied the Welsh medium referred to as "Lewis" was able to play and **levitate** several musical instruments, including a tambourine which it was possible to photograph in mid-air (Mowbray, p. 49). A musical medium referred to as "Thayer," from Wisconsin held séances in full light with "a square drum and two drum sticks, a guitar, three table bells of various sizes, and a rubber whistling ball" which were all played both singly and simultaneously seemingly without any human intervention (*Human Nature*, pp. 208–209). Although not actually performing herself the medium Miss Nina Francis conveyed information about **Beethoven**, Verdi and **Wagner** through her spirit control George R. Sims, the author and journalist who had died in 1922 (*Prediction*, p. 456).

A so-called vaudeville "musical medium" was Magdeleine G. (c. 1878–?) who was born in Tbilisi to Russian and Swiss parents who were both dancers. An article in *The Royal Magazine* (Dark, pp. 387–390) was devoted to her together with illustrations. She was trained in music and dancing and her "act" was to perform in a hypnotized state according to a chosen character from a musical genre, including the opera, allegedly unknown to her in a spellbinding and "transcendental" way (Price, pp. 268–269). She was tested by Charles Richet, Baron von Schrenck-Notzing, F.W.H. Myers, Colonal de Rochas and others. Schrenck-Notzing was so impressed with her that he wrote a book about her, *Die Traumtänzerin Magdeline G.* (1904) (Price, 269).

One of the most unusual investigations of a medium, referred to as "Rosemary," was embarked on by the composer and researcher Dr. Frederic H. Wood (1880–1963). She was said to have channeled messages from an ancient Egyptian princess who communicated in ancient Egyptian, which Wood and A.J. Howard Hulme worked to translate into English. Of particular interest was the music that was also conveyed through the spirit guide

"Vola." The music was recorded which was allegedly sung by sailors as they travelled along the Nile on a boat which she also described. She conveyed a popular **dance** tune from ancient Egypt which was similarly recorded and analyzed by Wood. He described the tunes as using modes which "were evidently in use in Egypt three thousand years ago, and they are still to be found in the folk-tunes of the Near East, as well as in those of most European nations" (Wood, pp. 57–62). The identity of "Rosemary" was actually Miss Ivy C. Beaumont (ca. 1895–1961).

(The further exploits of musical mediums can be read about in the works of Emma Harding Britten and Archibald Campbell Holms—see bibliography).

Britten, Emma Hardinge (1869). *The History of Modern American Spiritualism*. London: Burns.
Carr, Bernard, and Kathy Korner (1993). "Two Cases of Morbid Imagination and Precognition." *Psi Researcher* 10 (Summer): 5–6.
Carr, Jean (1978). "Encore from Sir Thomas Beecham." *Sunday Mirror*, March 26.
Crowell, Eugen (1875). *The Identity of Primitive Christianity and Modern Spiritualism*. Vol. I. New York: Author.
Dark, Sidney (1904). T"he Musical Medium." *The Royal Magazine*, September. London.
Freedland, Nat (1972). *The Occult Explosion*. London: Michael Joseph.
Human Nature. (1871). Vol. 5: 208–209. London.
Leaf, Horace (1950). "Sound in Relation to Mediumship." *Two Worlds* 63 (April 8): 651.
Maynard, Nettie Colburn (1917). *Was Abraham Lincoln a Spiritualist?* Chicago: Progressive Thinker.
McCarthy, Maud (1920). "Psychic Music." *The Two Worlds* 33 (April 9): 228.
Medhurst, R.G., and Mary Rose Barrington (1970). "Incantation." *Man, Myth and Magic*. Vol. 4. London: Purnell.
Mowbray, Major C.H. (1947). *Transition*. London: L.S.A.
Prediction (1936). "Musicians in the Spheres." Vol. I, no. 10 (November).
Price, Harry (1936). *Confessions of a Ghost-Hunter*. London: Putnam.
Rogo, D. Scott (1970). *NAD*. New York: University Books.
Willin, Melvyn J. (2005). *Music, Witchcraft and the Paranormal*. Ely: Melrose.
Wood, Frederic H. Wood (1939). *The Egyptian Miracle*. London: Rider.

Menotti, Gian Carlo

Gian Carlo Menotti (1911–2007) was an Italian composer who was noted for his popular operas. One such work was *The Medium* (1946) commissioned by Columbia University. It was inspired by his attendance at a séance with a baroness who believed herself to be in contact with her dead daughter. In the opera the medium, Madame Flora, is a fraudulent alcoholic and the work provides a somewhat morbid atmosphere for the fake psychic activity (*Psychic News*, p. 11).

Psychic News (2016). "Broadway opera about medium is reborn." December: p. 11.

Mesmer, Franz Anton

Franz Anton Mesmer (1734–1815) is known for his work in animal magnetism which can be argued led to hypnotism in the hands of other scientists. He was a medical doctor and an amateur musician (playing the glass harmonica) both of which suited his style of **healing**. What is less well-known was his acquaintance with Gluck, Haydn and **Mozart**—the latter's singspiel *Bastien und Bastienne* was thought to have first been performed in Mesmer's garden (Horden, p. 326). Mesmer also met Benjamin Franklin in 1779, who was interested to hear him play the glass harmonica (Crabtree, 1993). The place of music in his rituals directed the "magnetic fluid" into the correct places to counteract the imbalance of the afflicted humor. "Magnetism runs through nineteenth-century esotericism like the powerful unifying force it was claimed to be" (Horden, p. 329) and with it the vital music was more than an accompaniment, but rather an integral part of what many people believed to be a supernatural force.

The American psychologist Julian Jaynes (1920–1997) summed up the twentieth-century reaction to hypnosis as "the black sheep of the family of problems which constitute psychology.... It wanders in and out of laboratories and carnivals and clinics and village halls like an unwanted anomaly" (Jaynes, p. 379).

Crabtree, Adam (1993). *From Mesmer to Freud*. New Haven: Yale University Press.
Horden, Peregrine, ed. (2000). *Music as Medicine*. Aldershot: Ashgate.
Jaynes, Julian (1976). *The Origin of Consciousness in the Breakdown of the Bicameral Mind*. Boston: Houghton Mifflin.

Middleham Castle

Middleham Castle is situated in North Yorkshire, England, and was built in the eleventh century. It was the birthplace of Richard III's son Edward and a favorite abode of the king of England. During a visit by the Richard III Society music was heard for a number of minutes by several members of the society and then again later: "the same music suddenly struck up again, seemingly much nearer and louder, again for about a minute. There was clearly no question of **hoax**, and all obvious normal explanations seemed to be ruled out ... the music still sounded vaguely muffled, as though one had been standing there, say in the late fifteenth century, with the doors and windows of the great hall shut, and the minstrels had suddenly struck up in the gallery" (Dening, pp. 131–132).

Dening, John, and R.E. Collins (1996). *Secret History: The Truth about Richard III & the Princes*. Lavenham: Lavenham Press.

Middleham Castle in North Yorkshire has associations with the English King Richard III as well as with mysterious music being heard on several occasions (Jeanette Teare/Shutterstock.com).

Minsden Chapel

All that remains of the fourteenth-century Minsden Chapel, in Hertfordshire, England, are a few ruins. The author Elliott O' Donnell (1872–1965) spoke about having "heard sweet music" there on one occasion which started with the tolling of the lost **bells** (cited in O' Dell, p. 33). The investigator Damien O'Dell and the author both visited the site separately and did not witness anything paranormal, but Peter Underwood believed he may have heard a snatch of music which he couldn't account for during a visit.

O'Dell, Damien (2009). *Paranormal Hertfordshire*. Stroud: Amberley.

Moore, Sir Patrick

Sir Patrick Alfred Caldwell-Moore (1923–2012) was a celebrated English astronomer and researcher. He related that during an evening at his home having dinner with friends they all heard "a sound of music—not a tune, but concerted rippling chords, not random" (St. Aubyn and Hanbury, p. 115). He ran to the music room to find the **piano** lid closed and nobody there which baffled both him and his guests, but the event was never repeated in the future. In private correspondence with the author, he confirmed the story and stressed that he didn't find it in any way "spooky."

St. Aubyn, Astrid, and Zahra Hanbury (1996). *Ghostly Encounters*. London: Robson.

Morris Dances

It has been written that the music and dances of the Morris are ritual ceremonies that can bring luck, **healing** and fertility to those that associate with them as observers or participants. They "inherit a pagan tradition, which has persisted, especially among country people … and while they are taking part in the ritual, the young men are not of this world; they are superhumans" (Kennedy, p. 1890). Although the tradition of Cotswold and Border Morris dancing and music is well known to English audiences, its equivalent can be found throughout Europe—in Romania the *Calusari* dancers "produce a cathartic effect on any spectator exposed to the [music and dance] medicine which is now being constantly distilled and dispensed" (Kennedy, p. 1891). The shadowy figure of the Fool and

Morris Dancing is shown here by the Border Morris Group Wicket Brood who inspire their audiences wherever they perform. They hail from Bricket Wood in Hertfordshire where Gerald Gardner held his coven meetings in the nineteen forties (courtesy Susan Bell).

sometimes an attendant beast or hobbyhorse with pagan overtones and the yearly springtime focus on the maypole draws further attention to the ritual's association with fertility. The historian Ronald Hutton alludes to an origin from "a courtly fool's entertainment" or the "Arabs of Spain" (Hutton, p. 262), but whatever the true origin there is something very **magic**al about the performance of a well-rehearsed Morris side at a suitably atmospheric outdoor location.

Kennedy, Douglas (1970). "Morris Dances." *Man, Myth and Magic* Volume V: 1890–1892.
Hutton, Ronald (1996). *The Stations of the Sun*. Oxford: Oxford University Press.

Moses, William Stainton

William Stainton Moses (1839–1892) was unusually both an English Anglican priest as well as a Spiritualist who produced a considerable amount of **automatic writing**. His notebooks were published in a series of *Proceedings* by the Society for Psychical Research wherein he wrote about one of his band of forty-nine spirit guides being the composer Mendelssohn. Unfortunately, the composer did not convey music to him, but mainly philosophical dialogue. The strongest musical connection with Moses were the sounds from a large number of different instruments that both he and the sitters in the **séances** witnessed on several occasions:

September 3 and 4th: Same circle. Manifestations … intensified. The musical sounds have reached seven, the new one being like the noise made by striking fine porcelain, but with a very decided ring in it. It is a very singular sound, and is made with great intensity. The three-stringed lyre is also very beautiful, more like the dropping of liquid on a metallic surface than anything else. But the sounds are all indescribable.

1. The sounds are very pure, and express feeling most wonderfully. They are most like a thick harp string.
2. The sound of an old Egyptian harp with four strings. There is little similarity to a stringed sound.
3. The lyre has only three strings. It is an old Egyptian instrument, and the sound is like dropping water on a steel plate, a sort of liquid sound, very intense. I am told it is very like the sound of a harmonium reed.
4. Sound of a seven-stringed lyre, very pretty rippling sound, but the strings do not seem to me to be arranged in harmonial progression.
5. Sound like a drum, very deep, a sort of pro-longed roll.
6. Makes a sound like the ringing of fine porcelain, only that the ring is very much more pronounced. This is a very intense sound.
7. The Welsh Harper makes a sound as of the highest strings of a harp, sharp and ringing.
8. In addition, there is the sound of a tambourine and a sort of flapping

sound like large wings. [Edited from the *Proceedings of the Society for Psychical Research* (1896–1897) XI, part 37, p. 54].

On other occasions the musical descriptions were somewhat strange: "There were also notes closely resembling that of a violoncello, sometimes of great strength and sonorousness, such as would be produced by placing a 'cello on the top of a drum. There were also **harp** and zither-like sounds; and notes like those of a clarionet, sometimes drawn out into a dismal wail" (Campbell Holms, p. 310). The attending spirits would identify themselves through various sounds: "Goyen produced pure sounds like of a thick harp string. Chom made the sound of an old Egyptian harp with four strings. Said used a three-stringed lyre. Roophal a seven-stringed one with a rippling sound [and] Kabbila's sound was like a drum, very deep, a sort of prolonged roll, etc." (Fodor, p. 354). He wrote several books under the pseudonym "M.A. (Oxon)" and was analytical of the messages and phenomena that came through to him and his friends when attending the séances.

(For details of Moses' books see the bibliography.)

Myers, Frederic William Henry. "The Notebooks of Moses, William Stainton." *Proceedings Society for Psychical Research*. 1893–1894. Volume IX, part 35 and 1896–1897. Volume XI, part 37.

Campbell, Holms Archibald (1925). *The Facts of Psychic Science and Philosophy*. London: Kegan Paul.

Fodor, Nandor (1934). *Encyclopedia of Psychic Science*. London: Arthurs Press.

Mozart, Wolfgang Amadeus

Johannes Chrysostomus Wolfgangus Theophilus Mozart (1756–1791) was born in Salzburg, Austria, into a musical family. He was an outstanding example of a musical **prodigy** and was tested by the lawyer and member of the Royal Society, Daines Barrington (1727–1800) for his exceptional skills in **London** when he was eight years old (Scott and Moffett, p, 175). The tests were to discover his sight-reading capabilities, his extemporization skills and other musical abilities, which proved to be "astonishing" and prompted the accolade of "**genius**." Mozart's prodigious memory was another facet of his musical talent possibly coming from an unconscious awareness and he spoke of his compositional process as emerging complete into his mind all at once (*gleich alles zusammen*) (cited in Inglis, p. 64). Whether genius has a normal, abnormal or paranormal aspect to it can be argued according to one's definition of the words themselves and one's own beliefs. However, what is not in question was his being named by several **musical mediums** who claimed to be making contact with him from the spirit world where he communicated music to them. Perhaps this was not so fanciful since his superpowers have been compared to that of the mythical Orpheus and the spirit-contacting abilities of the **shamans** (Flaherty, pp. 150–165).

Flaherty, Gloria (1992). *Shamanism and the Eighteenth Century*. Princeton: Princeton University Press.
Inglis, Brian (1987). *The Unknown Guest—The Mystery of Intuition*. London: Chatto & Windus.
Scott, Donald, and Adrienne Moffett (1977). "The Development of Early Musical Talent in Famous Composers: A Biographical Review." *Music and the Brain*. Ed. Macdonald Critchley and R.A. Henson. London: Heinemann.

Mozart Effect

The original concept of what was later to be called the "Mozart Effect" was devised by **Alfred Tomatis** who found that the music of **Mozart** had a more calming effect on people's brains than other composers (Campbell, p. 27). In 1993 at the University of California, Gordon Shaw and Frances Rauscher, an expert on music cognition, studied the effects on college students of listening to the first ten minutes of the Mozart Sonata for Two **Pianos** in D Major (K.448) and the results suggested that a brief period of spatial enhancement occurred after the music had been listened to (Rauscher, p. 611). The idea that listening to Mozart's music increased one's intelligence level was promoted, despite the evidence being weak for such an assumption. There is considerable controversy as to whether the Mozart Effect actually exists at all and if it does whether it is simply a function of the brain responding to music (Hallam, 1996) or whether there are outside and currently unknown influences at play. Michael Linton, the head of the Division of Music Theory and Composition at Middle Tennessee State University, has written that the proponent of the effect, Don Campbell, provides evidence which is "usually anecdotal, and even this he misinterprets. Some things he gets completely wrong.... If Mozart's music were able to improve health, why was Mozart himself so frequently sick?" (https://www.firstthings.com/article/1999/03/the-mozart-effect). Other commentators have expressed a similar spirit of disbelief: "The Mozart effect is an example of how science and the media mix in our world. A suggestion in a few paragraphs in a scientific journal becomes a universal truth in a matter of months, eventually believed even by the scientists who initially recognized how their work had been distorted and exaggerated by the media" (Carroll, pp. 234–235).

Campbell, Don (1997). *The Mozart Effect*. London: Hodder & Stoughton.
Carroll, Robert Todd (2003). *The Skeptic's Dictionary*. Hoboken: John Wiley & Sons.
Hallam, Susan (1996). "Does music make you sharp?" *The Daily Telegraph*, 28 February.
Rauscher, Frances H., L. Gordon Shaw, and Catherine N. Ky (1993). "Music and Spatial Task Performance." *Nature* 365 (6447): 611.

Music of the Spheres

The Music of the Spheres (also called Harmony of the Spheres and *Musica Universalis*) equates the correlation of the moon, sun and planets as a form of inaudible music. The original concept is generally thought to have been devised by **Pythagoras** who actually heard the musical intervals leading to a system of cosmic and musical harmony. Nicolaus Copernicus also alluded to "non-solid celestial spheres" (www.crystalinks. com/musicspheres). **Johannes Kepler** extended the ideas in his *Harmonice Mundi* in 1619 and disputed some of **Robert Fludd**'s own opinions about the theory of harmony. In the twentieth century the author David Tame linked the "...vibrations from the heavens" with astrology which he believed "is rapidly emerging from the misty realms of superstition, newspaper columns and ignorant laughter, to establish itself as a valid science" (Tame, p. 234).

Tame, David (1984). *The Secret Power of Music*. Wellingborough: Turnstone Press.

    For an exhaustive study of the phenomena see Godwin, Joscelyn (1992). *Harmony of the Spheres: Source Book of Pythgorean Tradition in Music: Source Book of Agorean Tradition in Music*. Rochester: Inner Traditions Bear and Company.

Mysticism

Mysticism conveys a vast number of different interpretations and manifestations according to belief systems and periods in time. Music has often been an essential part of such experiences which were and still are beyond any normal understanding. Eastern traditions bring a mystical approach to their music through the overriding importance of the single sound or note—as in Japanese koto music—or the properties of the **ragas** in Indian music and the mystical nature of **Sufi** music has been explored at length (Friedlander, pp. 127–143) notably through the teaching of **Hazrat Inayat Khan**. Western mystics such as **Henry Suso** and Richard Rolle (the "Father of English Mysticism") heard music from what they believed to be **angel**ic sources and the mystics St. Guthlac, St. Therese de Lisieux and St. Chad all had music phenomena associated with them (Rogo, pp. 86–89). In more modern times Evelyn Underhill recorded accounts of paranormally produced music (Underhill, pp. 76–78) and **Nelsa Chaplin, Helen Bonny** and Attila von Sealay also underwent what they described as mystical experiences with accompanying music.

    In the early part of the twenty-first century the *Journal of the Music and Psyche Network* was founded by the composer Maxwell Steer which approached the issues of music and mysticism in depth from a variety

of viewpoints from knowledgeable writers. These included "Music and
Magic" (Steer, Vol. 1, pp. 19–26); "Music and the Paranormal" (Willin,
Vol. 1, pp. 74–84); "Music and the Metaphysical" (Harvey, Vol. 2, pp. 9–13);
"**Pythagorean** Aspects of Music" (Phillips, Vol. 3, pp. 33–58); and "Some
musings on *Anahata **nada***" (Perry, Vol. 4, pp. 9–15). Many further exam-
ples can be found in Joscelyn Godwin (1987).

Friedlander, Shems (1992). *Music by Nezih Uzel in The Whirling Dervishes*. New York: State
    University of New York Press.
Harvey, Jonathan (2003). "Music and the Metaphysical." *Journal of the Music and Psyche Net-
    work* 2. Tisbury, Wilts.
Perry, Frank (2001). "Pathways to Magic." *Journal of the Music and Psyche Network*1. Tisbury,
    Wilts.
Phillips, Stephen M. (2005). "Some musings on *Anahata nada*." *Journal of the Music and Psyche
    Network* 4. Tisbury, Wilts.
Steer, Maxwell (2001). "Pathways to Magic." *Journal of the Music and Psyche Network* 1. Tis-
    bury, Wilts.
Underhill, Evelyn (1955). *Mysticism*. Boston: E.P. Dutton.
Willin, Melvyn J. (2001). "Music and the Paranormal." *Journal of the Music and Psyche Net-
    work*. 1. Tisbury, Wilts.

NAD

NAD (or NADA) is a Sanskrit word with different meanings, but its
use here signifies "transcendental, astral, psychic, or paranormal music"
(Rogo, 1970) from no apparent source. In its ability to affect consciousness
it has also been referred to as "a divine science of psycho-sonics" (Stewart,
p. 104). Sometimes the words "Nada-Brahma" are used which implies the
deity of Brahma within a sound or celestial musical interpretation. Perhaps
the experience of NAD can be, at least partially, explained by the concept of
transcendental music:

> Perhaps the "music of the spheres" is some sort of property of the higher
> spheres—spiritual realms existing within the Universe that interweave with
> the physical world in which we live. Perhaps this is the realm we enter when we
> die. When a person comes close to death, perhaps a rift opens between our ter-
> restrial dimension and the Great Beyond, so that the patient can momentarily
> experience its pleasures and music. People sharing the intimacy of death with a
> close friend or relative could perhaps share in the experience. People enjoying
> out-of-body experiences might perceive the music, since a similar rift in the fab-
> ric of reality could easily take place during these mysterious excursions [Rogo,
> 1990, pp. 104–105].

The American parapsychologist D. Scott **Rogo** brought the word
into use with his two volumes devoted to such music (Rogo, 1970; 1972).
They contain a wealth of information about such varied musical anomalies as **near-death experiences**, musical **hallucinations**, transcendental

music and other related phenomena from a wide range of sources. He arranged the books in a case-by-case procedure, but of particular interest were the examples that he investigated personally. The opening case was given to him by his friend **Raymond Bayless** who claimed as a teenager to have heard "celestial" music which he remembered for the rest of his life (Rogo, pp. 14–15). As to the phenomena itself the mathematician and mystically minded Michael Whiteman (1906–2007) was well-versed in music and referred to such phenomena as "other-world experiences" in his diaries (archives of the Society for Psychical Research). **Out-of-body** musical experiences are also described within these books and notably from the studies of **Robert Crookall** (see bibliography for details). The state of NAD does not necessarily only occur in **altered states of consciousness** as for example, when a Mr. Barnes was lying on the floor of a plane when for more than half a minute he heard fantastic music (cited in Rogo, p. 36). NAD encompasses **near-death experiences** which have been extensively researched by **Ernesto Bozzano** and **William Barrett**.

At the conclusion of Rogo's second NAD book (Rogo, 1972, pp. 163–165) he expands on the ancient doctrines and the use of NAD indicating the "base sound of the universe" and he follows this with a combined list of cases from the two books. However, useful though this is, it does not provide either details of the phenomena witnessed or their original sources. Therefore, Appendix 2 at the end of this encyclopedia redresses this defect and expands and corrects where necessary.

Rogo, D. Scott (1970). *NAD*. New York: University Books.
Rogo, D. Scott (1972). *NAD. Volume 2*. New York: University Books.
Rogo, D. Scott (1990). *Beyond Reality*. Northants: Aquarian Press.
Stewart, Bob (1988). *Where Is St George?* London: Blandford Press.

Nadabrahmananda Saraswati, Swami

Nadabrahmananda Saraswati, Swami (1896–?) was an Indian Hindu musician and teacher who developed the energy of music and yoga through the psychic power of sound vibrations. He played various instruments and was a masterly vocal performer. He allegedly directed sounds to various parts of his body and was also said to suspend respiration for nearly half an hour in a state of trance, when playing the tabla. He also used sound vibrations for **healing** purposes (occulthealth.com/nadabrahmananda-saraswati-swami). There is video footage available purporting to showing him undergoing scientific testing (youtube.com/watch?v=4Ax0mG999lo).

Nanteos

Nanteos is a mansion house built in the eighteenth century on the site of an eleventh-century building near Aberystwyth in Wales. It is said to be haunted by a "Grey Lady" as well as **harp** music from no known source. There have been many witnesses from a variety of places as well as the family and friends of the owners (Underwood, p. 94).

Underwood, Peter (1993). *The Ghosthunters Almanac.* Orpington: Eric Dobby.

Near-Death Experiences (NDEs)

"Music is associated with death and around the time of death in a whole lot of fascinating ways" (Clarke, 2009). Composers have spoken of these experiences from both a personal and musical perspective. A prime example of the latter is **Elgar's** *The Dream of Gerontius* which can be cited as a fine example of what some people have witnessed in their near-death state which they have recounted on being resuscitated. **Arnold Schönberg** composed his String Trio op. 45 immediately following a cardiac arrest and while still in hospital. Composers have believed in an **altered state of consciousness** being accessed for their creative **inspiration** and the NDE is possibly the ultimate such altered state other than actual death. There is disagreement as to the origin of the experiences with arguments on both sides as to its chemical or electrical attributes in contrast to spiritual definitions (Willin, pp. 3–4). The psychologist Dr. Susan Blackmore favors a physiological approach (Blackmore, 1993), but many cases can be found in Scott **Rogo's** "NAD" books (1970; 1972); **Bozzano's** *Musica Trascendentale* (1943); and **William Barrett's** *Death-Bed Visions* (1926) which also include examples of actual **deathbed music** being heard. The publications *Light, Fate* and the journals of both Society for Psychical Research and the American Society for Psychical Research also provide many examples. More recently Margot Grey "found in a UK study that 11% of NDErs heard the **'music of the spheres'** [and used words such as] transcendental, unearthly harmonic beauty, angelic, sublimely beautiful" (cited in Willin, p. 6). In the twentieth and twenty-first centuries the author investigated cases such as **Tony Cicoria**, who started playing the **piano** after having been struck by lightning and **David Ditchfield** who started composing after having almost being killed in a rail accident. A similar claim is made by Marcey Hamm, who claims considerable **healing** results from her music (marceyhammmusic.com) which uses slow and sustained synthesized concordant homophonic sounds. The Canadian sound therapist Giles Bèdard was on the brink of death with Crohn's disease in 1973 when he had his NDE: "What I remembered the most is the music I heard when I was out of my body. It was fascinating. It was hard to tell how long the experience lasted. It could have been five seconds or half an hour" (*Psychic News*, p. 16). There are many cases still in evidence up to the present times which are studied by scientists such as Bruce Greyson, the professor emeritus of psychiatry and neurobehavioral sciences at the University of Virginia; Penny Sartori, an expert medical researcher in the field; Sam Parnia, director of the Human Consciousness Project at the University of Southampton; and Peter Fenwick, a neuropsychiatrist and neurophysiologist. The author was in contact with the composer **John Tavener** and violinist **Paul Robertson** near to their times of death, both of whom experienced NDEs involving music. After appealing to the public for further instances a number of examples were sent to him from throughout the UK with similar experiences that people had reported in the past, namely "angelic," "waves of sound," and "all encompassing" music (private correspondence).

Blackmore, Susan (1993). *Dying to Live*. London: Grafton.
Clarke, Eric, Heather Professor of Music, Oxford University. (2009). Private correspondence.
Psychic News (2016). "Does 'Music from Heaven' Accompany Us into the Next Life?" October: 14–17.
Willin, Melvyn J. (2011). "Music and Death: An Exploration of the Place Music Has at the Time of Human Death, with Special Emphasis on the Near-Death-Experience." *The Paranormal Review* 58 (April).

Nebraska Wesleyan University

A case of alleged haunting was reported by the American psychologist Gardner Murphy (1895–1979) at this private Methodist university in Lincoln in 1963. A secretary, Mrs. Coleen Buterbaugh, heard the sound of a marimba being played followed by an unpleasant odor and the sight of a strangely dressed woman that faded before her. It was later discovered that a woman who fitted the description given by Mrs. Buterbauch had died in the same place in 1936 (Roy, p. 1716).

Roy, Archie (1982). "Living in the Past." *The Unexplained* 86. London: Orbis.

Odiham Castle

The ruins of the thirteenth-century Odiham Castle are situated on the banks of the Basingstoke Canal in Hampshire, England, and it has always been known as "King John's Castle" because of its association with him and Magna Carta. The investigator Peter Underwood related that many of the locals had heard piping music there as well as Alasdair Alpin MacGregor (1899–1970), the celebrated writer, and his wife (Underwood, p. 21).

Underwood, Peter (1996). *Ghosts & Haunted Places*. London: Piatkus.

Old Soar Manor

Old Soar Manor, Borough Green, Kent, England is a thirteenth-century dwelling with a long history of haunting attached to it. The residents of the adjacent eighteenth-century farmhouse have reported hearing "church music" when the Manor was empty at the time (Underwood, p. 177).

Underwood, Peter (1984). *This Haunted Isle*. London: Harrap Limited.

Old Stocks Inn

The Old Stocks Inn is to be found in Stow-on-the-Wold in Gloucestershire, England. It is a restored coaching inn which has reports attached to it from the twentieth century of a singing ghost called "George" and **piano** music from an unknown source. It has been modernized and no phenomena has been reported recently (www.hauntedhostelries.uk/haunted-inns/south-west/cotswold/the-old-stocks-inn).

Out-of-Body Experiences (OOBEs)

Out-of-body experiences (OOBEs) can also be linked with **near-death experiences** albeit without the critical element of approaching death—if indeed death was actually approaching. There are further arguments that the imagination is responsible for the belief in exiting the body and that astral projection, or any other description, really does not happen. Scientists have undertaken experiments to try and ascertain whether hidden objects, number patterns or other checkpoints can be discovered which would not be possible without some form of withdrawal from the body (Blackmore, pp. 193–195). According to skeptics the sensations of leaving the body can arise through lucid **dream**ing, physical exhaustion, **drugs** or alcohol and mental techniques such as **ganzfeld** and sensory deprivation, whereas others argue that a soul or etheric body is responsible for the activity (Muldoon, 1936). The musician Luis Perez believes that the music he perceives comes from an astral plane and he is also visited from the beings within **UFOs** via dream-like experiences (O' Neill, pp. 34–35).

There are many, many musical examples to be found in books such as the NAD books, the multiple works of Joscelyn Godwin (see bibliography) and other sources devoted to NDEs. Many of the musical experiences stem from religious accounts and use suitably holy terminology to define them—"celestial," "heavenly," "angelic" and so on. However, what has been described inadequately as a **"hallucination"** does not necessarily involve reliance on a belief system. From the many examples one edited and representative sample must suffice:

> It was early one summer's morning that I heard the music. I had ... slept very soundly.... But suddenly I was awake and there was music, wonderful music.... I saw the large house across the way, perhaps fifty feet away.... The music could not have come from there. It came from the air outside the window. It poured in, seemingly against my face.... I felt spellbound. I did not try to move. But I listened, and this is what I heard: A very large group of instruments being played in a way I had never heard music played before. It was as though the instruments were not far apart.... I have thought about this music with sincere effort, trying to decide what instruments must have played it, but I have never come to a conclusion.... No one instrument played solo at any time. ..But I felt there were many because of the variety of tones. There were no wild clashes of sound, no beating of drums, no shrill high tones. But there was definite melody, wonderful harmony ... which seemed an endless song without words.... This music was of an intensity most unusual. It had meaning and great beauty. Not charm as some music, but a beauty that enthralled me [Rogo, p. 99].

Blackmore, Susan (1983). *Beyond the Body: An Investigation of Out-of-the-Body Experiences.* London: Granada.
Muldoon, S. (1936). *The Case for Astral Projection.* Chicago: Ariel Press.
O'Neill, Terry (1999). "Luis Perez: Music from the Astral Plane." *Fate* (April): 34–35.
Rogo, D. Scott (1990). *Beyond Reality.* Northamptonshire: Aquarian Press.

    See wikipedia.org/wiki/Out-of-body experience for multiple examples of non-musical OOBE studies.

Outsider Music

Outsider Music is the work of Irwin Chusid (1951–), an American journalist and record producer. His creation *Songs in the Key of Z. The Curious Universe of Outsider Music* consists of a book of the same name and CDs which have been described as follows: "At the farthest reaches of our culture, there exists an anarchic tribe of visionaries whose works are likely to be dismissed by casual listeners as evidence of a pathological condition—gross and incurable incompetence, willful neglect of form, delusional thinking, or utter madness" (Honigman, p. 42). The music sounds anything but normal and although not coming from paranormal sources, other than the "creativity" of the performers and composers, its content is certainly bizarre! Artists include The Shaggs, Jandek, Jack Mudurian and Captain Beefheart.

Honigman, A. (2001). "Songs in the Key of Z." *Fate* (July): 42.

Paganini, Niccolò

The famous Italian violinist, guitarist and composer Nicolò Paganini (1782–1840) was known in his day as an outstanding **violin** virtuoso, who was also a friend of **Berlioz**. The violinist **Florizel von Reuter** believed himself to be in spirit contact with Paganini and wrote the full details of this communication in his book *The Psychical Experiences of a Musician* (Reuter, 1928) with a foreword by Sir Arthur Conan Doyle. Paganini recounted many details of his life through Reuter and in another book (Reuter, p. 91) he gave details of **Beethoven**'s death and entry into the spirit realm. Interestingly he added a note to say that the tribute to Beethoven "was written by Nicolo in English in order ... to save us the additional strain which the transmission of these thoughts in his own speech would have involved" (Reuter, p. 94).

Reuter, Florizel von (1928). *The Psychical Experiences of a Musician*. London: Simpkin Marshall.
Reuter, Florizel von (1931). *A Musician's Talks with Unseen Friends*. London: Rider & Co.

Palladino, Eusapia

Eusapia Palladino (1854–1918) was an Italian medium who produced physical phenomena and was investigated extensively by numerous psychical researchers when she was observed to be faking the phenomena on many occasions. However, she was also seen to levitate both a mandolin above her head behind her and also a small accordion. Dr. Ercole Chiaia sought her out in 1886 and contacted the Italian psychiatrist and criminologist Cesare Lombroso, requesting Lombroso's help in determining whether or not she possessed some sort of new physical force. He disclosed that she played on musical instruments including "organs, **bells** and tambourines" without her seemingly touching them (www.americanhauntingsink.com/wonder): "One of the most remarkable manifestations, however, was the playing of the mandolin, on at least two occasions. The instrument sounded in the cabinet first of all—distinct twangings of the strings being heard, in response to pickings of Eusapia's fingers on the hand of one of her controllers. The mandolin then floated out of the cabinet, on to the séance table, where, in full view of all, nothing touching it, it continued to play for nearly a minute…. Eusapia was at the time in deep trance" (Fodor, 1934).

Carrington, Hereward, and John Meader (1912). *Death: Its Causes and Phenomena*. New York: Funk & Wagnalls.

Parapsychology

The Cambridge English Dictionary defines parapsychology as "the study of mental abilities, such as knowing the future or telepathy that seem to go against or be outside the known laws of nature and science" (dictionary. cambridge.org/dictionary/english/parapsychology). In reality the subject encompasses more than this since university departments researching parapsychology, such as in **Edinburgh** in Scotland and Northampton in England, often study concepts such as **magic** and deception that are strongly allied to the subject as well as mainstream psychology. The word was initially used in connection with psychical research, but with a greater emphasis on laboratory-based exploration. Links to the paranormal and specifically musical phenomena can be found in **ganzfeld** studies when music was employed as the target for extra sensory perception (ESP). These would include the following experiments: (Keil, 1965, pp. 35–44); (Willin, 1996a, pp. 1–17); (Willin, 1996b, pp. 103–108); (Parra and Villanueva, 2004, pp. 114–127). The results of these tests did not produce any significant data linking music with the ability of subjects to experience telepathy, despite a few seemingly positive examples in the author's own experiment (Willin, 1996b, 1–17).

Skeptics tend to label parapsychology as "pseudo-science" together with a number of other studies in which there is controversy as to their legitimacy (Hines, 1988), but the level of professionalism that is usually maintained in its study in universities around the world would suggest the subject is far from being pseudo-scientific.

Hines, Terence (1988). *Pseudoscience and the Paranormal*. New York: Prometheus.
Keill, H.H.J. (1965). "A GESP Test with Favorite Musical Targets." *Journal of Parapsychology* 29: 35–44.
Parra, Alejandro, and Jorge Villanueva (2004). "Are Musical Themes Better Than Visual Images as ESP-Targets? An Experimental Study Using the Ganzfeld Technique." *Australian Journal of Parapsychology* 4, no. 2, 114–127.
Willin, Melvyn J. (1996a). "A Ganzfeld Experiment using Musical Targets." *Journal of the Society for Psychical Research* 61, no. 842: 1–17.
Willin, Melvyn J. (1996b). "A Ganzfeld Experiment Using Musical Targets with Previous High Scorers from the General Population." *Journal of the Society for Psychical Research* 61, no. 842: 1–17.

Parrott, Ian

Ian Parrott (1916–2012) was an English composer and musicologist who held the Gregynog Chair of Music at the University of Aberystwyth for many years. During this period he devoted a considerable amount of time to the music of **Rosemary Brown** and to the **Versailles** time slip where music was allegedly heard from unknown sources. From a position of considerable musical knowledge he defended Brown's music and one piece in particular: "Undoubtedly the most spectacular piece, **Liszt**'s *Grübelei*, was partly 'dictated' (29 May 1969) with BBC TV engineers, etc., in the room—quite a remarkably successful occasion" (Parrott, p. 11). He also used his skills in musical analysis to try and decipher the actual music that was heard by the witness Eleanor Jourdain during her "adventure" at Versailles (Parrott, 1966).

Parrott experienced his own extra-sensory input when he visited the temple of Luxor in Egypt during the Second World War. He felt that the main theme of the symphonic impression "Luxor" which he had subsequently composed had "come" to him in a completely unknown way and he was told by the musicologist Dr. Frederic Wood that the Lydian mode melody "was almost certainly of the period of the eighteenth dynasty, more than three thousand years ago" (cited in Inglis, p. 70).

Inglis, Brian (1987). *The Unknown Guest—The Mystery of Intuition*. London: Chatto &Windus.
Parrott, Ian (1966). *The Music of "An Adventure."* London: Regency Press.
Parrott, Ian (1978). *The Music of Rosemary Brown*. London: Regency Press.

Penfield, Wilder

Wilder Graves Penfield (1891–1976) was an American brain surgeon who undertook experiments into the hallucinatory activity of the brain notably through temporal lobe stimulation. He discovered that during this **surgery** the use of electrodes on the area produced **hallucinations** of music, which was not physically present, but may have been the reproduction of a past experience. In different circumstances this may have led to belief in a paranormal source. Examples of the music "heard" were "White Christmas," "Hush-a-Bye Baby," "The War March of the Priests" (Mendelssohn), hymn tunes, organ and orchestral music (Penfield & Perot, pp. 595–696). Some of his other findings had links to sensations of déjà-vu and OOBEs.

Penfield, Wilder, and Phanor Perot (1963). "The Brain's Record of Auditory and Visual Experience: A Final Summary and Discussion." *Brain* 86, no. 4 (December).

Pettibone Tavern

The original Pettibone Tavern was built by Jonathan Pettibone in Simsbury, Connecticut, in 1788. It has been remodeled over the centuries but was known as a haunted location from before and since the 1970s. A detailed report was made by three employees who witnessed the sound of a woman singing from inside the building after it had been securely locked and then checked again for intruders. The singing lasted several minutes and seemed to emanate from different parts of the tavern. It is currently known as Abigail's Grille and Wine Bar and the alleged music does not seem to have returned.

Groh, Richard (2002). "The Singing Ghost of Pettibone Tavern." *Fate* (September): 36–38.

Phantasms of the Living

Phantasms of the Living (1886) was an early two-volume work on the history of psychical research by **Edmund Gurney**, Frederic W.H. Myers and Frank Podmore of considerable importance documenting over seven hundred cases of ghosts and related phenomena with a viewpoint of telepathy being relevant to the information discovered. The books contain many examples of musical **hallucinations** which have been quoted by other authors as well as in this current work. Some of the examples fit into the category of remarkable coincidences as when an army officer discovered an old and somewhat obscure manuscript and at the same moment another officer (actually a colonel) started to hum the same piece for reasons which he could not explain (Gurney, Vol. I, pp. 234–235). In another example a bell was heard tolling on board a ship which could only by heard by one sailor, who believed it was an omen of bad news to follow (Gurney, Vol. II, p. 127). Collective musical hallucinations are especially important, notably when nobody present suggests that music of a specific type has been mentioned. When the daughter of the Sewell family was terminally ill in 1885 a number of people present heard what they described as an "Aeolian **harp**" playing (Gurney, Vol. II, pp. 221–223).

Gurney, Edmund, Frederic W.H. Myers, and Frank Podmore (1886). *Phantasms of the Living.* 2 vols. London: Trübner.

Piano

The piano has been a favorite source of alleged paranormal music since its arrival in the world of music in the eighteenth century and notably

during its heyday in the late nineteenth century and throughout the twentieth century. Its capacity to move seemingly of its own accord was witnessed
by **Abraham Lincoln** and this activity was seen at other times especially
during the nineteenth century. Dr. F.L.H. Willis recounted an experience
at a séance when "he was impressed to go to the piano and play, though he
had no knowledge of music; and the piano, which was a heavy grand, rose
and fell, keeping time with the music; and it continued to sway after five
men got on top of it…. Musical instruments played untouched in his presence and materialization occurred" (Campbell Holms, p. 344). Piano music
was heard in a building in Leicester which had originally been used as a
music shop. However, in 1980 several people heard piano music sounding
from the building which was firmly locked up and in darkness (Cutting,
p. 24). In the 1960s a professional family living in Sussex, England, heard
piano music in their house when they did not possess an instrument and
there was no obvious sound source (Moss, p. 64).

Mediums claiming to be in contact with dead composers and performers have often been drawn to the keyboard by their contacts from the
spirit world (Willin, 2005). One such manifestation occurred at the **Tweedale** rectory during the night of January 29, 1934, when the Rev. Charles
Tweedale's daughter Marjorie heard a piano playing when the piano was
"out of repair at the time" (Tweedale, p. 194). The psychic investigator
Harry Price suggested one possible reason why a piano would be thought to
be played by unseen hands:

> At about 11. 45 I was awakened by the church bells ringing in the New Year. The
> little church was only about two hundred yards from the house in which I was
> staying. As I lay awake listening to them, I fancied…. I could hear sweet music
> doming from the dining room, which was immediately below my bedcham-
> ber. ..I could distinctly hear faint chords as from a harp or zither. Then I remem-
> bered that in the apartment below me was a piano, and it occurred to me that
> someone might be twanging the strings, producing a sort of pizzicato effect….
> Actually, the explanation was quite simple. I discovered that certain notes from
> the piano recurred always during a particular peal from the bells, and this gave
> me the clue to the "ghostly music." The wires of the piano were vibrating in sym-
> pathy with the noisy bells [Price, p. 38].

Others have turned to the piano/ keyboard after life threatening events in
their lives such as **Tony Cicoria** and **David Ditchfield** or the instrument
has been a focus in the lives of musical **savants**.

One bizarre episode happened in Kent, England, in 2005 when an
unknown man was found wandering the streets of a local town (Sheerness)
who seemed unable to speak but could play the piano. He was taken to a
psychiatric hospital and numerous probably exaggerated stories arose as to
his identity and musical capability (Jack, pp. 286–290). It would seem that

he may have been a German national and was taken back to his homeland in due course suitably "cured" (kentonline, 3 June 2020).

An unusual report of piano music being heard was sent to the author by Ms. Divina Swan who reported that while she was in the bath, she heard her own piano being played at a far higher standard than usual and that no one else was in the house at the time. When she went to investigate the music stopped, but when she returned to the bathroom, the music started up once more "of the utmost beauty" (private correspondence).

Campbell Holms, Archibald (1925). *The Facts of Psychic Science and Philosophy*. London: Kegan Paul.
Cutting, Angela (1982). "Mysterious Music." *Leicestershire Ghost Stories*. Blabby, Leicester.
Jack, Albert (2007). *Albert Jack's Ten-Minute Mysteries*. London: Penguin Books.
www.kentonline.co.uk/sheerness/news/the-story-of-the-worlds-most-famous-missing-man-228062.
Moss, Peter (1977). *Ghosts Over Britain*. London: BCA.
Price, Harry (1936). *Confessions of a Ghost-Hunter*. London: Putnam.
Tweedale, Charles (1940b). *News from the Next World*. London: Werner Laurier.
Willin, Melvyn J. (2005). *Music, Witchcraft and the Paranormal*. Ely: Melrose.

Piper, Leonora

Leonora Piper (1857–1950) was an American trance medium who was investigated at length by numerous psychical researchers and other scientists. The Harvard psychologist William James described her as his "one white crow" to illustrate that if there is just one person or happening that is beyond normal apprehension, then one can no longer insist that the alleged phenomena cannot exist, or that "all crows are black" (Nemrow, pp. 309–324). Her two most famous spirit guides were a French doctor referred to as "Phinuit" and "G. P." who was alleged to be the spirit of George Pellew, a friend of one of her investigators, Richard Hodgson, who had died in 1892. One of Piper's early spirit guides was J.S. **Bach**, who had also been the guide to her mentor a blind medium called Mr. Cocke (Hodgson, p. 46). Bach had allegedly formed a "band" to make contact with her, but he soon announced that he and the other guides would withdraw to allow all the energies to be focused on Phinuit (Sage, 1904). Unfortunately, Bach did not present anything to confirm his true identity during his encounters with Mrs. Piper.

The Society for Psychical Research investigator Richard Hodgson (1855–1905) undertook a serious examination of her claims of spirit communication resulting in detailed notes recording some of her **séances**. In Boston in 1893 she sat for the Rev. and Mrs. Sutton whose daughter had died six weeks earlier. In addition to numerous verified details of the child being conveyed to the sitters she also sang a song which she had known "through the entranced medium" and another song could be heard in a childlike voice from the medium's mouth. These were allegedly the only two songs the child had fully known in life (cited in Rogo, p. 31).

Hodgson, Richard (1892). "Mrs. Piper's Early Trances." *Proceedings of the Society for Psychical Research* 8.
Nemrow, L.A. (2019). "One White Crow." Attributed to Henry James. *Essays in Criticism* LXIX, no. 3 (July).
Rogo, D. Scott (1986). *Life After Death*. London: Guild.
Sage, Michael (1904). *Mrs. Piper & the Society for Psychical Research*. New York: Scott-Thaw.

Plants and Music

The subject of plants' response to music must be treated with caution since there are many spurious claims some of which could be firmly placed in the world of fiction. Other assertions, including those by the biochemist Linda Long, are involved with *sound* rather than *music* which therefore precludes them from this survey. However, in January 1988, the Japanese geneticist Susumu Ohno found that the notes derived from genetic codes resembled music from the "Baroque and Romantic eras" (*Fortean Times*, p. 8). Furthermore, sound has been suggested as a cause of the formation of crop circles with "trilling" sounds being recorded during some activity (Silva, p. 16).

There is sometimes the possibility for the claims made for music affecting plants being caused by other factors such as breath or temperature fluctuations. **Cleve Backster** undertook work with a polygraph which he believed indicated that plants responded to music, which was taken up with a best-selling book written by Peter Tompkins and Christopher Bird: *The Secret Life of Plants* (Tompkins and Bird, pp. 145–162). They devoted a complete section to "Tuned to the **Music of the Spheres**" where they discussed the experiments of T.C. Singh, the head of the botany department at the University of Annamalai, near Madras. His assistant played the **violin** in the vicinity of *hydrilla* which responded positively as was also the case with the playing of **ragas**. In Milwaukee, Ontario, Illinois, and other places they related similar instances with a variety of plants and crops. Dorothy Retallack, an organist and mezzo soprano, undertook an extensive university study from 1968 to 1971 at Temple Buell College, in Colorado which led to her own book on the subject (Retallack, 1973). Her results suggested that even though the plants had a liking for J.S. **Bach**, their favorite was the sitar playing of ragas by Ravi Shankar. Folk and country and western music showed no different reactions to the plants being subjected to silence, but jazz was again a popular choice for them (cited in Berendt, pp. 79–80). The author David Tame devotes a chapter to the subject in his book *The Secret*

Power of Music (Tame, pp. 141–145) where he draws attention to the adverse effects of some music on "'beans, squash (marrow), corn, morning glory and coleus' … Within ten days, the plants exposed to Led Zeppelin and Vanilla Fudge were all leaning away from the speaker. After three weeks they were stunted and dying. The beans exposed to the 'new music' [contemporary avant-garde atonal music] leaned 15 degrees from the speaker…. The plants left in silence had the longest roots and grew the highest" (Tame, p. 143).

Inevitably not everyone agrees with these findings! Arthur Galston and Clifford Slayman heavily criticized the information conveyed in the Tompkins and Bird book (Galston and Slayman, 1981) and Lisa Summer similarly attacks both their work and others in a scathing attack with accusations of "unsubstantiated reports based upon uncontrolled experiments, random observations, and anecdotal reports"; "dubious research"; and "bad science" (Summer, pp. 119, 120, 122).

Berendt, J. (1987). *Nada Brahma: The World Is Sound*. London: East West.
Fortean Times (2001). "Plant Music." No. 150 (September): 8.
Galston, Arthur, and Clifford Slayman (1981). "Plant Sensitivity and Sensation." *Science and the Paranormal*. New York: Scribner's.
Rettalack, Dorothy (1973). *The Sound of Music and Plants*. Santa Monica: De Vorss.
Silva, Freddy (2005). "Crop Circles … Created by Sound?" *Fate* (February): 12–21.
Summer, Lisa (1996). *Music—The New Age Elixir*. New York: Prometheus Books.
Tame, David (1984). *The Secret Power of Music*. Wellingborough: Turnstone Press.
Tompkins, Peter, and Christopher Bird (1973). *The Secret Life of Plants*. New York: Harper and Row.

Poling Priory

St. John's Priory, known locally as "Poling Priory," is situated in Sussex, England, and is said to date back to the twelfth century. "Many residents of the house have frequently reported hearing ghostly music and voices…. One authority verified the **chant**ing as ancient **Gregorian** music used at funeral services" (Underwood, p. 186).

Underwood, Peter (1971). *Gazetteer of British Ghosts*. London: Souvenir Press.

Pool of the Harper

Llandyssul is a small town in Wales where a harper allegedly drowned in a part of the River Teifi, known as the "Pool of the Harper." It is said that his music can sometimes be heard there still, but no other details have been found (Hippisley Coxe, p. 148).

Hippisley Coxe, Antony D. (1973). *Haunted Britain*. London: Pan Books.

Possession

The concept of possession is open to different interpretations according to history and cultures. The German philosopher and psychologist Traugott Konstantin Oesterreich (1880–1949) defined it as "a state ... in which the normal individuality is temporarily replaced by another and leaves no memory on return to the normal ... [often with] intense motor and emotional excitement" (Oesterreich, p. 39). He recounted rituals where the supernatural language of music was used by a goye-player, a **violin**ist or a guitar player to drive out the *babaku* that possessed a sick man (Oesterreich, pp. 134–135). Gilbert Rouget, Peter Cooke and Jan Platvoet have written about the subject at length pertaining to African cultures in particular (Rouget, 1985; Cooke, 2000; Platvoet, 2000) and Gary Tomlinson explores the subject from the area of Renaissance **magic** with reference to **tarantism** (Tomlinson, pp. 145–188). The impact of music upon this **altered state of consciousness** should not be underestimated. It is used in **exorcism** to dispel spirits and as a means of provoking possession and has long been associated with **shaman**istic trances and the Dionysiac cult of ancient Greece (Oesterreich, p. 396 index). Ethnomusicology shows an interest in the subject which frequently appears in its literature (for example, Jankowsky, pp. 185–208).

Cooke, Peter R. (2000). "Appeasing the Spirits: Music, Possession, Divination and Healing in Busoga, Eastern Uganda." *Indigenous Religious Musics*. Eds. Ralls-MacLeod and Harvey. Aldershot: Ashgate.

Jankowsky, Richard C. (2007). "Music, Spirit Possession and the In-Between: Ethnomusicological Inquiry and the Challenge of Trance." *Ethnomusicology Forum* 16, no. 2 (November). Taylor & Francis.

Oesterreich, Traugott Konstantin (1930). *Possession: Demoniacal and Other*. London: Kegan Paul.

Platvoet, Jan G. (2000). "Chasing Off God: Spirit Possession in a Sharing Society." *Indigenous Religious Musics*. Eds. Ralls-MacLeod and Harvey. Aldershot: Ashgate.

Rouget, Gilbert (1985). *Music and Trance: A Theory of the Relations Between Music and Possession*. Chicago: University of Chicago Press.

Tomlinson, Gary. (1993). *Music in Renaissance Magic*. Chicago: University of Chicago.

Premonitions

Premonitions have long been an investigative feature of psychical research and sometimes they embrace the world of music. The composers **Saint-Saëns** and **Liszt** both experienced them as well as the singer **Galli-Marie** and premonitory bagpipe music has been heard in Scottish castles such as **Cortachy**, to announce impending deaths. Other cases are less well-known such as an example in the village of Cookham near the River Thames when a boy felt compelled for no apparent reason to play a funeral march at a joyful party to celebrate an engagement. The next day he was found dead in the river (Godefroi, pp. 366–367). The spirit of the **violin** maker Stradivarius allegedly gave the Reverend **Tweedale** confirmatory premonitions which he devoted to two chapters of his book (Tweedale, pp. 143–218).

Godefroi, Katherine (1923). "Premonitions Through the Medium of Music." *Occult Review* XXXVII, no. 4 (April): 364–368.
Tweedale, Charles (1940b). *News from the Next World*. London: Werner Laurier.

Prince of Wales Inn

The Prince of Wales is an inn at Kenfig in Mid-Glamorgan, Wales. In 1982 the landlord claimed to have heard organ music playing there when there was no organ present. Electrical engineer John Marke and industrial chemist Allan Jenkins decided to investigate and they set-up recording equipment to test the veracity of the claim. They believed that the sounds they recorded sounded like, among other things, organ music which had been activated by the electrodes they had attached to the stone walls overnight (Bord, p. 191). The author has heard the alleged organ sounds which, in his opinion, do not sound like an organ and according to the BBC Sound Workshop engineer John Hunt, feedback is a more likely answer to the mystery (Willin, p. 127).

Bord, Janet, and Colin (1989). *Modern Mysteries of the World*. London: BCA.
Willin, Melvyn J. (2005). *Music, Witchcraft and the Paranormal*. Ely: Melrose.

Prodigies

Questions inevitably arise concerning the paranormality of child prodigies whether they are musical or otherwise. The condition is generally thought to be at least abnormal and with varying degrees of exceptional capability which sometimes move into the realm of the paranormal, or at the very least are perceived as such. The phenomenal performing aptitude of **Pepito Arriola, Mozart** and **Virgil Fox** have been referred to, but the examples of **Rubinstein, Paganini**, Mendelssohn and **Saint-Saëns** might also be highlighted. Some prodigies, despite a spectacular start to their careers, did not progress in the ways of the above. These included Charles Wesley (1757–1834)—son of the founder of Methodism—also Samuel Wesley (1766–1837) and William Crotch (1775–1847) (Scott and Moffett, pp. 174–201). In the twenty-first century the performers' list would include Emily Bear, Yuja Wang, Brianna Kahane, Kang Eunju, Noah Gray Cabey,

Umi Garett, Yu Pyol Mi, Sungha Yung and Jackie Evancho. (www.youtube.com/watch?v=EV1j8F0-FsU) and the remarkable composer, pianist and **violin**ist Alma Deutscher. Once child prodigies move into their teens and adulthood, they usually lose the title "prodigy" and become mainstream musicians in their own right.

Scott, Donald, and Adrienne Moffett (1977). "The Development of Early Musical Talent in Famous Composers: A Biographical Review." *Music and the Brain*. Eds. Macdonald Critchley and R.A. Henson. London: Heinemann.

Puccini, Giacomo

Giacomo Antonio Domenico Michele Secondo Maria Puccini (1858–1924) was a famous Italian composer of mainly operas. His conversations with **Arthur Abell** revealed his belief in the "supernatural influence which qualifies me to receive Divine truths" (Abell, p. 116). He spoke at length about the "vibration to pass from the dynamo, which the soul-center is, into my consciousness, and the inspired ideas are born" and how "that higher Power we call God" (Abell, p. 116–118) allowed him to access **inspiration** which he then formed into the music.

Abell, Arthur M. (1955). *Talks with Great Composers*. London: Psychic Book Club.

Purse Caundle Manor

Purse Caundle Manor, a fifteenth-century manor house in Dorset, England has been the scene of the unknown **chant**ing of plainsong. It was the original site of Athelney Abbey which was recorded in the Domesday Book in 1086 (Legg, p. 35).

Legg, Rodney (1969). *A Guide to Dorset Ghosts*. Bournemouth: Dorset.

Pythagoras

Pythagoras of Samos (c. 570–c. 495 BCE) was an ancient Greek philosopher whose work had a lasting influence on mathematics and music. Unfortunately, his works did not survive, and the researcher is therefore reliant on the writings of his followers and subsequent scholars. Iamblichus of Chalcis (CE c. 250–c. 325) provided much of the detail (Iamblichis, 1818). One learns from him and others that he "distinguished three sorts of music in his philosophy ... *musica instrumentalis*, the ordinary music; ...

musica humana, the continuous but unheard music … resonance between the soul and the body; and *musica mundana*, the music made by the cosmos itself, which would come to be known as the **music of the spheres**" (cited in James, p. 31). Pythagoras believed not only in the direct interaction of number, music and the cosmos, but also that music could act as a force of **healing** of the body and mind. The story related by **Boethius** of his passing by a brazier's shop and hearing the relations between the sounds caused by hammering on the iron caused him to experiment with the division of sounds leading to the invention of the monochord and the subsequent system of intervals. Pythagoras opened his own academy at Crotona in Italy, between Tarsus and Sicily and his teaching was of such intensity that his students "were sufficiently conditioned that such inner faculties as extra sensory perception and clairvoyance would rapidly assert themselves" (Pepper and Willcock, p. 21).

Iamblichus (1818). *Life of Pythagoras or Pythagoric Life*. Trans. Thomas Taylor. London: A.J. Valpy.
James, Jamie (1995). *The Music of the Spheres*. London: Abacus.
Pepper, Elizabeth, and John Willcock (1994). *Magic and Mystical Sites*. Grand Rapids: Phanes Press.

Rachmaninoff, Sergei

Sergei Vasilyevich Rachmaninoff (1873–1943) was a Russian composer and pianist. After a disastrous performance of his first symphony in St. Petersburg he suffered a nervous breakdown that stunted his composition. Following a period of training in auto-suggestion by his hypnotist Nikolai Dahl (1860–1939) he returned to composition with his second **piano** concerto and described his **inspiration** "as he looked at rain-soaked foliage or a sunset the music would swirl to him: 'All the voices at once. Not a bit here, a bit there. All. The whole grows. Whence it came, how it began, how can I say? It came up within me, was entertained, written down'" (cited in Ostrander and Schroeder, p. 166). He dedicated the work to his hypnotist.

Ostrander, Sheila, and Lynn Schroeder (1973). *PSI. Psychic Discoveries Behind the Iron Curtain*. London: Sphere.

Ragas

Ragas are "the melodic basis of Indian classical music on which the musicians improvise. Each raga has definite melodic qualities that distinguish it from all other ragas. It is assumed that the ragas create an emotional impact on the listener" (Shankar, p. 157). The paranormal and emotional power of ragas has been written about by Ravi Shankar (1920–2012), the world-famous sitar player and singer and specific examples of paranormality can be found in other literature. For instance, "it is said that some could light fires or the oil lamps by singing one raga, or bring rain, melt stones, cause flowers to blossom, and attract ferocious wild **animals**—even snakes and tigers—to a peaceful, quiet circle in a forest around a singing musician" (cited in Berendt, p. 154). An example of a famine being diverted in Bengal by the singing of an unspecified raga has been written about as well as an anecdotal story of the **magic**al effects of the *Dipaka raga* (also referred to as *Deepak* and *Dupak*) played by the Indian musician "Tan Sen" in causing a river to boil and an adversary to burst into flames (cited in Tame, pp. 172–173).

Berendt, J. (1987). *Nada Brahma: The World Is Sound.* London: East West.
Shankar, Ravi (1992). *Ravi Shankar. My Music. My Life.* New Delhi: Vikas.
Tame, David (1984). *The Secret Power of Music.* Wellingborough: Turnstone Press.

Raikov, Vladimir

Vladimir Leonidovich Raïkov (1934–2007) was a Russian psychotherapist and hypnotist about whose methods of auto-suggestion many controversial claims have been made. Using his own form of regression technique, and notably through past art masters, he attempted to evoke talent in people that was dormant but within them. The parapsychologist Leonid Vasiliev (1891–1966) believed that "man's psychic and creative faculties have much in common" (cited in Ostrander and Schroeder, p. 158). Raikov also applied his techniques to musical performance and he "reincarnated" the **violin**ist Fritz Kreisler in a student at the Moscow Conservatory of Music, who started to play in Kreisler's style which he then "consolidated in his conscious state" (Ostrander and Schroeder, p. 163). Details of his other experiments on students were published in the *Psychoneurological Dispensary*, no. 3, Moscow (no date) claiming "significant" results, however, the *International Journal of Clinical and Experimental Hypnosis*, 1976, Vol. XXIV, No. 3. 258–268, maintained there were several unanswered questions which needed to be resolved before the "startling" results could be verified.

Raikov's techniques were also used by the physiologist William Benjamin Carpenter (1813–1885) who "described the case of a factory girl whose musical ability was ordinarily limited, but who was able under hypnotism to provide an imitation of Jenny Lind's singing ... so instantaneously and correctly, as to both words and music, that it was difficult to distinguish the two voices" (cited in Inglis, p. 113). A pilot experiment was conducted by the author in 1998 in an imitation of Raikov's techniques using a mature music student as the subject and a British qualified hypnotist. The result was that although the subject played better during the hypnotized sessions, she did not display an ability wildly in excess of her normal capability and subsequently did not display anything worthy of paranormality.

Inglis, Brian (1990). *Trance*. London: Grafton Books.
Ostrander, Sheila, and Lynn Schroeder (1973). *PSI. Psychic Discoveries Behind the Iron Curtain*. London: Sphere.

Raymond

Raymond was the name of the well-known book written by the physicist Sir Oliver Lodge (1851–1940) to commemorate his son Raymond's (1889–1915) death in the First World War and it describes his contact with the family in spirit form through séance activity. On one notable occasion music was an intriguing part of the encounter: "However, I got the table ready near the **piano**, and Honor came to it, and the instant she placed her hands on it, it began to rock. I put my hands on too. We asked if it was Raymond, and if he had been waiting, and he said 'Yes.' He seemed to wish to listen to the music, and kept time with it gently. And after a song was over that he liked, he very distinctly and decidedly applauded [the table] was determined to edge itself close to the piano, though we said we must pull it back and did so" (Lodge, pp. 222–223). On a different occasion Raymond communicated, "There are places on my sphere where they can listen to beautiful music when they choose" (Lodge, 234).

Lodge, Sir Oliver (1916). *Raymond or Life and Death*. London: Methuen.

Reincarnation

Reincarnation, or the return from having lived in one or more previous lives, has been studied by numerous serious researchers—Ian Stevenson (1918–2007) was the most prominent—and is an integral part of many worldwide **religion**s. Stevenson mentioned in private correspondence that he had heard of musical **prodigies** mainly from Southern India, who were said to have derived their abilities from previous lives and one specific case was that of Bishen Chand Kapoor who showed an ability to play the tablas without having received any instruction in how to do so (Stevenson, p. 199). **Richard Wagner** seemed to be a believer and Gustav Mahler affirmed that "we all return; it is this certainty that gives meaning to life, and it does not make the slightest difference whether or not in a later incarnation we remember the former life" (Specht, p. 39). The composer Jean Sibelius allegedly spoke to his friends about "remembrances of previous lives" (cited in Christie-Murray, pp. 78–79). Worthy of mention is a well-researched novel by Mary Montaño (1995) that recounts the possible intertwining of the lives of **Mozart** and Sussmayr with the pianist William Kapell (1922–1953) and Montaño. Other proposals for reincarnation have included Ray Charles returning as Matthew Whitaker; Aida Overton Walker as Whitney Houston; and **Richard Strauss** as Alma Deutscher (www.reincarnationresearch.com/category/celebrity-reincarnation-cases/music).

The technique known as past-life regression has been used by hypnotists and hypnotherapists since the first half of the twentieth century and it came to considerable prominence through the seemingly spectacular results of Arnall Bloxham which were published in the 1970s. In a hypnotic state normal members of the public seemed to acquire information that they had previously not had any knowledge of and relived their experiences in previous lives. Sometimes people believed themselves to have previously had musical talents. One such example was the English singer and composer Lynsey de Paul (1948–2014) who believed she played the harpsichord at the age of ten in one incarnation and possibly the **piano** in another which led to her capability in playing the piano. The celebrated ballet dancer Wayne Sleep (1948–) also undertook regression and found himself to be a professional **violinist** playing in everything from Irish music sessions to a Royal Albert Hall gala (Everett, pp. 85–96).

Christie-Murray, David (1988). *Reincarnation*. Bridport: Prism Press.
Everett, Lee (1997). *Celebrity Regressions*. London: Foulsham.
Montaño, Mary (1995). *Loving Mozart*. Albuquerque: Cantus Verus Books.
Specht, Richard (1913). *Gustav Mahler*. Berlin: Schuster and Loeffler.
Stevenson, Ian (1988). *Cases of the Reincarnation Type, Vol. 1, 10 Cases in India*. Charlottesville: University of Virginia Press.

Religion

Religion and music have been bound together since primitive man first tried to communicate with invisible forces through "rude musical sounds" (Harrington-Edwards, p. 257). Most religions have integrated music into their rituals and worship. In ancient Greece the cults of Apollo and Orpheus used music in their rites and notably the Orphic Hymns were used for **magic**al purposes when **chant**ed or sung with appropriate melodies according to Giovanni Pico della Mirandola (1463–1494) (olympianismos.forumotion.com/t159-melodies-for-the-orphic-hymns). In Indian culture Brahma gave music to the populace; Judaism and Christianity assimilate music into their services; a main feature of Sufism is its music; pagans past and present use music for communication with nature and their gods and goddesses. The list is far from complete. Paranormality within the music of many religions is never far away. The **altered states of consciousness** of the Sufi and the **shamans**' chants use music to communicate with their respective deities as can be witnessed in **voodoo** rituals and Buddhist chants. It has even been written that the Akashic Records recorded that "melody is the cry of Man to God, Harmony is the answer of God to Man" (Scott, p. 152). The Native American Indian *ghost dance* with its accompanying music brings together music, religion and paranormality which can also be observed in Druid rituals when rattles or *sistra* and **trumpets** reminiscent of the Scandinavian *lurer* were used in summoning the gods during religious ceremonies (Green, p. 63).

Green, Miranda J. (2005). *Exploring the World of the Druids*. London: Thames & Hudson.
Harrington Edwards, John (1904). *God and Music*. London: J.M. Dent.
Scott, Cyril (1958). *Music: Its Secret Influence Throughout the Ages*. London: Aquarian Press.

Reuter, Florizel von

Florizel von Reuter (1890–1985) was an American virtuoso violinist and composer who spent most of his life in Germany and from 1931 to 1933 was professor of violin at the Vienna Music Academy. He claimed to have written numerous works including operas and orchestral music, but his main focus was the **violin** (Reuter, p. 7). He first became intrigued with psychic matters through his mother's use of a planchette—referred to as an "Additor"—to make psychic contact with deceased musicians, especially **Paganini** and Pablo de Sarasate, but other musicians, composers and even literary figures also made contact, including Giuseppe Tartini (1692–1770), Joseph Joachim (1831–1907) and Honoré de

Florizel von Reuter was a concert violinist who believed himself to be in touch from beyond the grave with the violinist and composer Paganini (Wikimedia Commons).

Balzac (1799–1850). While practicing a difficult part of Paganini's *La Campanella* he was compelled to adopt entirely new fingerings as if guided by an external intelligence: "Suddenly, without any premeditation, while playing a difficult passage my fingers seemed to be impelled to abandon suddenly the fingering I had used for years, the substitution of a perfectly different fingering taking place as naturally as if it had been a simple passage instead of a very complicated one ... in the course of the ensuing hour I received at least a dozen new ideas in nuancing, fingering, and bowing, the effect being as though the suggestions were given me through telepathy, or that my bow and fingers were being controlled by another Intelligence than my own" (Reuter, pp. 76–77). Reuter's philosophical exchanges with the spirits were described in his book *A Musician's Talks with Unseen Friends* (Reuter, 1931).

Reuter, Florizel von (1928). *Psychic Experiences of a Musician*. London: Simpkin
Reuter, Florizel von (1931). *A Musician's Talks with Unseen Friends*. London: Rider.

Richmond Castle

Richmond Castle is situated in North Yorkshire, England, and was built in the eleventh century. A legend maintains that at the end of the eighteenth century a tunnel was discovered leading away from the castle and a drummer boy was ordered to enter it and play his drum to allow the soldiers to know where he was under the ground and thereby follow his route. The drumming stopped at Easby Wood on the way towards Easby Abbey and the drummer boy was never seen again (Richmond Castle, publicity flyer). It is said that his drumming can still be heard on occasions.

Robertson, Paul

The **violin**ist Paul Robertson (1952–2016) was the leader and founder of the Medici String Quartet. Believing that "the ancient philosophers taught that the soul was enticed into the body by means of music" (Robertson, 1996, p. 19) he spent a large amount of his time in the pursuit of the combination of music, mind and the spirit. It was augmented notably through the music experiences he underwent in a **coma** after suffering a burst aorta in 2008. He explored this in his book *Soundscapes. A Musician's Journey Through Life and Death* (Robertson, 2016, 2016). In conversation with the author Robertson spoke of the music he heard during what he described as his "**near-death experience**" (private conversation) and its connection with similar experiences had by the composer **John Tavener** (*Psychic News*, pp. 16–17). He hosted a series of three one-hour television programs on Channel 4 called *Music and the Mind* in May 1996 and wrote an article about them in the magazine *Caduceus* (Spring, 1996).

Psychic News (2016). "Does 'Music from Heaven' Accompany Us into the Next Life?" October: 14–17.
Robertson, Paul (1996). "Music and the Mind." *Caduceus* 31 (Spring): 17–20.
Robertson, Paul (2016). *Soundscapes. A Musician's Journey Through Life and Death*. London: Faber and Faber.

Rogo, D. Scott

Douglas Scott Rogo (1950–1990) was a musician and psychical researcher who wrote several books about **parapsychology**-based subjects including its connections with music. His best-known works were his two *NAD* volumes (1970; 1972) which have been referred to throughout this volume. His ideas on transcendental music could best be explained in his own words: "When a person hears transcendental music, it is impossible to verify that the percipient did actually hear it" (Rogo, pp. 18–19). His book *Phone Calls from the Dead* (1979) written with **Raymond Bayless** was highly controversial and may have either prompted or explained later examples of such phenomena, for instance, when Maggy Harsch-Fishbach was allegedly telephoned by the composer Scott Joplin on August 11, 1992, who had died in 1917 (*Psychic News*, p. 3).

Psychic News (1995). "Scott Joplin Phones from Beyond." February 25: 3.
Rogo, D. Scott (1972). *NAD. Volume 2*. New York: University Books.
Rogo, D. Scott, and Raymond Bayless (1979). *Phone Calls from the Dead*. Englewood Cliffs: Prentice Hall.

[For a list of his cases see Appendix 2.]

Rubinstein, Anton

Anton Rubinstein (1829–1894) was a famous Russian pianist and composer who on his deathbed, it was claimed, visited his pupil Lillian Nichia from within what might have been a nightmare to convey his death to her. They had made a pact six years before agreeing that whoever died first would contact the other (Prince, pp. 265–266). The account first appeared in *Harper's Magazine*, in December 1912.

Prince, Walter Franklin (1928). *Noted Witnesses for Psychic Occurrences*. Boston: Boston Society for Psychical Research.

Rudhyar, Dane

Dane Rudhyar (1895–1985), aka Daniel Chennevière, was a French composer and astrologer who attempted to imbue in his music what was **magic**al and sacred. He spent much of his time in the USA and was heavily influenced by his detailed study of astrology as well as the music of **Scriabin** and the **Theosophical** movement. He wrote: "Music is a myth in which the actors are tones uttered by the … transformative-regenerative power of the One life—the sacred tone of cosmic being" (cited in Gann, p. 380). He stressed the importance of space in music as advocated by Eastern thought processes and believed that composers should be **mediums** and magicians.

Gann, Kyle (2005). "Spirituality in Music." *Music Magazine* (June): 378–388.

Rumi, Jalālu'ddīn

Jalālu'ddīn Rūmī (1207–1273) was the Persian Islamic founder in Konya, Turkey of the Mevlevī Order of Sufis, better known as the "whirling **dervishes**" (Godwin, pp. 88–90). Their dancing was said to symbolize the movements of the heavenly spheres and the music through the nay reed flute, his favorite instrument, possessed **magic**al or spiritual qualities (Schimmel, pp. 210–222).

Godwin, Joscelyn (1987b). *Music, Mysticism and Magic.* London: Arkana.
Schimmel, Annemarie (1993). *The Triumphal Sun.* Albany: State University of New York Press.

St. Albans Abbey

Officially the Cathedral & Abbey Church of Saint Alban, it dates back to the eleventh century and was built near to the site of the execution of the first Christian martyr in England, Alban, during the Roman occupation. There have been several stories concerning anomalous music at the Abbey including a bell tolling in the belfry when the **bells** had been removed during the Second World War and the organ playing by itself with a "glorious burst of singing" (Puttick, p. 13). A well-documented case occurred prior to this concerning the *Albanus Mass* written by Robert Fayrfax during the reign of Henry VIII:

> To commemorate the 400th anniversary of Fayrfax's death, the mass was performed in a concert at the Abbey on October 20th 1921. It was after this event that Canon George Glossop claimed to have heard the music previously "in the middle of the night on more than one occasion." His wife vouched for his

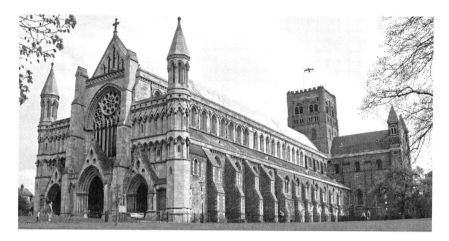

The Cathedral and Abbey Church of St Alban has been the site of numerous musical manifestations of unknown origin witnessed by reliable witnesses (HiltonT/Shutterstock.com).

sincerity and his daughter also claimed to have heard the same music. There have been several other reports of choral music being heard from the Abbey at about 2 a.m., the most recently quoted taking place in 1983. A letter to Dr B. Rose, the Master of Music at the Abbey, prompted the reply that he knew of the story but having been at the Abbey for nine years he had received no experience of any "ghostly" music [Willin, pp. 117–118].

There are other witnesses to music being heard there—a Mrs. P. (identity disguised) "heard the sounds of the most beautiful music and choral accompaniment that I have ever experienced" when the doors were locked and there was nobody within (Carrington and Thresher, p. 2). Again, during the Second World War, a firewatcher heard the *Albanus Mass* when he was on duty there; music has also been heard coming from the Abbey when empty from a nearby café; and a group of people also heard "simply heavenly strains" coming from the building in the middle of the night (Carrington and Thresher, pp. 7–9).

Carrington, Beryl, and Muriel Thresher (n.d.). *The Ghost Book. St Albans' Favourite Haunts.* St. Albans.

Willin, Melvyn J. (2005). *Music, Witchcraft and the Paranormal.* Ely: Melrose.

St. Andrew's Church (Langenhoe, England)

The fourteenth-century church of St. Andrew in Langenhoe, Essex, England, was demolished in 1962 after it had been damaged and rebuilt after an earthquake in 1884—an unusual event for the English countryside.

However, in 1937 the Rev. Ernest Merryweather was the rector and he experienced various phenomena which he believed to be paranormal during his incumbency there (Dening, 2000). In September 1950 a musical incident consisted of "the clear sound of a feminine voice in full song, seemingly down the west end of the church" (Dening, p. 64)—no one was there at the time. The singing was also heard by a local gypsy and two workmen on different occasions. Although none of the witnesses could make out the words of the song, it seemed to them that the language could have been Latin. An investigation was carried out by the Rev. John Dening who was impressed with the veracity of the manifestations.

Dening, John (2000). *The Restless Spirits of Langenhoe*. Lavenham: Lavenham Press.

St. Andrew's Church (Norwich, England)

St. Andrew's Church in Norwich, Norfolk, England, has one musical anomaly attached to it that was witnessed by the reliable witness and author Joan Forman. During a visit to the church and while inside the building she heard the organ playing when there was no one else present except herself (Forman, p. 127).

Forman, Joan (1985). *Haunted East Anglia*. Norwich: Jarrold.

St. Donat's Castle

St. Donat's Castle is situated in South Glamorgan, Wales and it was built in the fourteenth century. It is currently the home of a United World College. "Many teachers, students, historical researchers, visitors and local people are convinced, from personal experience, that St Donat's is indeed haunted" (Underwood, p. 103) by various phenomena including inexplicable **piano** music.

Underwood, Peter (1993). *The Ghosthunters Almanac*. Orpington: Eric Dobby.

St. Gluvias' Church

St. Gluvias' Church, Penryn, Cornwall, England, had a legend attached to it which stated that the church **bell** tolled on the anniversary every year of the death of a bell ringer who had died at sea. Two investigators, George Truscott and Dr. Blamey, decided to stay the night there and arrived separately. Blamey was "curiously disinclined to talk" (McEwan, p. 18) so no verbal contact took place. During the night the bell did indeed toll of its own accord. Blamey noticed it but Truscott didn't respond. The next day Blamey was informed that Truscott had actually died the afternoon before their visit.

McEwan, Graham J. (1989). *Haunted Churches of England.* London: Robert Hale.

St. Ives Bay

St. Ives Bay in Cornwall, England, is the location for another example of "phantom **bells**" being heard in the vicinity of the bay which seem to emanate from "way out at sea" (Underwood, pp. 197–198). There have not been any recent accounts.

Underwood, Peter (1971). *Gazetteer of British Ghosts.* London: Souvenir Press.

St. John the Apostle

The Church of St. John the Apostle in Torquay, Devon, England, "has long been reputed to be haunted by a phantom organist whose music could be heard echoing through the building when it was locked up and empty" (McEwan, p. 29). In reality the rector the Rev. B.G. Burr told Graham McEwan that a "blind parish clerk who used to play the organ for his own amusement without bothering to put on the lights" (McEwan, p. 29) was almost certainly responsible for the story.

McEwan, Graham J. (1989). *Haunted Churches of England.* London: Robert Hale.

St. Margaret's Church (Bowers Gifford, England)

Parts of St. Margaret's Church in Bowers Gifford, Essex, England, date from the fourteenth century and it is situated in an isolated location. It has been named as a site for unaccountable organ music heard at night when the building is empty. This has been witnessed by different people throughout the mid-twentieth century, but there are no recent (2021) reports (Payne, pp. 14–15).

Payne, Jessie (1995). *A Ghost Hunter's Guide to Essex.* Norfolk: Ian Henry.

St. Margaret's Church (East Wellow, England)

St. Margaret's Church in East Wellow, Hampshire, England, dates from at least the thirteenth century and has the distinction of being the burial place of Florence Nightingale. The author Graham McEwan visited the church in 1988 with his wife and a friend when two of them mentioned having heard the sounds of what seemed to be plainsong lasting about twenty seconds. There were no other buildings nearby or any other obvious source of the sound (McEwan, pp. 135–136).

McEwan, Graham J. (1989). *Haunted Churches of England*. London: Robert Hale.

St. Mary's Church (Avenbury, England)

There are very few details to be found about the haunted music heard in the derelict church of St. Mary's at Avenbury in Herefordshire, England. There have been stories of phantom organ music being heard, but nothing has been substantiated. This is similarly true of **bells** that allegedly ring by themselves when a death occurs. The rural and somewhat desolate location probably lends itself to suggesting ghostly presences in suitably gloomy weather conditions. A letter from the Reverend Prebendary, Mr. W. Gould, to the author has a few scant details and a previous vicar, the Reverend Archer-Shepherd, wrote that "some telepathic or auto-suggestive, or other natural cause may have acted on their auditory nerves, setting up sensations which were transmitted by the brain into external sounds" (private correspondence).

For further details see www.haunted-britain.com.

St. Mary's Church (Beaminster, England)

The Church of St. Mary in Beaminster, Dorset, England, was used as a schoolroom in the eighteenth century. An account from *The Gentleman's Magazine* in 1774 (cited in Legg, p. 14) provided details of the appearance of an apparition as well as a sound like a "congregation singing psalms" which was witnessed by a group of schoolboys. The ghost was believed to be that of one John Daniel who had been dead for more than seven weeks at the time.

Legg, Rodney (1969). *A Guide to Dorset Ghosts*. Bournemouth: Dorset.

St. Mary's Church (Hassingham, England)

St. Mary's Church, Hassingham in Norfolk, England, was the scene of organ music being heard from inside the church when a family stopped there sometime in the last century. When they entered the church, the music stopped, and it appeared to be empty. No further information was forthcoming (www.paranormaldatabase.com/norfolk).

St. Mary's Church (Hendon, England)

The Church of St. Mary in Hendon, **London,** built in the eleventh century lays claim to the sound of the **chant**ing of Benedictine monks who lived there before Henry VIII's Dissolution of the Monasteries (Hallam, p. 147). It has not been possible to verify any recent phenomena there.

Hallam, Jack (1975). *Ghosts of London.* London: Wolfe.

St. Mary's Church (Lawford, England)

St. Mary's Church, Lawford, Essex, in England dates from before the twelfth century. In 1940 a young lady was passing by the church late one night when she heard what sounded like a choir singing in the church which was fully lit. Somewhat surprised, she returned the next day and learned from the caretaker that the power had been disconnected because of wartime restrictions and the choir had been disbanded for some time (Downes, p. 76) The author contacted the Rector who humorously informed him that "we have had some 'ghastly' music in our time, but I am afraid I am not aware of anything 'ghostly'" (private correspondence).

Downes, Wesley (2009). *Memories of an Essex Ghosthunter.* Newbury: Countryside.

St. Mary's Church (Reigate, England)

The twelfth-century Church of St. Mary in Reigate, England, was the scene of a musical "haunting" in 1975: "It's said that a Mrs Bell first heard a choir singing inside the building in 1975 late in the evening although inside was pitch black and the church had been locked up ... many people have heard the sounds of singing when passing the vacant building" (howard-cundey2.wpdev2.com/general/ghost-stories-of-reigate).

St. Mary and All Saints' Church

St. Mary and All Saints' Church in Fotheringhay, Northamptonshire, England, was the scene of an intriguing incident of a possible musical

hallucination in August 1976 when the church was visited by a school-teacher, Mr. John Priest, and his wife: "As the couple approached the church door, to their considerable surprise they heard the clear sound of a strange, rather primitive kind of martial music with **trumpet** fanfares and **drums**. Thinking that there must be a rehearsal for something going on in the church, they were hesitant about entering, but, on surreptitiously opening the door and peering in, they found, to their amazement, that there was no one whatsoever in the building.... The couple, greatly puzzled decided to retrace their steps to the churchyard gate, and continued to hear the music for most of the way" (Dening, pp. 135–136). Dening suggested that since the date was probably exactly five hundred years since a ceremony to re-inter the bodies of Richard Duke of York and Edmund was held there with considerable pomp, it was likely that an auditory time-slip had occurred during the visit of the Priests in 1976.

A local retired policeman also reported that he and his cousin had visited the church and the cousin heard what sounded like "monks **chanting**" while the church was empty (Dening, p. 136). Dening received a letter from another person who visited the church when it was empty, but they both heard chanting coming from it which stopped when they entered.

Dening, John (1996). *Secret History. The Truth about Richard III & the Princes.* Lavenham Press.

St. Michael's Church

St. Michael's Church is situated on the site of Didlington Hall in Norfolk, England. On the night of November 14, 1965, the experienced Police Constable Williams was doing his rounds nearby when he heard the sound of a distant bell. He realized that the bell's sound was coming from the church. When he entered the churchyard, the bell stopped tolling immediately and he could find no one there. He later learned that the previous owner of the Hall had died at the same time as he had heard the bell tolling (McEwan, pp. 96–97).

McEwan, Graham J. (1989). *Haunted Churches of England.* London: Robert Hale.

St. Nectan's Glen

St. Nectan's Glen is a beautiful wooded valley area with cascading waterfalls in Cornwall, England near to the mysterious castle of Tintagel which has connections with Arthurian Britain. Saint Nectan, a local saint, allegedly lived in a hermitage there and a silver bell has been heard ringing as well as monks **chant**ing and "beautiful organ music emanating from an empty building" (Underwood, p. 16).

Underwood, Peter (1983). *Ghosts of Cornwall.* Bodmin: Bossiney.

St. Nicholas' Church

St. Nicholas' Church, Pyrford, Surrey, in England is a twelfth-century building which was the scene of an alleged time-slip during the twentieth century. A Mrs. Turrell-Clarke found herself while attending evensong there to be "back in the thirteenth-century church, listening to monks **chant**ing" (Forman, 647). She later discovered that the church's interior was correct according to her "vision."

Forman, Joan (1981). "When Time Slips." *The Unexplained* 33. London: Orbis.

St. Peter's Church (Cambridgeshire, England)

It has been alleged that the voice of a soprano has been heard at various times in the Church of St. Peter, Babraham, in Cambridgeshire, England, when no such person was discovered there as well as the scent of female perfume. The organist Mr. C. Ingrey was interviewed by a reporter from the *Cambridge Evening News* in 1989 about the haunting and he later learned that a previous organist's wife had been a soprano. The author spoke to Mr. Ingrey in 1997 and he confirmed that he had heard the soprano himself and smelled the perfume, but he did not recognize the aria she was singing since it only lasted a few seconds. "A spectral lady was seen once, but she was outside the church walls flitting between the graves" (Matthews, p. 15).

Matthews, Rupert (1994). *Haunted Cambridge.* Andover: Pitkin Pictorials.

St. Peter's Church (Northamptonshire, England)

St. Peter's Church, Lutton in Northamptonshire, England, was built in the eleventh century. Organ music was heard by a man as he approached the building, but there was no one inside the church at the time (Forman, p. 127).

Forman, Joan (1985). *Haunted East Anglia.* Norwich: Jarrold.

St. Peter and St. Paul's Church

St. Peter and St. Paul's Church, Caister in Lincolnshire, England, has stood on its present site since the eleventh century with various additions. A number of references to organ music being heard including it being recorded on tape (Hippisley Coxe, p. 141) prompted the author to contact an organist from the church. Mr. D. Naylor kindly replied to his enquiry: "The ghostly music to which you refer is easily explained. Many years ago I regularly went to play the organ late at night without switching any lights on, except for the console. You can imagine, therefore how the rumors started, especially with a boarding school close by! There have, of course, been no subsequent tales reported" (private correspondence).

Hippisley Coxe, Antony D. (1973). *Haunted Britain*. London: Pan Books Ltd.

Saint-Saëns, Camille

Charles Camille Saint-Saëns (1835–1921) was a French child **prodigy** and a renowned pianist and composer. He was subject to psychic experiences including what he believed to be a **premonition** concerning his application to the Académie des Beaux-Arts involving the Egyptian lions that adorn the façade of the Institute. He wrote: "I shall present myself again when the lions turn around. Sometime afterwards the lions were turned" (cited in Prince, p. 255). He also believed himself to have telepathic powers, but of more consequence was his sensing of the death of his friend Henri Regnault who was hundreds of miles away. The impression of his death "exploded in his mind into the mournful theme for the opening of his hauntingly beautiful *Requiem*" (cited in Panati, p. 137), despite the fact that at the time he and his fellow soldiers were dining joyfully on what was the last day of the Franco-German war. He confirmed this in a letter dated January 1871 to the astronomer and psychical researcher Camille Flammarion.

Panati, Charles (1974). *Supersenses*. London: Jonathan Cape.
Prince, Walter Franklin (1928). *Noted Witnesses for Psychic Occurrences*. Boston: Boston Society for Psychical Research.

Sandford Orcas Manor House

The present manor house was built in the Tudor period and stands on a much older site which was mentioned in the Domesday Book. It was investigated by three researchers from the now obsolete Paraphysical Laboratory under the leadership of Benson Herbert (1912–1991) who believed that it was haunted (cited in Legg, p.36). The tenants from 1965 to 1979 Colonel Francis Claridge and his wife claimed to have heard harpsichord or spinet music emanating from the gatehouse. The previous owner Sir Mervin Medlycott had not heard or seen anything unusual while he lived there.

Legg, Rodney (1969). *A Guide to Dorset Ghosts*. Bournemouth: Dorset.

Sangoma

The Sangoma are practitioners of traditional medicine in Southern Africa and have similarities to **shamans**. They use divination, **chant**ing, **drum**ming and **dance** to achieve varying degrees of trance whereby an ancestor or another spirit can take **possession** of their body and communicate directly with the patient. There is an emphasis on spirituality which is often at odds with traditional western medical practices. (For further reading and detailed information see Cumes, 2004.)

Cumes, David M. (2004). *Africa in My Bones*. Claremont: New Africa.

Savants

According to the Cambridge University Dictionary a savant is "a person with a high level of knowledge or skill, especially someone who is less able in other ways: There are musical savants who are very awkward physically—until they sit at the **piano**" (dictionary.cambridge.org/dictionary/english/savant). Several musical savants are discussed in this manuscript including **Blind Tom, Ellen Boudreaux, Harriet G.** and **Leslie Lemke**. Many others have also been studied who display musical skills which would have been described as "paranormal" in the past, but with the greater understanding of brain patterns, can now be understood more even if far from fully. One such case was that of a musical savant referred to as Eddie (Bonafe) who was studied by Leon Miller, a psychologist specializing in childhood disability at the University of Illinois (cited in Mithen, pp. 40–41). Eddie possessed phenomenal skills of harmonization, improvisation and transposition at the keyboard when only five years old (Miller, 1989) and was subsequently given piano lessons by Nancy Newman who was amazed by his ability. Another example, from a different source, was Martin: "When I met him in 1984, he told me that he knew more than two thousand operas, as well as the Messiah, the Christmas Oratorio, and all of **Bach**'s cantatas. I brought along scores of some of these, and tested him as best I could, I found I was unable to fault him. And it was not just the melodies that he remembered. He had learned, from listening to performances, what every instrument played, what every voice sang. When I played him a piece by **Debussy** that he had never heard, he was able to repeat it, almost flawlessly on the piano. He then transposed it into different keys and extemporized on it a little, in a Debussyan way" (Sacks, p. 152). The interested reader would benefit from also studying Geza Révész's study of the musical savant Erwin Nyiregyházi (Révész, 1970).

Miller, Leon K. (1989). *Musical Savants: Exceptional skill in the Mentally Retarded*. Mahwah: Lawrence Erlbaum.
Mithen, Steven (2005). *The Singing Neanderthals*. London: Weidenfeld & Nicolson.
Révész, Erwin Nyiregyházi (1970). *The Psychology of a Musical Prodigy*. New York: Greenwood Press.

Sawston Hall

Sawston Hall is a sixteenth-century mansion situated in Cambridgeshire, England, which has several stories of hauntings associated with it. In 1930 a member of the Huddleston family, the owners, reported hearing "spinet or harpsichord music" (Poole, p. 14) and more recently during the filming of *The Nightcomers* (an adaptation of Henry James' *The Turn of the Screw*), two security men claimed to have heard music being played in the chapel when it was deserted (Forman, p. 87). In February and March 1983 members of the Cambridge University Society for Psychical Research undertook serious investigations there, but only recorded a few seconds of music which they believed could have originated from a radio signal (Cornell, 1984).

Cornell, A.D. (1984). "Research Report of the Cambridge University Society for Psychical Research." *Journal of the Society for Psychical Research*. No. 52, 797.
Forman, Joan (1985). *Haunted East Anglia*. Norwich: Jarrold.
Poole, Keith B. (1995). *Britain's Haunted Heritage*. Leicester: Magna Books.

Schipa, Tito

Tito Schipa (1889–1965) was an Italian singer who was noted for his lyrical tenor voice in operatic roles. He claimed to have had two psychical experiences, including one where he saw the apparition of a woman whom he did not know, but who was recognized by others as having died on the night that the apparition appeared. The other involved an audible instruction to search a part of a room in an inn where he was sleeping which resulted in him finding a hitherto lost will. In 1919, he was initiated into the Scottish

Rite Freemasonry, but it is not known whether he participated in any esoteric practices therein.

Prince, Walter Franklin (1928). *Noted Witnesses for Psychic Occurrences*. Boston: Boston Society for Psychical Research.

Schoenberg, Arnold

Arnold Schoenberg (1874–1951) (or Schönberg) was an Austrian composer who became famous for his use of the atonal system of composition and was generally accepted as the leader of the Second Viennese School. He was interested in esoteric subjects and was also very superstitious; however, it is the circumstance of the composing of his String Trio op. 45 which is of particular interest. It was commissioned by the Music Department of Harvard University in 1946, but a heart attack caused him to attempt to reproduce the sensations in music which were believed to reflect common aspects of **near-death experiences**, namely calmness; meeting with others; and "a profound transcendental experience" (cited in Corazza & Terreni, pp. 47–51). He completed the work in hospital three weeks later.

Corazza, Ornella, and Maria Francesca Terreni (2005). "NDE in Music: An Aesthetic-Musical Analysis of String-Trio by Arnold Schönberg, in F. Cariglia, "Life After Life," 1975–2005: *30 years of NDE*, IX International Symposium of the Near-Death Experience.

Schopenhauer, Arthur

Arthur Schopenhauer (1788–1860) was a German philosopher and in his famous book *The World as Will and Representation* (1818/19) he expounded on many subjects including music which he considered to be apart from the other arts through its all-encompassing effect on man's innermost nature: "Music stands quite alone. It is cut off from all the other arts…. It does not express a particular and definite joy, sorrow, anguish, horror, delight or mood of peace, but joy, sorrow, anguish, horror, peace of mind themselves, in the abstract, in their essential nature, without accessories, and therefore without their customary motives" (cited in Beaizley, p. 5). His beliefs probably stemmed from his metaphysical and esoteric interests (Alperson, pp. 155–166) which were further manifested in works by **Wagner**, **Schoenberg** and Mahler. Schopenhauer's influences in music can also be found in aesthetics and music journals (Dunton Green, pp. 199–206) and even music books (Storr, pp. 128–149).

Alperson, Philip (1981). "Schopenhauer and Musical Revelation." *The Journal of Aesthetics and Art Criticism* 40, no. 2 (Winter). Wiley.

Beaizley, Andrew (1996). "An Echo of the Voices of Eternity." *The Christian Parapsychologist* 12, no. 1 (March): 2–8.

Dunton Green, L. (1930). "Schopenhauer and Music." *The Musical Quarterly* 16, no. 2 (April). OUP.

Schopenhauer, Arthur (1818/19 & 1969). *The World as Will and Representation.* Trans. E.J. Payne. New York: Dover.

Storr, Anthony (1992). *Music and the Mind.* London: HarperCollins.

Schumann, Robert

Robert Alexander Schumann (1810–1856) was a German pianist and composer who suffered from both angelic and demonic visions towards the end of his life as well as a form of tinnitus with a single note "A" sounding in his head. He also attempted suicide. The circumstances of the conveyance of his **violin** concerto to **Jelly d'Aranyi** have already been discussed, but there is a further link with him and paranormal music manifestations. He wrote to Clara Wieck—later to become his wife—in 1838 telling her that while composing a **piano** suite he had visions of a funeral, coffins and "sorrowing faces." The title came into his head of *Leichenphantasie* ("Funeral Fantasy") and he was overcome with sadness while writing it. Unexpectedly a letter arrived saying his brother had just died. Schumann changed the title to *Nachtstücke* after pressure from Clara (cited in Prince, p. 257) but maintained the opening section as a "Funeral Procession." The *Geistervariationen* (*Ghost Variations*), or *Theme and Variations in E-flat major for piano* (1854) was Schumann's last piano work and the variations were composed in the time leading up to his admission to an asylum for the insane (Seiffert, 1995). He claimed to have heard entities that conveyed to him both angelic and demonic music and that he was being dragged down to hell.

Prince, Walter Franklin (1928). *Noted Witnesses for Psychic Occurrences.* Boston: Boston Society for Psychical Research.

Seiffert, Wolf-Dieter (1995). Preface to *Thema mit Variationen (Geistervariation)* (PDF). G. Henle Verlag.

Scole Experiment

The Scole Experiment was named after the village Scole in Norfolk, England where a series of **séances** were held between 1993 and 1998. The alleged psychic phenomena caused considerable controversy with believers maintaining that proof of contact with entities was forthcoming, while skeptics proposed fraud or misinterpretation as the origin of the phenomena. A supporter of the paranormality of the phenomena was Dr. Hans

Schaer, a Swiss lawyer, who sat with the group on several occasions. At one of these sittings in Ibiza he hoped that musical contact would be made with the spirits. He brought a **trumpet** along for this purpose and a few indistinct bugle-like sounds were made as well as "a real blast." The sound of **drum**ming was also heard (Solomon, pp. 238–241). On another occasion a part of **Rachmaninov**'s Second **Piano** Concerto was heard playing from a tape recorder. One of the Society for Psychical Research investigators, Montague Keen, claimed that the music had particular significance for him and that he had not mentioned this to anyone else present (Solomon, p. 107). The author attended one such séance and was given musical information of no relevance or applicability to his situation.

Solomon, Grant, and Jane (1999). *The Scole Experiment*. London: Piatkus.

Scott, Cyril

Cyril Meir Scott (1879–1970) was an English composer and occultist whose music might be described as late-Romantic, but with hints of impressionism and the exotic. In the field of the occult, he wrote prodigiously and inevitably devoted considerable energy into his studies of music and the esoteric. He claimed that **Nelsa Chaplin** was the pupil/disciple of the Himalayan mahatma Master Koot Humi and that she was the source and **inspiration** for his knowledge which he wrote about in *Music: Its Secret Influence Throughout the Ages* (1969). Furthermore, he believed that Koot Humi "in a former life had been the great philosopher and musician, **Pythagoras** the Sage" (Scott, p. 36). He drew attention to the "sense of 'between the notes' which is essential to the portrayal of [what he called] Deva-music" (Scott, 133). In this respect he was particularly enamored by **Scriabin**'s music. Some of the chapters in his book provide an abundance of much that is firmly within the ranks of paranormality in music. For instance:

The Esoteric Source of this Book.
The Effects of Sound and Music.
Musicians and the Higher Powers.
The Occult Constitution of Man.
César Franck, the Bridge between the Humans and the Devas.
Musicians and their Subtler Bodies.
The Music and Character of the Ancient Egyptians.
The Music of the Future [Scott, contents].

Scott was a supporter of the **Theosophy** Society having heard Annie Besant (1847–1933), the head of the Society, lecture on his area of interest.

In the last paragraph of his book, in the chapter on "The Music of the Future," he related a message from Koot Hoomi: "Today, as we enter this new Age, we seek, primarily through the medium of *inspired* music, to diffuse the spirit of unification and brotherhood, and thus quicken the vibration of this planet" (Scott, p. 204). American readers will be pleased to read that "America will be particularly responsive to this new music, for that great continent is the cradle of the coming race" (Scott, p. 201).

Cyril Scott was a British composer who was totally immersed in esoteric music and literature (Wikimedia Commons).

Scott, Cyril (1958). *Music. Its Secret Influence Throughout the Ages.* London: Aquarian Press.

Scriabin, Alexander Nikolayevich

Alexander Nikolayevich Scriabin (1872–1915) was a Russian composer and pianist whose music was influenced by **synesthesia** (the blending of the sensations of perception) and his intense mystical beliefs. His Fifth Symphony *Prometheus: The Poem of Fire* involved the use of a "color organ" (Schonberg, p. 497) and his "mystic chord"—when based on a "C" sounding as C, F♯, B♭, E, A, D—was evident in his music in different forms and with different pitches within the same intervallic structure. **Cyril Scott** thought that *Prometheus* "reaches a climax expressive of unutterable grandeur, but it is a grandeur incomparable with anything we have seen or experienced on earth" (Scott, p. 134). *Mysterium* was an unfinished musical work, exploiting all the senses, requiring an orchestra, a large choir, special visual effects, dancers and incense. The place of performance was to be a cathedral, but with effects that would change its architectural impact. Scriabin wrote of it: "I shall not die. I shall suffocate in ecstasy after the *Mysterium*" (Panati, p. 158). Scott wrote that Scriabin's early death may have been ascribed to "Dark Forces" that he was not able to combat since his **inspirational** Devas were "restricted to their own planes" (Scott, p. 133).

Panati, Charles (1974). *Supersenses.* London: Jonathan Cape.
Schonberg, Harold C. (1970). "Mysticism and Melancholy, Scriabin and Rachmaninoff." *The Lives of the Great Composers.* New York: Norton.
Scott, Cyril (1958). *Music: Its Secret Influence Throughout the Ages.* London: Aquarian Press.

Séances

Music is used in séances as a source of background sound—skeptics would argue its use is to disguise the sound of fraudulent activity—and often to produce an initial encouraging environment for the communication from spirits and spirit guides (personal experience). When its origin or production is unknown it becomes anomalous in nature. This can be through performances seemingly without physical contact, as in the examples of the **Davenports**, D.D. **Home** and **Stella C.** or when there is no known basis for the music as in the cases of D.D. Home, **William Stainton Moses** and Mina Crandon. The effect of a medium being taken over by a spirit musician in a séance can be very dramatic as was evident with **Indridi Indridason**, Catherine Mettler, **Jesse Shepard** and **George Aubert**. A more recent example was a spirit communicator referred to as "Frances" who sang with "incredible power and purity" in a séance in 1996 (Hume, p. 4). Whatever the source of the music or its performance it always seems to conform to the accepted traditions of what would be expected in a western-based society, namely tonal, melodic and adhering to accepted rhythmic and harmonic patterns.

Hume, Steve (1996). "A Musical Soirée with the Swift Circle." *Noah's Ark Newsletter* 4, no. 70 (May): 4–7.

Sennen Cove

Sennen Cove is a small coastal village in Cornwall, England, which has long been reputed to be the area where phantom **bells** can be heard at various times. One witness, a Mr. Stanley Baron, is one of many who have heard "the long, low pealing of distant and muffled bells" which gradually diminish with the coming of dawn (Underwood, pp. 83–84).

Underwood, Peter (1983). *Ghosts of Cornwall.* Bodmin: Bossiney.

Shamans

The word "shaman" originates from the Tungusc word "saman" from Siberia and is one of many different words to indicate a person who "through trance and ecstasy, enters other states of being to that in which he or she usually lives, returning with news from which all of humanity can benefit" (Matthews, p. 6). Shamanism can be found throughout the world with regional differences according to its importance in society and geographical location. For instance, the Korean shamans are mainly women who sing and **dance** to percussion music which is played by "her instrumental accompanists" (Howard, 2000a, p. 56) and the Mongolian shamans use overtone singing as well as the drum and a horse head **fiddle** (*morin xuur*) (Lee, p. 48). The Waro Indians in Venezuela sing in an ecstatic trance and also use a gourd rattle for their spirit communication (cited in Devereux, pp. 39–40). Music is essential to the ritual allowing the shamans to lose themselves and thereby find their soul with the spirits encountered as active participants. Rouget draws attention to the importance of the shaman going into trance through his or her own musical performance and therefore at variance with some states of **possession** (Rouget, p. 126). Even the classicist and Society for Psychical Research past president E.R. Dodds differentiated between the two states' definitions as far back as the ancient Greeks (Dodds, 1951). Although **drums** of many varieties are the main instruments used, other percussive instruments can fulfill the same functions in inducing spirit contact through rhythmic intensity. The ancient Celtic bodhran is an especially magical tool which often has painted symbolic designs painted on it. During the late eighteenth century, it was noted "that Christianity had had a disastrous influence" on shamanism and that "the race was almost extinct" (Flaherty, p. 92). During Stalin's persecution of the shamans in Siberia shamans remained mainly hidden, but examples of **healing** still prevailed as when a man became ill and an "old woman" was summoned who was known to be a shaman but not named as such. She "took down a frying pan

Shamanism has claimed to contact spiritual entities for many centuries and in many cultures. It is still practiced today as can be seen by this Mongolian performer undertaking a winter ritual (CW Pix/Shutterstock.com).

… and beat it with a wooden spoon" (Howard, 2000b p. 360) to achieve the journey to the spirit world. The **magic** can be further enhanced by the use of dance, alcohol and hallucinogenic **drugs** and the end result from the shamanic songs can relate to healing as well as "conjuring a lunar eclipse, aiding whale hunters, or preventing rain through rituals" (Rouget, p. 131). The world of the shaman is almost certainly enmeshed with the paranormal power of music.

Devereux, Paul (2001). *Stone Age Soundtracks*. London: Vega.
Dodds, E.R. (1951). *The Greeks and the Irrational*. Berkeley: University of California Press.
Flaherty, Gloria (1992). *Shamanism and the Eighteenth Century*. Princeton: Princeton University Press.
Howard. Keith (2000a). "Sacred and Profane: Music in Korean Shaman Rituals." *Indigenous Religious Musics*. Eds. Ralls-MacLeod and Harvey. Aldershot: Ashgate.
Howard, Keith (2000b). "Shamanism, Music, and the Soul Train." *Music as Medicine*. Ed. Hordern Peregrine. Aldershot: Ashgate.
Lee, Brian (n.d.). "Overtone Singing." *Caduceus* 40: 48–49.
Matthews, John (1991). *The Celtic Shaman*. Shaftesbury: Element.
Rouget, Gilbert (1985). *Music and Trance. A Theory of the Relations Between Music and Possession*. Chicago: University of Chicago Press.

Shepard, Jesse

Jesse Shepard (1848–1927) was believed to be the finest **musical medium** of the late nineteenth century and early twentieth century. He claimed to having been visited by a spirit who advised him about developing his singing voice and later exceptional ability on the **piano** and knowledge of obscure languages while in trance. He was feted around the civilized world but having retired from his **musical medium**ship he moved to **London** and died in poverty there.

His full name was Benjamin Henry Jesse Francis Grierson Shepard and though born in Birkenhead, England of Scottish/Irish descent he was taken to the United States at a very early age and grew up there in Illinois. He started to play the piano at the age of twelve but little else is known of his early childhood. In 1869 while attending the theater in St. Louis, a spirit called "Rachel" came to him with advice to develop his singing (Shepard, 1870). He decided to journey to Paris where he earned his living by displaying his exceptional musical gifts and in similar ways to D.D. **Home**. His popularity led to numerous invitations from high society and the support of wealthy patrons. He first visited California in 1876 where he performed at an old mission in San Diego. Shepard was so impressed with the place that he later returned there and built a grand mansion known as the Villa Montezuma. During the years leading up to the mid–1880s he travelled to London, Berlin and even Australia. His patrons included the Queens of

Denmark and Hanover, Prince Phillip of Bourbon and Braganza, Princess Marie of Hanover and the Viscountess Combermere (Wisniewski, 1894). In 1885, Shepard met Lawrence W. Tonner, who became his secretary and friend for over forty years, and they lived together in the Villa Montezuma. He became more involved in **Spiritualism** from this time and converted his house into a center for grand receptions, but he started to turn away from music and turned towards literary ventures and he also developed ties with the Catholic Church. He changed his name to "Francis Grierson" as a nom de plume and published essays in *The Golden Era*, a West Coast journal that published much of the early work of Mark Twain. His final years saw him dependent on Tonner for financial support and he was forced to sell the gifts that he had been presented with in his musical heyday. Shepard continued writing and gave occasional piano recitals. He settled in Los Angeles in 1920 but he became increasingly destitute. A benefit dinner was given for him on 29 May 1927 where he played the piano, but he died at the conclusion of the piece at the keyboard (Marble).

Shepard did not charge for his performances, and he did not publish the works he performed. One is therefore forced to rely on his and other people's testimonies as to their worth. He displayed paranormal capabilities notably through his singing voice; his ability to play the piano; and his knowledge of obscure foreign languages. Professor J. Niclassen, the organist and music critic of the *Fremdenblatt* of Hamburg spoke of his singing and playing in darkness:

> Soft, mysterious, sphere like tones, coming and going, fall on our ear … tone-pictures full of poetic charm. Most remarkable is the unfailing surety of touch, in spite of the darkness, especially in octave and wide jumps. Between short pauses, four or five selections followed one another, all completely different in character, giving the widest play to the imagination of the listeners. Suddenly one hears a basso of colossal register, the singer at the same time playing an accompaniment that makes the grand piano quiver, … while the mighty basso penetrated to bone and marrow … the accompaniment becomes more subdued, and to a melodious theme rises a soprano voice of sympathetic quality, which to about the second "G" has a youthful boyish character, but in the highest notes it becomes a decided soprano. A duet is now carried on alternately between a powerful basso and a beautiful soprano, which decidedly belongs to the most extraordinary manifestations in the realm of music [Campbell Holms, p. 239].

This ability to sing two parts simultaneously—soprano and bass—left his listeners profoundly shocked. During a visit to London, he gave a concert at one Lady Milford's abode where he played the grand piano inspired by **Beethoven** followed by an accompaniment to his singing in "a wonderful deep and sonorous basso, which a few minutes later was answered by a high and pure soprano of marvelous timbre and power" (*Light*, p. 200). Alexander Dumas spoke of him: "With your gifts you will find all doors open before you" (Campbell Holms, 1925). His ability on the piano was considered even more awe-inspiring and he seemed to be possessed by the spirits of many composers including **Mozart**, Beethoven, **Liszt**, and **Chopin**. A report documenting his piano playing at a séance in Paris on September 3, 1893, was written by Prince Wisniewski:

> After having secured the most complete obscurity we placed ourselves in a circle around the medium, seated before the piano. Hardly were the first chords struck when we saw lights appearing at every corner of the room.... The first piece played through Shepard was a fantasia of Thalberg's on the air from "Semiramide." This is unpublished, as is all of the music which is played by the spirits through Shepard. The second was a Rhapsody for four hands, played by Liszt and Thalberg with astounding fire, a sonority truly grand, and a masterly interpretation. Notwithstanding this extraordinarily complex technique, the harmony was admirable, and such as no one present had ever known paralleled, even by Liszt himself, whom I personally knew, and in whom passion and delicacy were united. In the circle were musicians who, like me, had heard the greatest pianists in Europe; but we can say that we never heard such truly super-natural executions [Wisniewski, p. 86].

On another occasion he played the piano through the spirit of **Berlioz**, who was not known to play the piano but rather the guitar, making the alleged feat even more incredible and especially when it was further stated that the piano lid was closed at the time (*Prediction*, p. 7).

Possibly the most detailed account of a musical séance, including a plan of where people sat and an illustration of the **harp** played (actually a zither), was provided by one J.S. Goebel on March 18, 1906. He listed some key features of the séance: Shepard advised that he could not guarantee phenomena that evening; there were nine sitters who held hands with each other with Shepard seated at the piano; the room was in darkness; a harp, which had been checked by the sitters was placed on the piano; the harp and the piano were played and Shepard also sang in a bass and soprano voice; the harp seemed to move about the room and touched/deposited itself upon several of the sitters; a Dutch song was requested which Shepard attempted to play on the piano, but the harp succeeded in playing it simultaneously; the musical activities finished with the *Egyptian March*; everyone agreed that the phenomena was not possible under normal circumstances (Goebel, pp. 236–242).

If the claims for his paramusicological abilities are true, then he was one of the most remarkable musicians to have existed and it is a tragedy that his performances were not recorded in professionally scrutinized musicological journals or on audio equipment.

[For further information about Shepard in addition to the references provided, the following list may be of use.]

Blavatsky, H.P. (1875). "A Word with the Singing Medium, Mr. Jesse Sheppard." *Boston Spiritual Scientist* 2 (July 8).
Campbell Holms, A. (1925). *The Facts of Psychic Science and Philosophy*. London: Kegan Paul.
Crane, C. (1987). "Jesse Shepard and the Spark of Genius." *The Journal of San Diego History* 33, nos. 2–3 (Spring–Summer).
Fodor, N. (1964). *Between Two Worlds: Amazing True Case-Histories of the Occult, the Mysterious, the Marvellous and the Supernatural*. West Nyack: Parker.
Gaddis, V.H. (1994). "Mystery of the Musical Medium." *Borderlands* 50, no. 3.
Goebel, J.S. (1906). "A Musical Séance with Physical Manifestations." *Annals of Psychical Science* IV, no. 22 (October): 236–242.
Grierson, F. (1899). *Modern Mysticism and Other Essays*. London: George Allen.
Grierson, F. (1901). *The Celtic Temperament and Other Essays*. London: George Allen.
Grierson, F. (1909). *The Valley of Shadows*. London: A. Constable.
Grierson, F. (1913). *The Invincible Alliance and Other Essays*. New York: John Lane.
Grierson, F. (1918). *Abraham Lincoln, the Practical Mystic*. New York: John Lane.
Light (1894). "Mr. Jesse Shepard." April 24.
Marble, Matt (n.d.). "The Illusioned Ear: Disembodied Sound & The Musical Séances of Francis Grierson." www.mattmarblemusic.com.
Prediction (1936). "Played Piano with Lid Shut—and Sang with Two Voices." Vol. 1, no. 1 (February).
Rogers, E. Dawson (1897). "Mr. Jesse Shepard." *The Two Worlds* X (March 26): 204.
Royal Magazine (1904).
Shepard, J. (1870). "How I Became a Musical Medium." *Medium and Daybreak Journal* (May 6). London.
Simonson, H.P. (1966): *Francis Grierson: A Biographical and Critical Study*. New York: Twayne.
Willin, M.J. (2019). "Jesse Shepard (Francis Grierson)." *Psi Encyclopedia*. London: The Society for Psychical Research. psi-encyclopedia.spr.ac.uk/articles/jesse-shepard-francis-grierson.
Wisniewski, Prince A. (1894). *The Journal of Light* (April 28). London.

Slade, Henry

Henry Slade (1835–1905) was an American medium who was noted for his slate-writing spirit messages and gained notoriety after he was condemned to prison for cheating. Another "trick" was the playing of an accordion with one hand while it was under a table in a similar, but not identical way to D.D. **Home**. Chung Ling Soo (1861–1918), the stage name of William Ellsworth Robinson, the famous magician and conjuror, revealed how he believed the trick was carried out:

> The accordion was taken by him from the table with his right hand, at the end containing the strap, the keys or notes at the other end being away from him. He thus held the accordion beneath the table, and his left hand was laid on top of the table, where it was always in plain view. Nevertheless, the accordion was heard to give forth melodious tunes, and at the conclusion was brought up on top of the table as held originally; the whole dodge consisting in turning the accordion end for end as it went under the table. The strap end being now downward, and held between the legs, the medium's hand grasped the keyboard

end, and worked the bellows and keys, holding the accordion firmly with the legs and working the hand, not with an arm movement, but mostly by a simple wrist movement. Of course, at the conclusion, the hand grasped the accordion at the strap end, and brought it up in this condition. Sometimes an accordion is tied with strings and sealed so the bellows cannot be worked. This is for the dark séance. Even in this condition the accordion is played by inserting a tube in the air-hole or valve and by the medium's using his lungs as bellows [Robinson, pp. 105–106].

Slade was also present during the alleged **levitation**, playing of a **piano** with no known source and executing tunes on it when in a trance state and under the control of a spirit guide called "Mr. Campbell" (Crowell, p. 165–167).

Crowell, Eugen (1875). *The Identity of Primitive Christianity and Modern Spiritualism.* Vol. I. New York: Author.
Robinson, William Ellsworth (1898). *Spirit Slate Writing and Kindred Phenomena.* New York: Munn & Company.

Snake Charmers

For many years the music played by a snake charmer on a pungi—a flute-like instrument with reeds that produce a piercing sound—was thought to be the cause of the snake's swaying and movement as if hypnotized by the music played. However, it is now known that the snake's lack of external ears does not allow it to hear music, but only be able to sense sound vibration. Its movement is caused by the swaying of the player which may imitate that of a predator. A detailed study of the subject has been made by John C. Murphy (2010).

Murphy, John C. (2010). *Secrets of the Snake Charmer.* New York: Bloomington.

Sound Phenomena

It can be argued that sound was the earliest form of communication and certainly before writing. The ears remain open unlike the eyes that are shut during sleep and through intention and they are also multi-directional. "We do not need an equivalent of light to hear—our ears work just as well after dark. We do not need a direct 'light of sight' to hear, at least for moderately loud sounds. And we do not have to be facing the direction of a sound to hear it" (Trubshaw, p. 103).

It has already been decided not to include sounds in this volume that do not mainly have a specific or at least near specific relationship with music. There are hundreds, even thousands, of books and articles relating to sound which contain references to music within their overview. Furthermore, some people's interpretation of the word "sound" might well be described by someone else as "music." Although the psychical researcher Rosalind Heywood (1895–1980) referred to her paranormal experiences as the "Singing," these were not strictly musical encounters, but actually sound phenomena (Heywood, pp. 191–198). An exception to these circumstances was to be found in an experiment conducted by the psychologist Richard Wiseman and others on May 31, 2003, in the Purcell Room, **London** (Blacklock, p. 56). During a concert of four music compositions, infrasound (approximately the frequency of 17 Hz) was applied to two of the pieces and at a later performance the other two pieces were chosen for this treatment. The presence of the infrasound resulted in 22 percent of respondents reporting feeling uneasy or nervous and Wiseman concluded that the results "suggested that infrasound boosted the number of strange experiences reported among the audience, even among those who were unaware of its presence" (richardwiseman.wordpress.com/).

Appendix 3 provides a small example of books that might be consulted for readers wishing to explore the sound-music hypothesis in more detail and especially infrasound research.

Blacklock, Mark (2003). "I Was a Sonic Experiment." *Fortean Times* 174 (September): 56.
Heywood, Rosalind (1978). *The Infinite Hive*. Middlesex: Penguin Books.
Trubshaw, Bob (2011). *Singing Up the Country*. Avebury: Heart of Albion Press.

Southend

According to a report published in *Psychic News*, January 1956, a harmonium played by itself in Richard and Olive Woodley's large Victorian flat in Southend-on-Sea, Essex, England, soon after they moved there. They discovered "three dust-covered harmoniums" on further exploration, but the nightly unknown music proved to be too much for them, and they subsequently departed (Payne, p. 78).

Payne, Jessie (1995). *A Ghost Hunter's Guide to Essex*. Norfolk: Ian Henry.

Spell-Craft

Spell-craft is an obvious derivative of **magic** practice which can use music in a variety of ways from a source of incidental background to being an integral part of the ceremony: "The most important use of song [or music] is in the ritual, the predominant Pagan form of worship and the central art-form of the movement.... Some covens have songs or **chants** for opening and closing the circle, for calling the quarters, or for invoking the deities.... Pagans also use songs as raw materials for spells and rituals" (Magliocco and Tannen, pp. 175–201). In ancient India many spells were sung and "the Indians of South America use powerful chants in virtually every magical ritual" (Guiley, p. 317). Whether the initiator is a solitary individual or the leader/ high priest/ess of a coven, personal choice is a major factor in the music's suitability for the intention of the spell. **Out-of-body experiences** and other **altered states of consciousness** are often claimed by participants during such rituals (Willin, pp. 185–191). "For the concentrated building-up of power required in spell-working, strongly rhythmic music can be effective—particularly if the music itself builds up as it develops" (Farrar and Farrar, p. 35). A sponsored academic study of spell-craft undertaken by the author (Willin, pp. 65–79) discovered that chant was an integral part of such activity which sometimes produced positive results. Other music that was used by covens was also specified from a number of direct contacts (private correspondence) which included music by Corvus Corax, Carolyn Hillyer, Loreena McKennitt, Endura and Dead Can Dance. If the powers of a spell are grounded in magic, then perhaps it is true that "the chief significance of sound is mystical ... it can release powers of the mind of which many people are unaware" (Parker and Parker, p. 51).

An example of a spell, not so much using music, as to create music, is related in *The Book of Power*: "Call the name of the genie El-Adrel and when you do, wear on your head a cap of metal. And he will come, and will speak to you from a pot of water that you have placed near you. Speak to him fairly, and he will cause you to hear what music you wish. And when you want the music to cease, call his name the other way about, and he will go away, and take the music. But you must not call him more than once a day" (Shah, no. 21).

Farrar, Janet, and Stewart (1990). *Spells and How They Work*. London: Hale.
Guiley, Rosemary Ellen (1999). *The Encyclopedia of Witches and Witchcraft*. New York: Checkmark Books.
Magliocco, Sabina, and Holly Tannen (1998). "The Real Old-Time Religion: Towards an Aesthetic of Neo-Pagan Song." *Journal of the Folklore Studies Association of Canada* 20: 1.
Parker, Derek, and Julia (1975). *The Power of Magic*. London: Beazley.
Shah, Idres (2009). *The Book of Power*. Master Aptolcater (author), Coleman Rydie (editor/publisher).
Willin, Melvyn J. (2004). *Music in Pagan and Witchcraft Ritual and Culture*. PhD. Thesis. University of Bristol.
Willin, Melvyn J. (2007). "Paranormal Phenomena in in British Witchcraft and Wiccan Culture with Special Reference to Spell-Craft." *Journal of the Society for Psychical Research* 71: 65–79.

Spinney Abbey

A farmhouse situated in Wicken, Cambridgeshire, England, is the location of a former priory that was inhabited in the seventeenth century by Henry Cromwell (1628–1674), son of the more famous Oliver Cromwell (1599–1658). In 1971 the owners of the Abbey told the psychical investigator and journalist Peter Haining (1940–2007) that they had heard the sound of Latin **chant**ing "clear as a bell, pure and sweet, all in Latin; and just where the old Chapel of the Abbey used to stand" (Haining, pp. 223–224). There were also visual manifestations.

Haining, Peter (2008). *The Mammoth Book of True Hauntings*. London: Constable & Robinson.

Spiritualism

The birth of the **religion** which became known as Spiritualism is generally believed to have arisen in Hydesville, New York, in 1848, when Margaret (1833–1893) and Catherine (1837–1892) Fox convinced their older sister Leah (1813–1890) and many others that they were communicating with spirits initially through raps, and later on, "music continued to hold a pivotal place" (Weisberg, p. 73). The amount of music allegedly produced by spirits and within Spiritualism is vast. Its many manifestations have already been encountered—playing instruments without touching them; compositions **channeled** by dead composers; **mediums** possessed by dead performers; and so on. "Harmonic sounds are heard, as of human voices, but more frequently resembling the tones of various musical instruments, among which those of the fife, **drum**, **trumpet**, guitar, **harp** and **piano** have been mysteriously and successfully represented, both with and without the instruments, and in either case without any apparent human or visible agency" (Curnow, p. 63). The famous naturalist Alfred Russel Wallace (1823–1903) witnessed the larger-than-life Mrs. Guppy produce musical sounds when there were no instruments present. She also produced apports of flowers and fruit and levitated considerable distances (cited in Fodor, p. 403). The allegedly exquisite music of D.D. **Home** has been described elsewhere, but a list drawn-up by Leslie Curnow (Curnow, p. 69) drew attention to less well-known mediums where musical phenomena occurred: Miss Bailey, Mrs. Cushman, Mrs. Annie Lord Chamberlin, Mr. J.R.M. Squire, Willy Turketine, Mrs. Everitt, William Eglinton and **Cecil Husk**.

In 1867 the London Dialectical Society was founded to scrutinize contemporary issues from a learned viewpoint. Two years later a committee was appointed to undertake a comprehensive investigation of Spiritualism and the results were published in 1871, which included numerous musical references which had previously not been brought to public attention. These included:

"The sounding of music and singing without any visible agency; three voices chanting a hymn, accompanied by music played on an accordion suspended in space, eight or nine feet off the ground...." At the passing away of an old servant of our household, a strain of solemn music, at about four in the morning, was, by the nurse and servants, heard in the room of the dying woman; the music lasting fully twenty minutes [p. 118].

An accordion was played in the air, Mr Home holding it by one strap, and not touching it in any other way. The room was fully lighted. Three or four persons, unknown to Mr Home, mentally wished for particular tunes and they were played [p. 128].

An accordion was mysteriously transported by Home to one Mr Coleman and it played a tune ("Angels ever bright and fair") when it landed upon his knee [pp. 138–139].

Further accordion phenomena were recorded [pp. 146–148; 205; 210; 249; 346] [London Dialectical Society, 1871].

The following list provides appropriate entries within the text that allude to Spiritualism and the bibliography contains considerable further reading material:

Aubert; Automatic music writing; Bozzano; Britten; Brown; Channeling; Chaplin; Crowley; D'Aranyi; Davenports; Drums; Eddy Brothers; Enticknap; Exorcism; Friml; Home; Husk; Indridason; Koons; Lill; Lincoln; Liszt; May; Mediums; Moses; Piper; Possession; Reuter; Sangoma; Scole; Séances; Shamans; Shepard; Slade; Stella C; Tamlin; Tweedale.

Curnow, Leslie (1925). *The Physical Phenomena of Spiritualism.* London: Two Worlds.
Fodor, Nandor (1934). *Encyclopedia of Psychic Science.* London: Arthurs Press.
London Dialectical Society (1871). *Report on Spiritualism.* London: Longmans, Green, Reader and Dyer.
Weisberg, Barbara (2005). *Talking to the Dead.* New York: HarperCollins.

Stainland

On New Year's Eve 1956 in a cottage in Stainland, near Halifax, England, a Mr. Albert Paradise observed what he believed to be an apparition walking towards his bed while playing a **violin**. Mr. Paradise did not describe the music in his account and after modernization the cottage did not reveal any further unaccountable activity (Spencer, pp. 113–114).

Spencer, John, and Anne (1992). *The Encyclopaedia of Ghosts and Spirits.* London: Book Club Associates.

Steiner, Rudolf

Rudolf Joseph Lorenz Steiner (1861–1925) was an Austrian philosopher and educationalist who became interested in **Theosophy** and esotericism before founding his own Anthroposophical Society in the early part of the twentieth century, which promoted a spiritual existence assimilating human knowledge and creativity as a form of **healing** and education. Music is at the very heart of Steiner's work: "a disease condition of the soul will … be spoken of in musical terms, as one would speak, for instance, of a **piano** that was out of tune" (Steiner, p. 349). His belief in an astral body took on undertones of neo-Platonicism and harked back to *musica mundane* and *musica humana* (cited in Horden, p. 330), but he went further, writing, "The musician, on the other hand, conjures up a still higher world. In the physical world he conjures up the Devachanic world. Indeed, the melodies and harmonies that speak to us from the works or our great masters are faithful copies of the Devachanic world. If we can obtain a shadow, a foretaste of the Devachanic world in anything, it is in the effects of the melodies and harmonies of music, in their effects on the human soul" (Steiner, p. 26). His influence remains in music **therapy** as well as in worldwide educational institutions numbering over one thousand.

Horden, Peregrine (2000). "Commentary on Part V, with Notes on Nineteenth-Century America and on mesmerism and Theosophy." *Music as Medicine*. Aldershot: Ashgate.

Steiner, Rudolf (1974). *Vom Wesen des Musikalischen*. Ed. Ernst Hagemann. Freiburg I, Br., Die Kommenden.

Steiner, Rudolf (1984). *The Essential Steiner*. Ed. R. McDermot. San Francisco: HarperCollins.

Stella C.

Stella Cranshaw (later Mrs. Leslie Deacon, d. 1950?) was discovered in the 1920s by the psychical researcher Harry Price (1881–1948) after a conversation on a train journey. She was a practicing nurse and was not interested in psychical research, but she agreed to be tested by Price. Her musical feats involved the playing of various instruments without touching them including a bell, harmonica, pan pipes and a zither which were surrounded with a gauze mesh to hinder physical access. Harry Price recorded a "sitting" with her and others in attendance including Eileen Garrett on May 7, 1923, when an "entity" manifested "upon a number of musical instruments" which included "a loud chord upon the mouth-organ" and "two or three notes upon the Pan pipes." Further musical demonstrations followed (Price, pp. 71–773). In March 1926 she sat in a séance attended by Professor Hans Driesch (1867–1941), the President of the Society for Psychical Research at the time, when "blue flashes were seen, and a sealed-off mouth organ produced musical notes" (Haynes, p. 123). She was married in 1928 and discontinued the experiments thereafter (Stemman, pp. 130–131).

Haynes, Renée (1982). *The Society for Psychical Research 1882–1982*. London: Macdonald.
Price, Harry (1925). *Stella C.* London: Hurst & Blackett.
Stemman, R. (1975). *Spirits and Spirit Worlds*. London: Aldus.

Stockhausen, Karlheinz

Karlheinz Stockhausen (1928–2007) was a German composer of controversial avant-garde and electronic music. He wrote about his views on music which placed it firmly into an esoteric or transcendental sphere: "with another music I can set my supranatural center in vibration ... this music awakens my consciousness for something I would otherwise repress.... Music should above all be a means to keep awake the connection of the soul with the other side.... Very few realize that every one of us basically needs music for self-**healing**.... Stockhausen's music is not Stockhausen, but this spirit which is using me" (cited in Godwin, pp. 289–294). He wrote, "I have dreamt several times that I came from Sirius and that I was trained there as a musician" (cited in Simmons, p. 34).

Godwin, Jocelyn (1987b). *Music, Mysticism and Magic*. London: Arkana.
Simmons, Ian (2009). "Mothership Connections." *Fortean Times* 244 (January): 30–35.

Strauss, Richard

Richard Georg Strauss (1864–1949) was a German composer of a large number of works including renowned operas and tone poems. In conversation with **Arthur Abell**, he disclosed many interesting thoughts about his reliance on "tapping the source of Infinite and Eternal energy from which you and I and all things proceed" (Abell, p. 86). He spoke of an "afflatus" that seemed to be without limit in its capacity for inspiring anyone who felt the creative urge within them and "being aided by a more than earthly Power" (Abell, pp. 106–107). Furthermore, he said he was dictated to by "Omnipotent Entities" (Harman and Rheingold, p. 46)

Abell, Arthur M. (1955). *Talks with Great Composers*. London: Psychic Book Club.
Harman, Willis, and Howard Rheingold (1984). *Higher Creativity*. New York: Tarcher/Putnam.

Stravinsky, Igor

Igor Fyodorovich Stravinsky (1882–1971) was a Russian composer whose most famous work was almost certainly the ballet *The Rite of Spring*. It was this composition that Stravinsky felt was dictated to him as if he had been the vessel through which the music manifested itself: "I had a fleeting vision which came to me as a complete surprise. I saw in imagination a solemn pagan rite: sage elders, seated in a circle, watched a young girl **dance** herself to death. They were sacrificing her to propitiate the god of spring" (Druskin, p. 39).

Druskin, Mikhail (1883). *Igor Stravinsky: His Life, Works, and Views*. Trans. Martin Cooper. Cambridge: Cambridge University Press.

Sufi Music

See **Dervishes; Khan; Hazrat Inayat; Mantras; Rumi; Jalālu'ddīn; Mysticism and Music; Tavener.**

Sundial Cottage

Sundial Cottage in Prestbury, Gloucestershire, England, is believed to house a resident ghost that plays the spinet on rare occasions (Brooks, p. 83). It is reported that the house was once used by a music teacher for giving lessons there, but an enquiry from the author to the owners a few years ago did not receive an answer, so perhaps there has not been any recent manifestations.

Brooks, J.A. (1992). *Ghosts and witches of the Cotswolds*. Norwich: Jarrold.

Sunken Bells

Sunken bells are referred to throughout the text from a variety of watery places. The reasons for their mysterious pealing has been ascribed to a number of sources ranging from the mythological and folkloristic involving mermaids or the **Devil**, to hallucinatory and natural. Some coastal villages' bells heard in the distance may have been mistaken for sunken bells and tides may have moved some bells usually secure in deep water on the seabed. A selection from the UK would include:

Seascapes

South Hayling Island, Hampshire/**Dunwich**, Suffolk/Nigg Bay, East. Highlands/**Aberdovey**, Gwynd/**St. Ives Bay**, Cornwall/**Forrabury**, Cornwall/Mount Bay, Cornwall/**Sennen Cove**, Cornwall/**Walton on the Naze**, Essex.

Lakes and Pools

Marden Pool, Herefordshire/Rostherne Mere, Cheshire/Llangorse Lake, Powys/**Cole Mere**, Shropshire/Tunstall Pool, Norfolk/Llyntarw Clatter, Powys.

Rivers, Broads and Creeks

Bosham, West Sussex.
(Further examples can be found in Ashliman, 2013–2019, and Willin, 2005.)

Ashliman, D.L., ed. (2013–2019). *Sunken Bells. Legends of Christiansen Type 7070*. Pitt.edu.
Willin, Melvyn J. (2005). *Music, Witchcraft and the Paranormal*. Ely: Melrose.

Surgical Procedures

Outside of medical journals and some New Age pronouncements there is very little literature exploring the relationship between music and its seeming power to overcome pain during surgical operating procedures. Psychic healers do not specifically use music as a form of hypnosis in their operations. However, there is certainly evidence to suggest that music has an effect on both patients and surgeons during operations (Rastipisheh, 2018), but how far it is purely therapeutic rather than having a direct physical influence is difficult to resolve. It has been suggested that suitable music "might reduce the need for large doses of anesthesia and would make the surgical procedure much safer" (Gardner, p. 95). Using music without anesthetic is a much bigger step to take. "In 1997, President Bill Clinton tore a tendon and required extensive surgery, which he chose to undergo without general anesthesia. The President instructed his surgeons to fill the operating room with country-western music" (cited in Campbell, p. 130). In the Channel 4 television program *Music and the Mind*, presented by **Paul Robertson** in 1996, the surgeon Ralph Spintge carried out operations that seemingly did not use anesthesia, but provided music for the patients who seemed to not feel the obvious pain they would normally have suffered.

Campbell, Don (1997). *The Mozart Effect*. London: Hodder & Stoughton.
Gardner, Kay (1990). *Sounding the Inner Landscape*. Rockport: Element.
Rastipisheh, Pegah, et al. (2018). "The Effects of Playing Music during Surgery on the Performance of the Surgical Team: A Systematic Review on Published Studies." *Proceedings of the 20th Congress of the International Ergonomics Association*: 245–253.

Suso, Henry

Henry Suso, aka Heinrich Seuse (c. 1295–1366), was a German mystic and monk. There was a link between his hearing of angelic music and the "reciprocal listening of **angels** and men in the Jewish tradition.... It also recalls the visions of Dante's *Paradiso*, in which **dance**, rather than music alone, figures as the expression of angelic worship" (cited in Godwin, p. 110). Suso's writings contain many incidents of angelic musical communication:

"The voice sang in tones sweet and loud ... the heavenly spirits began with loud voice to intone the beautiful responsory ... it seemed to him in a vision that he heard angelic strains and sweet heavenly melody" (cited in Godwin, pp. 111–112).

Godwin, Joscelyn (1987b). *Music, Mysticism and Magic*. London: Arkana.

Svengali Trio

The Svengali Trio was a vaudeville act that performed acts of telepathy in Europe and the USA from 1920 to 1925. "In their act, Hugo Lorenz (or Lorenzo) would move about the theater receiving whispered requests from the audience for specific musical selections or the names of celebrities. Without Hugo saying a word, the pianist, Elsie Terry, would break into the suggested melodies or the make-up artist, George Stuckenberg, would transform himself into a resemblance of the famous person named. They toured the world until around 1920" (geniimagazine.com/wiki/index.php?title=Svengali_Trio).

Synesthesia

Synesthesia is the sensory experience of perceiving color and music together and although it may not be definitively "paranormal" it is rare enough to be expressed as abnormal and not fully understood. Chromesthesia relates directly from sound to color. Inevitably there are problems encountered since composers see/relate different colors to different pitches, but this does not deny the bizarreness of the phenomenon. References were made to it as far back as the eighteenth century when the author and composer E.T.A. Hoffmann referred to its attributes which was used in the opera *The Tales of Hoffmann* (cited in Sacks, p. 166) and its use in metaphor may have provided earlier examples. Composers who have been synesthetes include **Alexander Scriabin**, Olivier Messiaen, György Ligeti, Jean Sibelius, **Franz Liszt**, Nikolai Rimsky-Korsakov and Michael Torke. Oliver Sacks devotes a complete chapter to the subject in his interesting book (Sacks, pp. 165–183) and Bulat M. Galeyev has published widely in the field (synesthesia.prometheus.kai.ru/sin1_e.htm). Håkon Austbø has written in depth about Messiaen's synesthesia (www.musicandpractice.org/volume-2/visualizing-visions-the-significance-of-messiaens-colours). He wrote that the Swiss artist Charles Blanc-Gatti, who apparently painted the sounds he heard from an organ, made a profound impact on Messiaen's impressions of the connections between colors and sounds.

Sacks, Oliver (2007). *Musicophilia*. London: Picador.

Talacre Arms

The Talacre Arms in Holywell, Wales, was a center for strange phenomena witnessed by several people in the 1970s which included poltergeist activity as well as **piano** music coming from an unknown source. The publican's dogs were particularly "spooked" by the activity (Playfair, p. 25).

Playfair, Guy Lyon (1985a). *The Haunted Pub Guide*. London: Harrap.

Tame, David

David Tame (1953–) is a British author and examiner of spirituality who has written at length about paranormality within the realm of music (Tame, 1984). He researches at length the effects of music on **plants** and other living organisms as well as its place in **magic**, esoteric and occult study. Another book is devoted the spirituality of **Beethoven** and his music (Tame, 1994). He has also conducted an interview with the musician Van Morrison and explored New Age music. However, some of his views have come under serious attack from the music therapist Lisa Summer (Summer, 1996).

Summer, Lisa (1996). *Music—The New Age Elixir*. New York: Prometheus Books.
Tame, David (1984). *The Secret Power of Music*. Wellingborough: Turnstone Press.
Tame, David (1994). *Beethoven and the Spiritual Path*. Wheaton: Quest Books.

Tamlin, Mrs.

Mrs. Sarah A. Tamlin was an attendee at a series of **séances** held in Auburn, New York, in the 1840s or 1850s during which time a guitar was heard to play "exquisite music" by itself in the dark sounding as if it was from afar (Capron, pp. 101–112) and sometimes the instrument passed over the assembled company's heads. Mrs. Tamlin soon became a medium herself and a variety of guitar music in particular manifested itself in her presence. In the *Revelations of a Spirit Medium* (Dingwall and Price, 1891) a specially made guitar was described with displaceable storage panels that could hide any devices or clothing that a medium might fraudulently make use of and a spring music box allowed music to sound from it perhaps while being waved in the air by means of a rod which could be attached to it (Dingwall and Price, p. 116).

Capron, E.W. (1855). *Modern Spiritualism: Its Facts and Fanaticisms; Its Consistencies and Contradictions*. Boston: Bela Marsh.
Dingwall, Eric J., and Harry Price, eds. (1922). "Facsimile Edition of *Revelations of a Spirit Medium* by A. Medium. St Paul Minnesota." London: Kegan Paul, Trench and Trubner.

Tarantism

The hysterical condition compelling people, often women, to **dance** wildly is "tarantism." It was known from about the fourteenth century onwards and although traditionally centered in Apulia in the southern region of Italy, it was known to be far more widespread than in just that small region. In the broad sense it might be thought of as having origins in Bacchanalian rites from ancient Greek/Roman times. Put simply, it was believed that the bite of the tarantula spider could only be cured by frenzied dancing: "These first dances are prolonged for several hours … which happens a dozen times during the day…. These dances usually continue for four days" (cited in Gentilcore, p. 259). Athanasius Kircher (1602–1680) explored the whole subject in depth in his *Magnes sive de Arte Magnetica* (1643) devoting four chapters to tarantism and its cure through music: "As described by Kircher, the music was played using various wind and plucked-string instruments—bagpipes, lyre, guitar, dulcimer, hurdy-gurdy—accompanied by tambourines and drums. Musical motifs tended to contrast low and high-pitched sounds, and made frequent use of semitones, thought to stimulate the nerves and muscles. As for mode, there was a clear preference for the Phrygian" (cited in Gentilcore, p. 262). As a dance form the tarantella has evolved away from its frenzied roots and has been used without a **healing** or paranormal undertone by many composers including **Beethoven, Chopin, Liszt** and Mendelssohn.

Gentilcore, David (2000). "Ritualized Illness and Music Therapy: Views of Tarantism in the Kingdom of Naples." *Music as Medicine*. Ed. Peregrine Hordern. Aldershot: Ashgate.

Tavener, John

Sir John Kenneth Tavener (1944–2013) was an English composer who came to prominence with the worldwide public after his *Song for Athene* was performed at the funeral of Princess Diana in 1997. The second half of his composing life was immersed in metaphysics and "it was necessary to move out of 'the Church'" back into the "market-place," to fill the *temeaos* [*temenos*] (an ancient Greek word meaning sacred space) (Tavener and Thekla, p. viii), notably after he joined the Russian Orthodox Church. He expressed his views about esoteric, exoteric and transcendental music in extensive conversations with Brian Keeble which were later published (Tavener, 1999). He claimed that in his piece *Mystagogia* he was "hardly able to tell where the notes have come from at all" (Tavener, p. 126). Tavener believed that **chant** was "the nearest we can get to the music that was breathed into man when God created the world" (Tavener, pp. 136–137), but he believed the chant was of a Byzantine nature rather than **Gregorian**. Nevertheless, even chant had to flow through the "fountainhead" of metaphysics (Tavener, p. 119) and he drew attention to the **music of the spheres** in his work *Agraphon*, which he loved more than any other. He also spoke of his love of Sufi music and many other influences. In an interview with Christian Tyler in 1994 he drew attention to the integral sacredness of music and the "singing chant of my soul" (Tyler, 1994). The author approached Tavener at a conference in **London** in 1996 and asked him whether his music came from within or from an external source. "After a long pause he answered that he thought it was a difficult question but that he thought it came from an external source, but worked through himself" (Willin, p. 66).

While in a **coma** and close to death he believed he was in some form of contact with the composer **Stravinsky**. He also shared experiences of **raga**s with **Paul Robertson** who was in a similar comatose state at the time (BBC 4 *Hearing Ragas*, 2012). Tavener's composition *Towards Silence* is important in illustrating the essence of his mind and beliefs. It was composed in 2007 for four string quartets and a large Tibetan bowl and it explores the nature of consciousness and the process of dying. It is a meditation on the four states of Atma (Hindu inner self or soul): the waking state, the dream state, deep sleep and that which is beyond and free from any mode of existence.

http://musicmindspirittrust.com/towards-silence.

Tavener, John (1999). *John Tavener. The Music of Silence. A Composer's Testament.* London: Faber and Faber.

Tavener, John, and Mother Thekla (1994). *Ikons.* London: HarperCollins.

Tyler, Christian (1994). "Musical Mystery Man." *The Financial Times* (February 5/6).

Willin, Melvyn J. (2005). *Music, Witchcraft and the Paranormal.* Ely: Melrose.

Tchaikovsky, Pyotr Ilyich

Pyotr Ilyich Tchaikovsky (1840–1893) was a Russian composer whose music has become famous through his ballets, symphonies and many other works. His letters revealed much of his sources of **inspiration** and the strange sensations he underwent during the compositional process: "I forget everything and behave like a madman. Everything within me starts pulsing and quivering; hardly have I begun the sketch ere one thought follows another" (cited in Inglis, p. 66). Concerning inspiration, he believed it came from the composer's soul and was a **magical** process.

He was the focus of **channeling** by a musical **medium** in the latter part of the twentieth century, but the music was not characteristic in any way of his actual music.

Inglis, Brian (1987). *The Unknown Guest—The Mystery of Intuition.* London: Chatto &Windus.

Theosophy

Theosophy is a **religion** that was founded in America in 1875 by Helena Petrovna Blavatsky (1831–1891) and Henry Steel Olcott (1832–1907). The basis of its structure is the integration of divinity and wisdom with a particular emphasis on esoteric Hinduism and Buddhism (Godwin, p. 4). There is a considerable amount of musical association attached to the religion and much of it from esoteric sources. Blavatsky herself was said to be a fine pianist receiving lessons from Ignaz Moscheles (1794–1870) in **London** and performing as a pianist under the pseudonym of "Madame Laura" (www.theosophy-ult.org.uk; theosophyart.org). There are many accounts of occult musical phenomena that were observed in the presence of Blavatsky. For instance, many times Olcott and others heard "exquisite music," which could be heard from any place of the room where they were located (cited in theosophyart.org). Theosophical doctrines were followed, or at the very least, appealed to a number of composers, both well-known and less renowned. Attention has already been drawn to **Alexander Scriabin** and **Cyril Scott**, but Gustav Holst, Oliver Messiaen and John Foulds were also said to hold similar beliefs, the last being married to the **violin**ist Maud

MacCarthy (1882–1967) who was a Theosophist and friend of Annie Besant (cited in theosophyart.org). **Emma Hardinge Britten** wrote several compositions and songs under the pseudonym "Ernest Reinhold" and Edmond Bailly (1850–1916) (born Henri-Edmond Limet) was a poet, musician, publisher, and one of the leading Theosophists in France. He was said to have restored an ancient Egyptian anthem and he wrote other pieces of esoteric music. The Italian composer Renato de Grandis (1927–2008) abandoned musical composition in 1987 and devoted himself to the doctrines of Theosophy (Hahn, 50–53). Luigi Carlo Filippo Russolo (1885–1947) the Italian painter and composer of "noise music" also held Theosophical beliefs (theosophyart.org). Charles Webster Leadbeater (1854–1934) an active Theosophist combined the "psycho-physical relations" of music, form and color in his extensive writings (Fotherby, p. 125).

Fotherby, Henry A. (1908). "Sound and Music in Their Physical and Psychical Relationship to Form, Light and Colour." *Annals of Psychical Science* VII, no. 39 (March): 119–138.
Godwin, Joscelyn (1995). *Music and the Occult.* New York: University of Rochester Press.
Hahn, Christoph (2010). "Sinfonische Lektüren aus einem unbekannten Archiv." *Neue Zeitschrift für Musik* 171, no. 5: 50–53. Mainz: Schott Music.
theosophyart.org/2019/11/07/theosophy-and-music/.
www.theosophy-ult.org.uk/wp-content/uploads/2014/06/Blavatsky-letters-to-Sinnett.pdf.

Therapy

There is a case to be made that music therapy should not be included in a book given a paranormal or anomalous focus. Indeed, Lisa Summer (Summer, 1996) argues convincingly that many claims for paranormality within music **healing** are bogus, whereby through implication, therapy should not be associated with the subject. However, other writers have drawn comparisons to the idea that music, therapy and the supernatural sometimes have common ground to share, notably from ancient sources. Primitive beliefs equated illness with **possession** by evils spirits or punishment by angry gods and although healing and therapy are closely linked, there are differences to be made. According to Dhyan Manish, "A therapist is an altruist who uses a technique, a method, a theory which allows the other person to heal by mentally understanding his or her own pathological problems. A healer is a spiritual being who uses his or her own energy to accompany other people in healing themselves by means of their own consciousness" (dhyanmanish.com). Indeed, one such author (Ted Andrews) has devoted a complete book to the subject of therapy that contains a host of "therapies" through listening to music to help a whole range of illnesses including circulation, digestion, glands, muscles, nerves, reproduction and respiration. One such [edited] list for the muscle system is:

Mahler, Symphony no. 1 in D major: use for recovery from muscle injury

Liszt, Hungarian Rhapsodies: strengthens and rejuvenates muscles

Kodaly, Peacock Variations: heals most major muscle groups

Wagner, Song of the Valkyries: use when muscles need a little stimulation

Elgar, Pomp and Circumstance: releases muscle tension due to sadness

Sousa, any of his marches: strengthens and uplifts muscles [Andrews, p. 164].

Another author (John Beaulieu) suggests, "The integration of an energy approach with current music therapy is important for the future growth of Music Therapy" (Beaulieu, p. 131) and he also promotes the use of "psychotherapy, guided imagery and bodywork." Judith Seelig combines music with yoga in her quest for universal consciousness. A curious claim is made by Edward Podolsky (1902–1965) who claimed that listening to music while eating had a direct effect on the digestive system and could therefore be used in a therapeutic way (cited in Bernard, pp. 48–49). Don Campbell devotes a chapter of his best-selling book *The Mozart Effect* (pp. 121–153) to the use of music therapy for rehabilitation. He draws attention to the fact that music therapy was first used in America in the nineteenth century and since then it has led to "awakenings" in the medical field with sometimes astonishing results. Kung Tai, a Chinese music therapist, "combines rhythm, *qi gong* exercise movements, and lyric writing.... In 1986, while meditating, Kung felt his body vanish and saw a golden light radiating from a lotus-shaped stage. He then heard a voice singing clear celestial music ... dramatic cases of spontaneous healing reportedly occurred" (Campbell, p. 139).

The literature for music therapy is vast, especially when discussing conventional information. However, Cathie Guzzetta (Dossey, pp. 263–288) and Joseph Moreno (Moreno, 167–185) both approach the subject from a less traditional angle—the former alluding to the "music of the soul" and the latter approaching the subject as both a therapist and a "contemporary **shaman**." Their references and bibliography provide further examples.

Andrews, Ted (1997). *Music Therapy for Non-Musicians*. Batavia: Dragonhawk.

Beaulieu, John (1987). *Music and Sound in the Healing Arts*. New York: Station Hill.

Bernard, Patrick (2004). *Music as Yoga*. San Rafael: Mandala.

Campbell, Don (1997). *The Mozart Effect*. London: Hodder & Stoughton.

dhyanmanish.com/?page_id=604&lang=en.

Guzzetta, Cathie E. (1988). "Music Therapy: Nursing the Music of the Soul." *Holistic Nursing: A Handbook for Practice* by B. Dossey, L. Keegan, C. Guzzetta and L. Kolkmeier. New York: Aspen, 263–288.

Moreno, Joseph J. (1997)." The Music Therapist: Creative Arts Therapist and Contemporary Shaman." *Music: Physician for Times to Come*. Wheaton: Quest.

Summer, Lisa (1996). *Music—The New Age Elixir*. New York: Prometheus Books.

Tomatis, Alfred

Alfred A. Tomatis (1920–2001) was a French otolaryngologist who received numerous awards for his ground-breaking work. He discovered that the ears were functioning several months before birth and that listening was therefore the first of the senses to be developed (cited in Leeds, p. 28). Among many **healing** advancements, "he formulated the law describing the feedback loop between the larynx and the ear" (Weeks, p. 42.), which became known as the "Tomatis Effect." His work was, and still is, surrounded with controversy because of his unorthodox and innovative ideas. Probably his most nonconformist research was the evidence he found for the effect that sound and music had directly on the human body, notably through **Gregorian chant**, which he believed was "an awakening of the field of consciousness" (Wilson, p. 23). Tomatis' experiments with curing monks' lethargy and other physical ailments in 1967 (Wilson, pp. 14–15) inevitably led to the birth of the **Mozart Effect** after he had highlighted Mozart's music as a source for re-charging people.

Leeds, Joshua (n.d.). "A Sympathetic Vibration." *Caduceus* 28: 27–30.
Weeks, Bradford S. (1993). "The Physician, the Ear and Sacred Music." *Music: Physician for Times to Come.* Ed. Don Campbell. Wheaton: Quest.
Wilson, Tim (1993). "The Healing Power of Voice and Ear." *Music: Physician for Times to Come.* Ed. Don Campbell. Wheaton: Quest.

Tourette's Syndrome

This medical condition is not paranormal as such, but in the past some of its manifestations were viewed as at least abnormal and the musical aspects that can arise from it are often very unusual. It was named after the French neurologist Gilles de la Tourette (1857–1904) who had been asked by Jean-Martin Charcot (1825–1893), director of the Salpêtrière Hospital, to undertake research into motor disorders. Probably the most famous composer to have arguably suffered from Tourette's Syndrome was **Mozart** (Ashoori and Jancovic, pp. 1171–1175), but there have been other less well-known musicians. The pianist Nick van Bloss found, for many years, that playing the **piano** allowed him to operate normally without the tics and grunts that he uttered in his usual daily life. (It is a fallacy that everyone with Tourette's Syndrome swears, except in cases of Coprolalia.) He believes that "Tourette's gifted me with a tremendous talent for music" (Palmer, pp. 56–59). Other examples of sufferers include John S. who felt music was both a blessing and a curse since it could alleviate or cause "a surge of tics"; Sydney A. used wild gesticulations to represent the music he heard; and Ray G. "was noted for his sudden and wild [drum] solos, which would often arise from a convulsive drum-hitting tic—but the tic could initiate a cascade of percussive speed and invention and elaboration" (Sacks, pp. 226–232).

Ashoori, Aidin, and Joseph Jancovic (2007). "Mozart's Movements and Behavior: A Case of Tourette's Syndrome?" *Journal of Neurology, Neurosurgery & Psychiatry* 78, no. 11 (November): 1171–1175.
Palmer, Sally (2007). "Inspiration or Affliction?" *Focus* (March). London.
Sacks, Oliver (2007). *Musicophilia*. London: Picador.

Trumpet

The trumpet has been referred to in numerous paranormal situations. It should not be confused with the speaking tube often referred to in **séances** for spirit communication which is also called a "trumpet." In demonology **Amdusias** favored the instrument and in mythology Asclepiades was said to have healed the deaf using it. It is a popular instrument in the **Bible** for heraldic purposes and similarly in **battlefield** re-enactments and at castles including **Calvados**, Castleconnell, **Fotheringhay**, and **Fyvie**. Allegedly it accompanied the paranormal **levitation** of large stones in Tibet, and it may have been associated with other buildings' constructions. **Pastor Pierre Jurieu** heard trumpet music during the persecution of the Huguenots in France in the seventeenth century and mysterious trumpet music was heard during the **Amherst Mystery**. Harry Martindale described hearing the sound of a trumpet while working in the Treasurer's House, in **York**, England, when a line of ghostly, but solid Roman soldiers walked through there in the 1950s (Mitchell, p. 122).

Mitchell, John V. (1996). *Ghosts of an Ancient City*. York: St. Peter's School.

Tweedale, Charles

Charles Lakeman Tweedale (?–1944) was an English Anglican minister and Spiritualist. He was the vicar of Weston Church in Yorkshire, and it was here that both he and his wife experienced numerous paranormal music phenomena. He believed that the great **violin** maker Stradivarius guided him in violin construction and the preparation of an unknown varnish to apply to the violin he was making, and he was also told details of Stradivarius' life that were unknown to him (cited Willin, pp. 58–60). Tweedale was first contacted by Stradivarius in December 1908 "when the family were in bed they were tossed about and lifted from the floor" (Hampson, p. 467). He recounted an event for October 24, 1910: "I was alone writing in my study. I distinctly hear a chord strummed on a violin hung up behind me. It was exactly as though a man's thumb had been passed across the strings sounding each note guitar-wise. The violin was in tune.... This sounding of the strings on the violin hanging in my study has occurred several times when I have been alone in the study" (Tweedale, p. 37). Tweedale's wife was contacted by the spirit of the soprano Adelina Patti (1843–1919) who caused her (Tweedale's wife) to sing beyond her normal capacity. Stradivarius also introduced the spirit of **Chopin** into the family circle on April 16, 1930, who took over Tweedale's daughter's hands when she was playing the **piano**. Ghostly music was heard at the vicarage which was witnessed by several other people: "we began to have musical sounds and instrumental manifestations of varied import … a strain of music began to sound from the top of the wardrobe. It was most beautiful, and the tone something like that of a musical box. It played a delightful air twice over, concluding with a fine chord. Nothing was seen. There was at that time no musical box in the house. [Tweedale continued concerning his wife] … she heard a violin playing from inside my study … when I was not in the house" (Tweedale, pp. 37–56).

Somewhat bizarrely Stradivarius also conveyed details of his meetings with other composers in rhyming verse as Tweedale's diary account for June 14, 1930, describes: "Mendelssohn beams all over his face and say we all 'Who can take his place'? Chopin walks around with glee for he sees some fun in me. **Handel**, dear soul, fills us all with awe, we never heard such melodies before" (Tweedale, p. 83). Chopin was also known to present some unconvincing couplets (July 22, 1931): "Chopin has a bit to say. Strad he always has his way. Chopin wants a book to make, or this house he will forsake" (Tweedale, p. 98).

The author visited Weston in 1996 and spoke to the inhabitant of the manor house located next to the church. He spoke of Tweedale as being thought to be "round the bend" (private conversation). Nevertheless, his violin was presented at an auction in **London** sometime in 1986 when it was estimated to sell for between two to three hundred pounds. It bore a label stating "the original varnish of Antonius Stradivarius has been applied" (Ortzen, 1986).

Hampson, Herbert (1949). "Violin Case 'walked' Across Room." *The Two Worlds* 63 (December 24): 467.
Ortzen, Tony (1986). "Under the Hammer." *Psychic News* (June 21).
Tweedale, Charles (1940b). *News from the Next World*. London: Werner Laurier.
Willin, Melvyn J. (2005). *Music, Witchcraft and the Paranormal*. Ely: Melrose.

Twmbarlwm Hill

Twmbarlwm is a hill that is situated just over a mile away from Risca in South Wales. Music from a seemingly unknown source has been heard there which received clarification from a local who related that she believed "the valley was acting as a funnel for the sound. The strange sounds that have been heard especially at night on Twmbarlwm, I think, are echoes from Cilfynydd Mountain.... Again a few weeks later, chatting to a neighbor they said that they'd heard an organ playing at the same place I had been. Further investigation showed that at that same time someone was playing the organ in Cwmcarn church and being a warm day, they had the door open. Personally, I think the atmospheric conditions have to be just right to experience the phenomenon" (www.twmbarlwm.co.uk/ghostly-music).

Ukulele

The ukulele is not the most common instrument to be associated with paranormal music, however, in 1989 a case was reported that one such instrument, signed by the famous performer George Formby, had started to play by itself in a shop in Bridgend, Mid–Glamorgan, Wales and the witness was very scared by its ghostly sounds (Sherwood, February 12, 1989).

Sherwood, Deborah (1989). "Help! I've a Spook in My Uke." *News of the World* (12 February).

Ur-Song

The Ur-song is the name given to a fundamental collection of notes that are believed to be universal in terms of infant music vocal production. In intervallic terms it can be represented by a descending minor 3rd as can be heard in songs such as the opening of "This Old Man" followed by an ascending perfect 4th. "In 1973 the composer and conductor Leonard Bernstein, in his Charles Eliot Norton lectures at Harvard, described the Ur-song of the world's children as an archetypal pattern.... Ur-song is the joint product of the physical laws of harmony, and of the innate, genetic pattern of all human beings" (cited in Tame, p. 230). The psychologist Howard Gardner (1943–) has also researched this intriguing subject (Gardner, pp. 70–71).

Gardner, Howard (1981). "Do Babies Sing a Universal Song?" *Psychology Today* (December): 70–77.
Tame, David (1984). *The Secret Power of Music*. Wellingborough: Turnstone Press.

Vaughan Williams, Ralph

Ralph Vaughan Williams (1872–1958) was an English composer who, despite often being thought of as a traditional, even old-fashioned, composer immersed in hymn tunes and folksongs, was nevertheless undoubtedly open to the mystical influences on his compositions. His essays, a musical autobiography and a detailed biography by his wife Ursula gave considerable credence to this aspect of his work. He believed the object of all art was "to obtain a partial revelation of that which is beyond human sense and faculties—of that which is spiritual … what lies beyond sense and knowledge" (Vaughan Williams, p. 122) and that it was bound up with **magic**. Vaughan Williams' notions of **mysticism** might be compared to the American poet Walt Whitman's (1919–1892) concept of transcendentalism and in his pursuit of the folk traditions of England he actually compared himself "to a psychical researcher who has actually seen a ghost" (Ursula Vaughan Williams, p. 100). His quasi-supernatural ideas have been compared to Jung's archetypes "buried in the unconscious, they are activated whenever we encounter them outside of ourselves" (Sutton, p. 42).

Sutton, David (2008). "Vaughan Williams: Toward the Unknown Region." *Fortean Times* 241 (October): 42.
Vaughan Williams, Ralph (1987). "The Letter and the Spirit." *National Music and Other Essays.* Oxford: Oxford University Press.
Vaughan Williams, Ursula (1964). *Ralph Vaughan Williams: A Biography.* Oxford: Oxford University Press.

Versailles

In 1901 Charlotte Anne Moberly (1846–1937) and Eleanor Jourdain (1863–1924)—the Principal and Vice-Principal, respectively, of St. Hugh's College for Women, Oxford—visited the Palace of Versailles as sightseers. They visited the Petit Trianon, the house and garden that Louis XVI had given to Marie Antoinette in 1774, but they became lost and somewhat depressed and disorientated. They encountered a number of people dressed in an old-fashioned and rather unusual way in an outside area where "everything suddenly looked unnatural, therefore unpleasant…. There were no effects of light and shade, and no wind stirred the trees. It was all intensely still" (Moberly and Jourdain, pp. 45–46). A number of different people responded to them, and they witnessed a French wedding party. They later learned that the date of their visit had coincided with the sacking of the Tuileries in 1792. They returned to the Petit Trianon the next year and while alone Jourdain noticed the topography was different and the style of dress people were wearing was again anachronistic. During a third visit in 1904 the details seemed different from before and they could not find the location or any similarly dressed people. In 1911 they published an account of their visits under the pseudonyms of Elizabeth Morison and Frances Lamont (1911).

What makes this case particularly interesting was the fact that Jourdain claimed to have heard music playing during her visit: "The crowd got scarce and drifted away, and then faint music as of a band, not far off, was audible. It was playing very light music with a good deal of repetition in it. Both voices and music were diminished in tone, as in a phonograph, unnaturally. The pitch of the band was lower than usual. The sounds were intermittent, and once more I felt the swish of a dress close by me.... On my return to Versailles I made careful enquiries as to whether the band had been playing there that day, but was told that though it was the usual day of the week, it had not played because it had played the day before, being New Year's Day" (Moberly and Jourdain, pp. 61–62). She also referred to having heard a "band of **violins**" the music of which she attempted to write out herself from memory (Bod. MS. Eng. Misc. C257, p. 130). Both ladies undertook considerable research to uncover the origin of the music and discovered a number of similarities in unpublished music held at the Conservatoire de Musique in Paris. The pieces included: *Dardanus—Oedipe a Colone*, no. 6 by Sacchini; *Rigaudons—Le Marechal Ferrand* 1767 by Philidor; and *Le Roi et le Fermier* by Monsigny (cited by Coleman, p. 50). Extensive research was undertaken by the composer and musicologist **Ian Parrott** (Parrott, 1966) who was convinced of the music's paranormal origin, but this view was opposed by the renowned musicians Ernest Newman and Sir Malcolm Sargent (Willin, p. 120). The Society for Psychical Research took a particular interest in the case and published several viewpoints in their journals (December 1967, volume 44, nos. 734/735/736; March 1968; and June 1968). The psychical researcher Andrew MacKenzie devoted a chapter of one of his books (MacKenzie, 124–156) to the investigation where he mentioned that a Mr.

Charlotte Moberly was the first Principal of St. Hugh's College, Oxford, and witnessed a time-slip at the Palace of Versailles (courtesy Mary Evans Picture Library).

Crooke had also heard "old music" at the same location when no one was present. Other interpretations have followed including Lucille Iremonger's critical account (1957). A far more skeptical approach to the musical recollection was published by the *Musical Times* of September 1, 1912, which created doubt as to the ability to remember twelve bars of a previously unknown piece and also, without perfect pitch, to be able to hear the music being played in a flat key which was "lower than usual" (cited in Sturge-Whiting, pp. 293–294). The story and the investigation were revitalized with further study in 2016 with the details of the original musicologist who studied the claims (Sir William Henry Hadow) being divulged: "He commented the music was more like something 'heard in a dream than music heard naturally with waking ears. There is something freakish and uncanny about it'" (cited in Lamont, p. 219).

Eleanor Jourdain was the Vice Principal of St Hugh's College, Oxford, and was the companion of Charlotte Moberly during their Versailles adventure. She also witnessed paranormally produced music there (courtesy Mary Evans Picture Library).

Coleman, Michael (1988). *The Ghosts of the Trianon*. Northants: Aquarian Press.
Iremonger, Lucille (1957). *The Ghosts of Versailles*. London: Faber and Faber.
Lamont, Marc (2016). *The Mysterious Paths of Versailles*. Bloomington: Xlibris.
MacKenzie, Andrew (1983). *Hauntings and Apparitions*. London: Granada.
Morison, Elizabeth, and Frances Lamont (1934) (original 1911). *An Adventure*. London: Macmillan.
Parrott, Ian (1966). *The Music of An Adventure*. London: Regency Press.
Sturge-Whiting, J.R. (1938). *The Mystery of Versailles*. London: Rider.
Willin, Melvyn J. (2005). *Music, Witchcraft and the Paranormal*. Ely: Melrose.

Violin/Fiddle

The violin or fiddle as it is also called in some folk circles is often associated with alleged paranormal phenomena. It has been quoted as the source of "ghostly" music in numerous locations including the **White Hart**, Chalfont St. Peter, the **Castle Hotel**, Taunton and **Stainland** in Halifax. Local fiddle players have been lost forever in legends while playing their instruments in caves at **Anstey** and Pendine in Wales and in a tunnel at **Binham Priory**. In the United States phantom violin music has been reported at the Julia Ideson Building, the public library, in Houston, Texas, after the death of a violin-playing employee. Another example can be found at Scott Run Bridge, south of St. Georges, Delaware, where an old man (Ebenezer) was accidently killed while playing his fiddle there. Further varied reports have been encountered at least as recently as the 1990s (Holloway, pp. 25–33).

The instrument was used in **séances** held by **Jonathan Koons** in the nineteenth century and the music for violin was the focus for **Florizel von Reuter's** communications with **Paganini** and also **Charles Tweedale's** spirit contact with Stradivarius. The much-repeated tale of Tartini's *Devil's Trill Sonata* has often been repeated, but less often has mention been made of **Leila Waddell's** playing in **Aleister Crowley's** rituals. Its connection with demons and the **Devil** has often been cited in references to ancient **witchcraft** Sabbaths. Margaret Murray reported that "the French witches were apparently appreciative of good music for they told de Lancre that 'they **dance** to the sound of the tambourine and the flute … sometimes with a violin'" (cited in Murray, p. 119).

Possibly the strangest concept purporting to involve the violin in an anomalous setting is the strange history of the funerary violin, which it is necessary to declare immediately is a complete **hoax** having been invented by the author Rohan Kriwaczek and published in 2006. Under the auspices of an invented Guild of Funerary Violins, established in 1580 by Elizabeth I, it tells the story of a league of musicians who introduced a new type of music to recognize the grief of those who mourned for their departed. "In a series of 'funerary purges,' the art of funerary violin was condemned as 'the music of the devil' and the Guild of Funerary Violinists driven into silence or clandestine activity. This is the music that, despite all attempts at suppression, has haunted Europe's collective unconscious for more than a century" (Kriwaczek, publicity). A detailed history was provided with references altogether running into over two hundred pages—all of which was invented!

[For another fictional (?) account involving the violin see Freakley, pp. 334–335].

Freakley, S. (1914). "The Haunted Violin." *The Two Worlds* 27 (July 3): 334–335.
Holloway, Lee (2004). "Spectral Violinists and Phantom Fiddlers." *Fate* (June): 25–33.
Kriwaczek, Rohan (2006). *The Incomplete History of the Art of Funerary Violin.* Richmond: Duckworth.
Murray, Margaret A. (1931). *The God of the Witches.* London: Sampson Low, Marston.

Voodoo

The word "voodoo" originates from "vodun" meaning "god, spirit or sacred object in the Fon language of West Africa. It is applied especially to the beliefs and practices found in Haiti, whose inhabitants are, for the most part, descendants of slaves imported from many parts of Africa, and by extension to similar practices in other Caribbean islands, in the Southern states of America, and in Brazil where plantation slavery was also customary" (Huxley, 2967). Although there is a perception that the **religion** is embroiled with black **magic**, curses, **spell-craft**, sacrifices, **possession** and zombies, it is far more involved than these practices suggest. Indeed, voodoo rituals make use of Roman Catholic conceptions including its saints and other elements. Music is an integral part of the ceremonies especially through the hypnotic effects of **drum** rhythms, **chants** and **dance**: "A rapid rhythm is beaten on metal **bells**; more than fifty

Voodoo has a mixed reputation in the west, but a fuller understanding of this belief system invites many interesting observations concerning the effects that music can have on its participants. This unidentified drummer is a Togolese performer (Anton_Ivanov/ Shutterstock.com).

people chant. Loud hand-clapping, the touching of rattle-instruments, drum beats cutting into the women's chants" (Chesi, p. 107). The rhythm associated with the *guédé loa* spirits of the cemetery and death consists of a syncopated: quaver, two semiquavers, semiquaver rest, two semiquavers, semiquaver rest on the leading drum and a counter rhythm of two semiquavers, quaver rest, six quavers (Hill and Marks, n.d.). Bowed-stringed instruments are also used known as *Ngomi* which are believed to be holy and may be decorated with Christian iconography or carvings.

The ethnomusicologist Gilbert Rouget rejected the "neurophysical effects of drumming on trance. He concludes that music's physiological and emotional effects are inseparable from patterns of collective representations and behavior" (Rouget, back cover).

Chesi, Gert (1980). *Voodoo: Africa's Secret Power*. Wörgl: Perlinger Verlag.
Hill, Richard, and Morton Marks. "Voodoo Trance Music: Ritual Drums of Haiti." *Lyrachord Discs*. New York.

Huxley, Francis (1970). "Voodoo." *Man, Myth and Magic* VII: 2967–2976.
Rouget, Gilbert (1985). *Music and Trance: A Theory of the Relations Between Music and Possession*. Chicago: University of Chicago Press.

Waddell, Leila

Leila Ida Nerissa Bathurst Waddell (1880–1932) was a violinist and the daughter of Irish immigrants in Australia. She was a favorite disciple of **Aleister Crowley**, who referred to her as "Laylah" notably in his *Book of Lies* (1912). He managed a group of seven female dancers and musicians, "The Ragged Ragtime Girls," on various tours at home and abroad which included Waddell. Before she joined Crowley and became involved in the occult, she was a **violin** teacher and performer in a **London** theater, however, it was her musical contributions to his "Rites of Eleusis" at the Caxton Hall that drew attention to her: "After a long pause, the figure enthroned [Waddell] took a violin and played with passion and feeling, like a master. We were thrilled to our very bones. Once again the figure took the violin and played … with such an intense feeling that in very deed most of us experienced the ecstasy which Crowley so earnestly seeked" (cited in King, p. 64). She was a practitioner in the occult in her own right, but eventually departed from the Crowley circle, returned to Australia and resumed her normal violin teaching activities until her death (theconversation.com/hidden-women-of-history-leila-waddell-australian-violinist-philosopher-of-magic-and-fearless-rebel-122402).

King, Francis (1987a). *The Magical World of Aleister Crowley*. London: Arrow Books.

Waggon and Horses

The Waggon and Horses is a public house at Millhouses near Sheffield in England that was a coaching inn as early as 1725. Customers have recounted stories about one landlord who didn't stay in the inn because of the ghostly **violin** music that persisted from an upstairs room when no one was there. There has not been any recent manifestations recorded.

Salim, Valerie (1983). *A Ghost Hunter's Guide to Sheffield*. Sheffield: Sheaf.

Wagner, Richard

Wilhelm Richard Wagner (1813–1883) was a German composer who many people believed to be a **genius** because of his innovatory operas and music-dramas which he wrote both the music and the librettos to, as well as his talents in theatrical management and prolific writing some of which caused considerable controversy because of its anti–Semitic and racist content. The author Emil Ludwig (1881–1948) thought Wagner was "the most dangerous of Germans" and believed that his music worked "upon the nervous system in a negative way whilst it 'transports the listener into a state of mystical ecstasy'" (cited in Summers, p. 284). He was a favorite composer of Adolf Hitler. Fortunately, the writings of **Arthur Abell** have allowed an insight into Wagner's extraordinary composing procedure which seemed to be far from normal. He compared his writing to the process that Shakespeare used when writing a scene from *A Midsummer Night's Dream*: "Doth glance from heaven to earth, from earth to heaven, and as imagination bodies forth, the forms of things unknown, the poet's pen turns them to shapes, and gives to airy nothing a local habitation and a name. Such tricks hath strong imagination"(cited in Abell, pp. 140–141).

In referring to *Rheingold* Wagner spoke of the semi-trance condition that allowed him to understand the essence of his own nature and that the vision of the rushing water was symbolic of his future creations—the stream of life that was to flow from him (Abell, p. 141).

His discussions about the power of **dreams** and the transcendental nature of music further explain Wagner's penetration into a **magic**al world for his **inspiration**. Connections have been made between Wagner and **Aleister Crowley** which inevitably places him further into an occult world (Allis, 2014), but his music has also been scrutinized scientifically for its anomalous effects "to learn more about the circumstances that favor anomalous deviations of a random event generator (REG), as described by the PEAR group in numerous scientific publications" (Vaitl, p. ii). (For an essay on Wagner and the occult see Adams, pp. 28–31).

Abell, Arthur M. (1955). *Talks with Great Composers*. London: Psychic Book Club.
Adams, Herbert (1919). "Wagner and Occultism." *Occult Review* XXX, no. 1: 28–31.
Allis, M.J. (2014) "The Diva and the Beast: Susan Strong and the Wagnerism of Aleister Crowley." *Forum for Modern Language Studies*. Oxford University Press.
Summers, Montague (1965). *Witchcraft and Black Magic*. London: Arrow.
Vaitl, Dieter (1998). "Anomalous Effects During Richard Wagner's Operas." *The Explorer* 14 (Fall): 4.

Walton-on-the-Naze

Walton-on-the-Naze is a seaside town in Essex, England that has a tradition of **sunken bells** being heard from beneath the waves at various times. The original church was swept away in 1798, but briefly reappeared during a storm in January 1928 (Payne, p. 22). The author has visited Walton on many occasions for the last sixty years and has not heard the bells or seen the church arising from the waves.

Payne, Jessie (1995). *A Ghost Hunter's Guide to Essex*. Norfolk: Ian Henry.

Warwick

Humber Avenue in Warwick, England was the scene of "over a hundred impromptu concerts," according to one Bill Duncan, but there was no one playing the plucked strings of the **piano** at the time (cited in Michell and Rickard, p.83). No further details have been discovered since this reported incident in *The News of the World*, 13 January 1974.

Michell, John, and Robert J.M. Rickard (1983). *Phenomena*. London: BCA.

Whalley Abbey

Whalley Abbey near Clitheroe in England has a gruesome history attached to it since the abbot John Paslew was tried and executed for treason either there or close by in 1537. "Witnesses have heard the singing of a *Te Deum* and have seen a procession of monks" (Guiley, p. 248). During a brief visit the author did not hear anything paranormal.

Guiley, Rosemary Ellen (1994). *The Guinness Encyclopedia of Ghosts and Spirits*. Enfield: Guinness.
Michell, John, and Robert J.M. Rickard (1983). *Phenomena*. London: BCA.

"Wheels Cottage"

"Wheels Cottage" is a property in Thundersley, Essex, in England which, according to the Latchford family, when they lived there, was the location of bugles being heard from an unknown source at "the time of the new moon" (Payne, pp. 92–93). Attempts were made to record the music but were not successful. Investigation discovered that the original owners' sons had both been buglers.

Payne, Jessie (1995). *A Ghost Hunter's Guide to Essex*. Norfolk: Ian Henry.

Whitby Abbey

The dramatic location of the ruins of Whitby Abbey on the Yorkshire coast, together with its connections with Bram Stoker's novel *Dracula*,

Whitby Abbey situated on the cliffs of the atmospheric town of Whitby, where Bram Stoker wrote *Dracula*, has its own legends of musical anomalies (author's photograph).

makes it a prime setting for tales of the paranormal—true and otherwise. It was built in the twelfth century on the site of a monastery founded by Abbess Hilda in ACE 657. It has been reported that the sounds of a choir have been heard echoing faintly in the ruins and notably "at the hour of dawn on old Christmas Day [January 7 to compensate for the calendar discrepancy when England and Scotland changed from the Julian to the Gregorian calendar in 1752]" (Harries, p. 35).

Harries, John (1974). *The Ghost Hunter's Road Book*. London: Rupert Crew.

White Hart Inn

The White Hart Inn is situated in the High Street of Chalfont St. Peter in Buckinghamshire, England and it is said to be haunted by a phantom **violin** player who has been named as Donald Ross, a former landlord of the public house in the 1920s. In 1989 the temporary landlords were frequently disturbed by this and other phenomena and departed without wishing to return (Brooks, pp. 76–77).

The German castle of Wildenstein, south of Bubendorf, has been investigated at length and found to be the focus of different types of paranormal music manifestations (Basel001/Shutterstock.com).

Wildenstein Castle

Wildenstein Castle is a thirteenth-century stronghold situated near Heilbronn, Germany. It was thoroughly investigated by the Freiburg Institute and commented on by the parapsychologist Dr. Hans Bender. Apart from legends various paranormal phenomena had been associated with it since about 1850. "Phantom music was heard in the castle ... on February 18, 1955" which was described "as if it was played on a child's **trumpet**" which was heard "for between thirty and forty minutes" (cited in MacKenzie, p. 81). Other musical manifestations included spinet music and what sounded like bagpipe music (cited in MacKenzie, pp. 81–82). The witnesses, which included Baron Maximillian and Anna von Zieten, a sister of Baron Goerg, claimed that neither of them were prone to **hallucinations**.

MacKenzie, Andrew (1987). *The Seen and the Unseen*. London: Weidenfeld and Nicolson.

Winchcombe Abbey

Very little remains of this eighth-century abbey in Gloucestershire, England; however, it has been claimed that the **chant**ing of monks has been heard around midnight and an apparition has been seen which resembled a monk "in a hollow near the cemetery..." (Hippisley Coxe, p. 93).

Hippisley Coxe, Antony D. (1973). *Haunted Britain*. London: Pan Books.

Witchcraft and Paganism

The belief system of witchcraft or in its often-designated modern description of wicca have somewhat different origins and emphases, but they nevertheless converge in the use of music for purposes which are outside of simple leisure and furthermore, music can often produce a number of circumstances which are firmly within the realm of anomalous, strange or beyond the normal. During the alleged witches' Sabbat (or Sabbath) it was written that music was provided as part of the perverted demonic ritual with a variety of instruments as were available and illustrated in sixteenth a seventeenth-century pamphlets (cited in Robbins, pp. 414–424). *The Discoverie of Witchcraft* by Reginald Scott, first published in 1584, took exception to the lies written by some of the witch hunters when they used such language as "the witches never faile to danse; and in their danse they sing these words; Har, har, divell, divell, danse here.... And whiles they sing and danse, everie one hath a broome in hir hand" (Scot, p. 24).

The use of music and **dance** in seventeenth-century gatherings as a form of alleged frenzied worshiping of devils and the like has often been quoted in the literature even up to the twentieth century: "There were often dances ... the choreography of hell, awkward jiggetings and lewd leapings, the muckibus caperings and bouncings.... The music well suits the movements. As there is an immortal melody and the 'Perfect Diapasons' of Heaven, so is there the horrid cacophony of hell. Music may be potent for evil, unloosing hideous passions and cruelty" (Summers, p. 284). The Egyptologist Margaret Murray gave a controversial primitive origin to witchcraft in drawing comparisons between a player/ dancer with the musical bow in the Paleolithic era and the music of the **Devil** in the same circumstances in Scotland. She also drew a strong connection between the use of the panpipes, named of course after the ancient Greek deity Pan, and their use by the Devil (cited in Crowther, p. 88).

With the onset of the Age of Enlightenment a more positive approach was set forth which nevertheless maintained the **magic**al effects of music. Although appearing in a children's story book *The Wind in the Willows* by the English author Kenneth Grahame (1859–1932), the appearance of Pan and his magical music emanates from Grahame's strongly-held pagan beliefs: "that glad piping broke on him like a wave, caught him up, and possessed him utterly" (Grahame, p. 113). The self-styled "King of the Witches" Alexander Sanders (1926–1988) referred to the "majesty of Pan's pipes" in a lecture he gave in 1986 (Sanders, p. 6).

Contemporary witchcraft practices and gatherings still use music to achieve **altered states of consciousness** involving magic and **spell-craft** and in some cases to enhance the attendance of archetypal presences typically referred to by numerous mythologically-based names—Pan, Hecate, Artemis, Diana etc. The founder of modern witchcraft Gerald Gardner writing about "Music Magic" related how playing a small **drum** with a monotonous rhythm produced unaccountable anger in an individual subjected to it which was beyond mere "suggestion" (Gardner, p. 120).

In a survey undertaken by the author eighty-eight practicing witches replied to a questionnaire asking about the use of music in ritual and eighty-nine percent claimed its integral use: "The purpose is to add a deeper dimension to the ritual being performed" (Willin, p. 236). The place of folk music in pagan ritual has also been highlighted: "Folk songs and music retain the roots of primitive magic and **religion**" (Stewart, p. 2) and perhaps even more importantly "the influence of Other-worldly beings on humans … act as cosmic symbols, or representations of apparent laws, which were eventually realized to exist through and beyond individual awareness and to be part of the basic pattern of existence" (Stewart, p. 44). Recorded music that is used by witches and pagans in rituals which is believed by them, at least in the first part of the twenty first century, to have magical effects includes:

> *Carolyn Hillyer & Nigel Shaw: Riven Inside* and *Echoes of the Ancient Forest*
> *Clannad: The Magical Ring* and *The Fairy Ring*
> *Dead Can Dance (Brendan Perry & Lisa Gerrard): Chant of the Paladin* and *The Wind that Shakes the Barley*
> *Enigma (Michael Cretu): MCMXC a. D*
> *Loreena McKennitt: Lost Souls* and *The Book of Secrets*
> *Omnia: Earth Warrior* and *Prayer*

[private correspondence].

Satanism, as established by the American Anton La Vey in 1966, also uses music in its rituals, but it bears no resemblance to the nature-based pagan music of contemporary witchcraft. It tends to use corruptions of church hymns arranged by La Vey himself—he was a trained musician playing second oboe in the San Francisco Symphony Orchestra as well as the organ for the Clyde Beatty Circus (Parker, pp. 254–257). His writings draw attention to the psychological power of music in general usage and away from any specific negative influences (La Vey, pp. 92). Trance inducing rhythms with references to Satan and the Devil in the words and music of some rock groups are similarly unrelated to genuine spiritually focused and desired pagan rituals, although some of the performances in the 1970s by the heavy metal group Black Sabbath seemed to aspire to "an authentic magical ceremony, probably derived from one of the textbooks known as the *grimoires*" (King, pp. 144–145). Notoriously heavy-metal rock music might be accused of causing aggressive behavior and "cosmic rock" has been promoted by such groups as Pink Floyd, Tangerine Dream and King Crimson (Drury and Tillett, p. 149).

Crowther, Patricia (1981). *Lid Off the Cauldron*. London: Muller.
Drury, Nevill, and Gregory Tillett (1997). *The Occult: A Sourcebook of Esoteric Wisdom*. New York: Saraband.
Gardner, Gerald B. (1999). *Witchcraft Today*. Thame: I-H-O Books.
Grahame, Kenneth (1997). *The Wind in the Willows*. London: Folio Society.
King, Francis X. (1987b). *Witchcraft and Demonology*. Middlesex: Hamlyn.
La Vey, Anton Szandor (2003). *The Satanic Witch*. Los Angeles: Feral House.
Parker, John (1993). *At the Heart of Darkness*. London: Sidgwick & Jackson.
Robbins, Rossell Hope (1959). *The Encyclopedia of Witchcraft and Demonology*. Middlesex: Hamlyn.
Sanders, Alex. (1986) Unpublished transcription. Archives: The Museum of Witchcraft, Boscastle, England.
Scot, Reginald (1972). *The Discoverie of Witchcraft*. New York: Dover Publications.
Stewart, R.J. (1987). *Music and the Elemental Psyche*. Wellingborough: Aquarian.
Summers, Montague (1965). *Witchcraft and Black Magic*. London: Arrow Books.
Willin, Melvyn J. (2005). *Music, Witchcraft and the Paranormal*. Ely: Melrose.

York

The city of York in England has often been referred to as the most haunted city in England, even Europe, and this has come about through its wealth of stories of apparitions and poltergeist activity that has been written about during the last hundred years (Mitchell, 1996). The most famous episode concerns Harry Martindale's (1935–2014) witnessing of a group of Roman soldiers coming through the wall of the Treasurer's House which he was initially alerted to by hearing a **trumpet** call from an unknown source. He was later cross-examined by experts in Roman history, and, unlike typical Hollywood representations, he described such items as their weapons and kit quite correctly. The author interviewed Martindale on several occasions, and he never deviated from his fascinating story which has subsequently been verified by other witnesses to the phenomena.

York also boasts other alleged paranormal musical phenomena. On an unspecified date ("some years ago") a policeman was on foot patrol one night when he heard music coming from the inside of St. Crux Church. It sounded like a funeral march being played on the organ. The music faded and he was aware of the door opening and the sound and sensation of a rustling dress brushed past him. The door closed and silence returned, much to his amazement (O'Donnell, pp. 87–88).

Mitchell, John V. (1996). *Ghosts of an Ancient City*. York: St. Peter's School.
O'Donnell, Elliott (1939). *Haunted Churches*. London: Quality Press.

Appendix 1

A Selection of References to Rosemary Brown

Abbreviations

JSPR   *Journal of the Society for Psychical Research*
PSPR   *Proceedings of the Society for Psychical Research*
PN   *Psychic News*

Alpha (1979a). "Concert Success." Issue 3 (July/August 1979): 2.

Alpha (1979b). "New Music from Old Masters." Issue 3 (July/August): 22–24.

Ansell, Danny (1987). "Musical Medium Plans New LP of Spirit Inspired Works." *PN*, December 5.

Bacon, Dorothy (1969). "Rosemary Brown." *Life*, June 9.

Banks-Smith, Nancy (1980). "Spirits from the Past." *The Guardian*, August 13.

Barrington, Mary Rose (1969). "Report of ESP Committee of the SPR." May 2.

Barry, Bill (1986). *PN*, 8 March.

Brown, Rosemary (1971a). "Life on the Other Side." *Sunday Mirror*, February 7: 10–11.

Brown, Rosemary (1971b). "Solved! The Riddle of the Unfinished Symphony." *Sunday Mirror*, February 14: 34.

Brown, Rosemary (1971c). *Unfinished Symphonies*. London: Souvenir Press.

Brown, Rosemary (1974). *Immortals at My Elbow*. London: Bachman and Turner.

Brown, Rosemary (1986). *Look Beyond Today*. New York: Bantam Press.

Brown, Thomas (2001). "Rosemary Brown Obituary." *The Independent*, November 21: 6.

Fagan, Keith (1970). "The Rosemary Brown Phenomenon." *Musical Opinion*, June: 469.

Harrison, Vernon (1972). "Correspondence." *JSPR* 46 (March): 51–52.

Harrison, Vernon (1994). "Some Parallel Cases: Appendix II." *PSPR* 58: 59–60.

Heywood, R. (1971). "Notes on Rosemary Brown." *JSPR* 46, no. 750 (December): 212–7.

Horder, Mervyn (1982). "In Her Own Write: A Note on Rosemary Brown." The Rosemary Brown Piano Album, Paxton, 1974. *JSPR* 51: 106.

Matthews, Denis (1969). "The Story of Rosemary Brown." *The Listener* (June 26): 897.

Mobbs, Kenneth (1974). "The Rosemary Brown Piano Album." *Music Journal ISM* 40, no. 3: 25.

Oakes, Philip (1970). "The Company She Keeps." *The Times* (April 5).

Oland, Sandra (1970). "Receiving Spirit Music Is Not Uncommon." *PN* (June 13): 5.

Ortzen, Tony (1986). "Musical Medium Plays Liszt Spirit Composition on TV Show." *PN* (July 26).

Osborn, Arthur W. (1972). "Correspondence." *JSPR* 46 (June): 103–104.

Parrott, Ian (1970). "I Accept Genuineness of Rosemary Brown's Mediumship." *PN* (May 23).

Picknett, Lynn (1981). "The Latest Works of Beethoven, Brahms and Liszt." *Unexplained* 18: 350–353.

Playfair, Guy Lyon (2002). "Rosemary Brown 1916–2001." *JSPR* 66.4, no. 869.

PN (1969a). "Record Has 11 New Works

from Famous 'Dead' Composers." April 26.

PN (1969b). "Thousands Hear Schubert's Spirit-Dictated Piano Composition on TV." June 4.

PN (1969c). "'Dead' Composer's New Work Heard on TV." June 7.

PN (1969d). "Behind the Scenes in Rosemary Brown's Psychic Life." June 28.

PN (1969e). "Rosemary's After-Life Music Causes Controversy in 'Life.'" August 9.

PN (1970a). "Scholar Stands by Famous Musician's Spirit Message." May 9.

PN (1970b). "Millions See Rosemary Brown on Dutch TV." June 20.

PN (1970c). "Rosemary Supplies Psychic Answers—but Not for 'Time.'" July 25: 7.

PN (1970d). "'Dead' Composers Speak to Their Musical Medium Rosemary Brown." October 24.

PN (1970e). "Rosemary Provides Fare for Famous Restaurant." December 12.

PN (1970f). "Beethoven Turns No Deaf Ear to His Medium." December 26.

PN (1971a). "Newspaper Serializes Rosemary Brown Story." January 30.

PN (1971b). "Rosemary Creates Record." January 31.

PN (1971c). "Music Medium Adds New Chapter to Psychic History." March 13.

PN (1978). "Famed Pianist Is Convinced of Survival and Spirit Communication." March 25.

PN (1979a). "'Dead' Composer Returns to Help Conductor of His Opera." March 10.

PN (1979b). "'Our Gracie' Returns with Cheering Song." October 13.

PN (1980a). "Concert Pianist Tells How Beethoven Supplies Eight Bars Missing from Work." March 8.

PN (1980b). "She Could Never Create All Her Spirit Scores." August 23.

PN (1982a). "Composer Who Praised Spirit Scripts Passes." May 22.

PN (1982b). "Composers Bring Harmony from the Spirit World." September 25.

PN (1983). "Schubert Sonata Has World Premiere." July 16.

PN (1984). "BBC Broadcasts Music from 'Dead' Composers." September 8.

PN (1986a). "Lennon Songs: Rosemary Puts Record Straight." March 8.

PN (1986b). "Written from Beyond." July 12: 3.

PN (1986c). "'Dead' Doctor Prescribes; 'Love is the only way' says John Lennon's Message." July 26.

Radford, Penny (1971). "Out of the Everywhere." The Times (October 25): 14.

Ratcliffe, Michael (1980). "Spirits from the Past." The Times (August 13).

Senior, Evan (1969). "Music from the Spheres." Music & Musicians (August).

Stemman, Roy (1975). Spirits and Spirit Worlds. London: Aldus Books, 122–123.

Trevelyan, Sir George (1969). "Rosemary Brown's Music." Correspondence.

Willin, Melvyn J. (1999). Paramusicology: An Investigation of Music and Paranormal Phenomena. PhD thesis. Music Department. University of Sheffield.

Willin, Melvyn J. (2005). Music, Witchcraft and the Paranormal. Ely: Melrose Press.

Appendix 2

The Cases Explored in
D. Scott Rogo's NAD Books

Abbreviations

JASPR	*Journal of the American Society for Psychical Research.*
JSPR	*Journal of the Society for Psychical Research.*
PSPR	*Proceedings of the American Society for Psychical Research.*
PSPR	*Proceedings of the Society for Psychical Research.*
Phantasms	*Phantasms of the Living* (1886) Gurney, Podmore and Myers.
Human Personality	*Human personality and its Survival of Bodily Death* (1903). Myers.
Dialectical	*Report on Spiritualism of the Committee of the London Dialectical Society,* 1873.
Fate	fate.mag.com.
Forum	*The Forum of Psychic and Scientific Research.*
NDE	Near-death experience
OOBE	Out-of-body experience
Hallucination	Music heard without claim of OOBE, NDE, or other explanation. Transcendental?

Name	Vol.	Case	Source	Details
A.C.F., Mrs.	1	34	*Psychic News* 1966	Deathbed. organ and voices
A.M.H., Miss	1	9	Owen, 1860	Dream telepathy. Piano
"Alice"	2	123	*JASPR* Aug. 1907	NDE singing heard
Anon.	2	148	*Light* 1921	Deathbed music heard
Anon.	2	150	Personal contact	Deathbed music heard
Anon.	2	153	Personal contact	Deathbed music heard
Artz, Karl	2	155	Personal contact	Deathbed music heard
B.R.G., Mrs.	2	128	Personal contact	OOBE music heard
Barnes, Carl J.	1	15	*Fate* July 1951	Hallucination in plane

Name	Vol.	Case	Source	Details
Barnett, E. W.	2	145	*JASPR* Vol. XII ?	NDE music heard
Bayless, Ray.	1	1	Personal contact	Childhood hallucination
Beggs, R. K.	1	79	*Fate* March 1960	NDE drowning. Music
Bell Witch	1	58	Ingram, 1961	Female choir hymn singing
Benincasa, Orsola	1	86	Thurston, 1955	Nun emits music
Blake, Mrs.	1	73	*PASPR* Vol. VII	Piano music from séance
Borley Church	1	99	Price, 1946	Choir singing and organ
"Bradley, John"	2	149	R. Digest May 1959	NDE then death-music
Bralley, Ross L.	2	127	Personal contact	Hallucination choir heard
Brook House	1	54	Stead, 1921	Female wailing and music
Brookes, Jesse	2	103	Personal contact	OOBE celestial music
Buffington, Ivan	2	141	Personal contact	OOBE or NDE music
Butler, W. E.	1	90	Butler, 1967	OOBE heavenly music
C., Alice Caroline	2	147	*JASPR* Vol. XII ?	Deathbed music
C., Mr.	1	48	Personal contact	Precognitive music heard
Castleconnell Castle	2	113	Owen, 1964	Voices, trumpets, drums
Chenoweth, Mrs.	1	69	*PASPR* 1925	Hallucination of organ
Colonel ---	1	38	*PSPR* Vol. III, p. 92	Deathbed singing heard
"Communicator"	1	97	Tubby, 1928	Singing heard while ill
Dter., Mrs. Sewell's	1	31	*Phantasms* Vol. II	Deathbed harp music
Dter., Mrs. Yates'	1	33	*Phantasms* Vol. II	After daughter's death
Davidson, L. A.	2	146	No details	Deathbed angels heard
Dedman, Harold	1	28	Personal contact	Childhood hallucination
Doyle's Correspond.	1	12	Doyle, 1930	Dream of NDE music
Dryden, Daisy	2	108	*JASPR* Vol. XII, no.6	Deathbed angels heard
Dyer, C. M.	1	82	Personal contact	Hallucination in bed
E.I.	1	39	*Phantasms* Vol. II	Post death singing heard
Edgerton, James C.	1	6	Muldoon, 1946	OOBE of single piano note
Elderly Guest	1	30	*Light* April 26, 1884	Hallucination at tea party
Eliot, George	2	124	Holt, 1914	NDE Aeolian harp heard

Name	Vol.	Case	Source	Details
Foote, Samuel	2	158	Foote, 1805	Precognition of death
Fred ---	1	94	Personal contact	NDE—month before death
Fulcher, Mabel	2	134	Personal contact	Hallucination of music
G., Ada	2	109	*Atlantic Mthly* 1879	Deathbed music heard
G., Mrs.	1	22	Personal contact	Choral music heard
Goethe, Wolfgang*	2	142	Bozzano, 1923	Deathbed music heard
Gooder, Edgar	1	23	Personal contact	Celestial choir heard
[* actually Johann]				
H., Anne	1	53	*PSPR* Vol. VI	Poltergeist and musical box
H.E.L.	1	40	*Human Personality*	Post death music heard
Haines, Elsie	1	24	Personal contact	Childhood hallucination
Hall, Prescott	1	5	*JASPR* Vol. X, 1916	
Hall, Ruth	1	78	*Fate* June 1960	OOBE of "glorious music"
Hamilton, Gail	2	144	Hamilton, 1896	NDE the deathbed angels
Haslam, Barbara	1	21	Personal contact	Hallucination in bed
Hatfield, Mrs. E.	1	10	Crookall, 1960	OOBE of music
Haunted Churchyard	1	59	Bennett, 1939	Hallucination wind band
Henley, M.E.	1	2	*Psychic News* 1955	OOBE "beautiful music"
Hicks, Charles E.	1	77	*Fate* April 1967	During a coma choir heard
Hill, Arthur	1	95	Personal contact	Deathbed music heard
Hinton, Ampner	1	55	Price, 1945	Hallucination of harmony
Hodgson's "Cousin"	2	125	Holt, 1914	Deathbed music heard
Home, D.D.	1	67	Home, 1864	Music heard around him
Home, D.D.	1	67	Adare, 1869	Harmonium or accordion
Home, D.D.	2	110	Home, 1864	Deathbed music heard
Home, D.D.	2	111	Home, 1864	Deathbed music heard
Hovanitz, Jeanne	2	115	Personal contact	Hallucination symphony
Hunter, David	1	98	Lang, 1894	Hallucination and ghost
Huntley, John	2	138	Hill, 1918	OOBE music heard
Hyams, Elizabeth	1	49	Personal contact	Music at death of a friend
Irvine, Mrs. M.E.	2	139	Hill, 1918	OOBE music heard

Name	Vol.	Case	Source	Details
J.M., Mrs.	2	119	*PSPR* Li 1905	Hallucination hymns heard
Jahenny, Marie	1	85	Thurston, 1955	Angelic music heard
Jencken, H. D.	1	35	*Dialectical*, 1873	Deathbed music
Jenkins, Sarah	1	42	*JSPR* Feb. 1893	After a funeral
Jobson, Mary	1	52	Crowe, 1848	Poltergeist and illness
Jobson, Mary	1	88	Clanny, 1841	Music from the medium
Jumièges, Abbey of	1	51	*JSPR* Vol. xviii.118	Hallucination monks chant
Kelley, S.H.	1	3	Crookall, 1964	NDE drowning
Kenealy, Dr.	2	154	Spicer, 1863	Deathbed music heard
Knutson, Kathleen	2	105	*Fate* July 1969	OOBE during illness music
L., Mrs.	2	142	*Phantasms* vol. ii	Deathbed singing/harp
L.C., Mrs.	1	26	Personal contact	Hallucination choral, organ
L.M., Mr. and Mrs.	2	122	*PSPR* Dec. 1905	Hallucination of singing
Lady C. and Z. T.	1	100	*Phantasms* 1884	Angel singing 2 witnesses
LaPat, Carl	2	136	Personal contact	OOBE symphony/ organ
Larcombe, M. A.	1	93	*Phantasms* 1882	Angels seen and heard
Lehmann, Rosamond	1	14	*Light* Summer 1962	OOBE symphonic music
"Lodge, Mary"	2	126	Hamilton, 1969	Medium and séance
Lonely Child	1	75	*Light* Sept. 1945	Hallucination when child
Louis XVII	2	143	Beauchesne, 1852	Deathbed music heard
Lowell, Arthur	2	152	*Light 1912*	Deathbed angels heard
MacComber, Mrs. C.	2	131	Personal contact	Hallucination of music
Madison, Betty	2	132	Personal contact	Hallucination of music
Madison, Betty	2	140	Personal contact	OOBE music heard
"Margery"	1	72	*PASPR* J.M. Bird	Various sounds in séance
Mason, Peggy	1	25	Personal contact	Hallucination childbirth
Milton, John	1	101	Summers, 1958	Quotes a poem—organ
Mitchell, Catherine	1	27	Personal contact	Dental "orchestral" music
Moberly & Jourdain	1	83	Moberly/Jourdain	Hallucination at Versailles
Moes, Dominica	1	84	Thurston, 1955	Angels and heavenly music
Montgomeryshire	2	120	*PSPR* Dec. 1905	Hallucination of music

Name	Vol.	Case	Source	Details
Mormelo, Rosemary	2	130	Personal contact	Hallucination of angels
Moses, W. Stainton	1	68	*Light* Jan. 28 1893	Fairy bells in séance
Moses, W. Stainton	1	68	*PSPR* Vols. IX/ XI	9 categories in séance
"Mystic"	1	16	*Fate* Nov./Dec. 1951	Hallucination—religious
Neilson, Peter	1	37	*Fate* October 1968	Angels on deathbed
Newsman, a	1	76	*Light* Sept. 1945	Hallucination orchestra
Old Sailor, an	2	107	Knight, 1969	Music in dream
Opfolter-Hull, L.	1	8	Personal contact	OOBE childbirth choir
Parker, Mr. and Mrs.	2	157	*Light* Sept. 1921	Deathbed music heard
Pattison, Nellie M.	2	137	Personal contact	Hallucination as driving
Pious Girl, a	2	112	*Zeitschrift*, 1933	Deathbed music heard
Pious Man, a	1	36	Gardner, 1911	Deathbed divine harmony
Polio Victim, a	2	106	*Fate* Aug. 1950	NDE music heard
Powell, Mrs. Emma	1	7	Personal contact	OOBE beautiful music
Powell, Mrs. Emma	1	47	Personal contact	Hallucination when ill
Ramsey, Florence	2	135	Personal contact	Hallucination while driving
Randall, Edward	2	102	Randall,	
Reine	1	71	Cornillier, 1921	Mediumistic celestial
Revell, M.	1	50	Personal contact	Premonition? Wailing
Ring, J. Willis	2	116	*Forum*, 1933	Deathbed music heard
Rinkowski, E.	2	156	Personal contact	Deathbed music heard
Rolle, Richard	1	66	Knowles, 1961	Mystical hallucination
Rooke, F. H.	2	151	*Light* 1921	Deathbed music heard
Roupp, Julia	1	80	Smith, 1965	NDE children singing
Rowe, P. B.	1	20	Personal contact	Hallucination choir
Russell, Grace	1	17	Personal contact	Hallucination on awaking
St. Chad	1	63	McKay, 1951	Religious NDE angels
St. Guthlac	1	60	Thurston, 1952	Deathbed angels
St. Joseph	1	64	Dingwall, 1947	Deathbed levitation/ music

Name	Vol.	Case	Source	Details
St. Therese	1	62	Yng. Husband, 1935	Deathbed concert heard
St. Veronica Giuliana	1	61	No details	Celestial choir "Victory"
Saint-Saëns, Camille	1	46	Flammarion, 1921	Premonition of death
Saint-Trond, Chris.	1	87	Thurston, 1955	Music sounds from inside
Salvanadin	1	89	Jacolliot, 1919	Fakir produces sounds
Salvation Army	1	43	D. Chronicle 1943	Hallucination 3 or 4 nights
Sanford, Joan	2	129	Personal contact	Hallucination of music
Schaeffer, Becky	2	133	Personal contact	Waking from sleep
Sealay, Attila von	1	74	Personal contact	Hallucination of flute
Sealay, Attila von	2	104	Personal contact	Hallucination of music
Servator	1	65	Underhill, 1955	OOBE and angels
Shopkeeper, a	1	81	Light Oct. 19, 1881	Deathbed organ music
"Sissy"	1	96	Light April 1900	Deathbed enchanting music
Skilton, J. W.	1	13	Human personality	OOBE heavenly music
Snowden, Kathleen	1	4	Crookall, 1964	OOBE ill in bed
Snow-Palmer, Gert.	1	11	Crookall, 1961	NDE music of pipe organ
Solmon Haunting	1	57	Price, 1945	Hallucination organ music
Stephens, William	1	44	Stead, no date	Hallucination during night
Swiss Boy, a	1	19	Jaffe, 1963	Hallucination while fishing
Taylor, Bayard	1	18	Prince, 1928	Hallucination chorus
Thelmar, E.	1	29	Thelmar, 1909	Hallucination Wagner?
Thompson-Gifford	1	70	Hyslop, 1919	Hallucination instrumental
Thunen, J.H. von	2	159	JSPR June 1899	Hallucination variety
Tweedale Haunting	2	118	Tweedale, 1940	Hallucination of singing
Ventresse, Edith	1	92	Personal contact	Hallucination children
Vicar, a	2	121	PSPR Dec. 1905	Hallucination of music
Vincent, Isabel	2	114	Pamphlet, 1689?	Trumpets and singing
Weymouth, A. B.	1	45	Hyslop, 1919	Hallucination singing
Willington Mill	1	56	JSPR Vol. v 1891–2	Hallucination hand-bell
Young Boy, a	1	91	Green, 1967	OOBE under chloroform

Appendix 3
Selected Books and Articles Devoted to the Sound-Music Hypotheses

Addis, L. (1999). *Of Mind and Music*. Ithaca: Cornell University Press.

Alder, Vera Stanley (1968). *The Finding of the Third Eye*. London: Rider & Company.

Allison, John (2003). "Soundless Music with a Haunting Refrain." *The Times* (September 8).

Andrews, T. (2003). *Sacred Sounds*. St. Paul: Llewellyn.

Beaulieu, J. (1987). *Music and Sound in the Healing Arts*. New York: Station Hill.

Berendt, J. (1987). *Nada Brahma: The World Is Sound*. London: East West.

Bernard, P. (2004). *Music as Yoga*. San Rafael: Mandala.

Blacklock, Mark (2003). "I Was a Sonic Experiment." *Fortean Times* 174 (September): 56.

Bonny, H., and Savary, L. (1990). *Music & Your Mind*. New York: Station Hill Press.

Budd, M. (1994). *Music and the Emotions*. London: Routledge.

Campbell, D. (1997). *The Mozart Effect*. London: Hodder and Stoughton.

Clarke, E. (2005). *Ways of Listening*. Oxford: Oxford University Press.

Collins, Paul (2001). "The Prophet of Sound." *Fortean Times* 145 (April): 40–45.

Critchley, M., and Henson, R., eds. (1977). *Music and the Brain*. London: Heinemann.

D' Angelo, J. (2000). *Healing with the Voice*. London: Thorsons.

Deutsch, Diana (2019). *Musical Illusions and Phantom Words: How Music and Speech Unlock Mysteries of the Brain*. New York: Oxford University Press.

Devereux, Paul (1999). *Places of Power*. London: Blandford.

Devereux, Paul (2001). *Stone Age Soundtracks*. London: Vega.

Dewhurst-Maddock, O. (1993). *Sound Therapy*. London: Gaia Books.

Diserens, C. (1926). *The Influence of Music on Behavior*. Princeton: Princeton University.

Draper, M. McCarthy (2001). *The Nature of Music*. New York: Riverhead Books.

Fischer, T., and Cory, L. (2015). *Animal Music*. London: Strange Attractor Press.

Fortean Times (2015a). "Sound This Out." 328 (June): 9.

Fortean Times (2015b). "Last Trumps and Hums." 329 (July): 4.

Gardner, K. (1997). *Sounding the Inner Landscape*. Shaftesbury: Element.

Gass, R. (1999). *Chanting*. New York: Broadway Books.

Godwin, J. (1987a). *Harmonies of Heaven and Earth*. London: Thames and Hudson.

Godwin, J. (1987b). *Music, Mysticism and Magic*. London: Arkana.

Godwin, J. (1989). *Cosmic Music*. Rochester: Inner Traditions.

Goldman, J. (1996). *Healing Sounds*. Shaftesbury: Element Books.

Henderson, Mark (2003). "Soundless Music with a Haunting Refrain." *The Times* (September 8): 3.

Hoffman, J. (1995). *Rhythmic Medicine*. Leawood: Jamillan Press.

James, J. (1995). *The Music of the Spheres*. London: Abacus.

Jones, Nelson (1997). "Music in Mind." *Prediction* (September): 60–62.

Jourdain, Robert (2002). *Music, the Brain, and Ecstasy.* New York: Quill.

Khan, H. (1996). *The Mysticism of Sound & Music.* Boston: Shambhala.

Maher, John M., and Briggs, Denise (1996). "On Sound." *Fate* (May): 26–29.

Maman, Fabien (1988). "The Technique of Pure Sound: Healing Mind, Body and Spirit." Interview with Jackie Young. *Caduceus* 5: 5–6.

Mannes, E. (2013). *The Power of Music: Pioneering Discoveries in the New Science of Song.* New York: Bloomsbury.

Mithen, S. (2006). *The Singing Neanderthals.* London: Orion.

Ortiz, J. (1997). *The Tao of Music.* Dublin: Newleaf.

Parsons, Steven (2012). "Infrasound and the Paranormal." *Journal of the Society for Psychical Research* 76.3, no. 908:150–174.

Parsons, S., and Cooper, C. (2015). *Paracoustics. Sound & the Paranormal.* Hove: White Crow.

Playfair, Guy Lyon, and Hill, Scott (1978). *The Cycles of Heaven.* London: Souvenir Press.

Reisberg, D., ed. (1992). *Auditory Imagery.* Mahwah: Erlbaum.

Ruland, H. (1992). *Expanding Tonal Awareness.* London: Rudolph Steiner Press.

Sargeant, Jack, and Sutton, David (2001).

"Sonic Warfare." *Fortean Times* 153 (December): 30–33.

Schoen, M. (1927). *The Effects of Music.* New York: Kegan Paul.

Sieveking, Paul (2000). "That's Not a Ghost, It's a Hum You Can't Hear." *The Sunday Telegraph* (September 3): 13.

Solomos, M. (2020). *From Music to Sound: The Emergence of Sound in 20th- and 21st-Century Music.* Abingdon: Routledge.

Stockhausen, K. (1989). *Towards a Cosmic Music.* Shaftesbury: Element.

Storr, A. (1992). *Music & the Mind.* London: HarperCollins.

Tame, D. (1984). *The Secret Power of Music.* Wellingborough: Turnstone Press.

Tandy, Vic (2000). "Something in the Cellar." *Journal of the Society for Psychical Research* 64: 129–140.

Tandy, Vic (2002). "A Litmus Test for Infrasound." *Journal of the Society for Psychical Research* 66.iii, Vol. 868: 167–174.

Trubshaw, Bob (2011). *Singing Up the Country.* Avebury: Heart of Albion Press.

Watson, Lyall (1974). *Supernature.* London: Hodder and Stoughton.

Whone, Herbert (1988). "Sound, a Healing Gift." *Caduceus* 5: 7–9.

Winkler, A. (2006). *O Let Us Howle Some Heavy Note.* Bloomington: Indiana University Press.

Bibliography

(see also Appendix 3)

Abell, Arthur M. (1955). *Talks with Great Composers.* London: Psychic Book Club.

Adams, Paul, Eddie Brazil, and Peter Underwood (2003). Stroud: The History Press.

Adare, Viscount (1869). *Experiences in Spiritualism with Mr. D. D. Home.* London: Thomas Scott.

Andrews, Ted (1997). *Music Therapy for Non-Musicians.* Batavia: Dragonhawk.

Andrews, Ted (2003). *Sacred Sounds.* St. Paul: Llewellyn.

Anson, Jay (1977). *The Amityville Horror: A True Story.* Englewood Cliffs: Prentice Hall.

Aubert, Georges (1920). *La médiumnité spirite de Georges Aubert exposée par lui-même avec les expériences faites sur lui par les savants de l'Institut Général Psychologie de février à mai 1905.* Paris.

Aveni, Anthony (1996). *Behind the Crystal Ball.* London: Boxtree.

Backster, Cleve (1968). "Evidence of a Primary Perception in Plant Life." *International Journal of Parapsychology* 10, no. 4 (Winter): 329–348.

Baigent, Michael, and Richard Leigh (1998). *The Elixir and the Stone.* London: Penguin.

Baillarger, Jules (1846). "Des hallucinations." *Memoires l' Academie Royale de Medicine* 12, 273–475.

Barrett, William (1926). *Death-Bed Visions.* London: Methuen.

Beauchesne, M.A. de (1852). *Louis XVII. Savie, son agonie, sa mort.* Paris: Plon Frères.

Beaulieu, John (1987). *Music and Sound in the Healing Arts.* New York: Station Hill.

Bell, David (1992). *Leicestershire Ghosts & Legends.* Newbury: Countryside.

Bennett, Sir Ernest (1939). *Apparitions and Haunted Houses.* London: Faber & Faber.

Berendt, J. (1987). *Nada Brahma: The World Is Sound.* London: East West.

Bernard, Patrick (2004). *Music as Yoga.* San Rafael: Mandala.

Blackmore, Susan (1993). *Dying to Live.* London: Grafton.

Blanche, C., and A. Beattie (2000). *The Power of Music.* London: Parkgate.

Bonny, Helen, and Louis Savary (1990). *Music & Your Mind.* New York: Station Hill Press.

Bord, Janet, and Colin (1989). *Modern Mysteries of the World.* London: BCA.

Bord, Janet, and Colin (1990). *Atlas of Magical Britain.* London: Sidgwick & Jackson.

Borgia, Anthony (1954). *Life in the World Unseen.* London: Odhams Press.

Bozzano, Ernesto (1923). *Phénomènes psychiques au moment de la mort.* Paris: Éditions de la B.P.S.

Bozzano, Ernesto (1943). *Musica trascendentale.* Verona: LAlbero.

Bracelin, Jack L. (1999). *Gerald Gardner: Witch.* Thame: I-H-O Books.

Brandon, Ruth (1984). *The Spiritualists.* London: Weidenfeld and Nicolson.

Britten, Emma Hardinge (1869). *History of Modern American Spiritualism.* London: Burns.

Britten, Emma Hardinge (1884). *Nineteenth Century Miracles.* Manchester: William Britten.

Britten, Emma Hardinge (1900). *Autobiography of Emma Hardinge Britten.* Mrs. Margaret Wilkinson, ed. London: John Heywood.

Brookesmith, Peter, ed. (1984). *Incredible Phenomena.* London: Orbis.

Brooks, J.A. (1990). *Britain's Haunted Heritage.* Norwich: Jarrold.

Brown, Rosemary (1971). *Unfinished Symphonies*. London: Souvenir Press.

Brown, Rosemary (1974). *Immortals at my elbow*. London: Bachman and Turner.

Brown, Rosemary (1986). *Look Beyond Today.* New York and London: Bantam Press.

Budd, M. (1994). *Music and the Emotions.* London: Routledge.

Burton, Jean (1948). *Heyday of a Wizard.* London: Harrap.

Butler, W. E. (1967). *The Magician, His Training and Work.* Northants: Aquarian Press.

Cammell, Charles Richard (1962). *Aleister Crowley.* New York: University Books.

Campbell, Don (1993). *Music: Physician for Times to Come.* Wheaton: Quest Books.

Campbell, Don (1997). *The Mozart Effect.* London: Hodder & Stoughton.

Campbell Holms, Archibald (1925). *The Facts of Psychic Science and Philosophy.* London: Kegan Paul.

Campling, C. (1997). *The Food of Love.* London: SCM.

Capron, E. W. (1855). *Modern Spiritualism: Its Facts and Fanaticisms; Its Consistencies and Contradictions.* Boston: Bela Marsh.

Carrington, Beryl, and Muriel Thresher (n.d.). *The Ghost Book. St Albans' Favourite Haunts.* St. Albans.

Carrington, Hereward, and John Meader (1912). *Death: Its Causes and Phenomena.* New York: Funk & Wagnalls.

Carroll, Robert Todd (2003). *The Skeptic's Dictionary.* Hoboken: John Wiley & Sons.

Castaneda, Carlos (1968). *The Teachings of Don Juan: A Yaqui Way of Knowledge.* London: Penguin.

Chapman, Colin (1990). *Shadows of the Supernatural.* Oxford: Lion.

Chesi, Gert (1980). *Voodoo: Africa's Secret Power.* Wörgl: Perlinger Verlag.

Chomet, Hector (1875). *The Influence of Music on Health and Life.* New York. G.P. Putnam's Sons.

Christie-Murray, David (1988). *Reincarnation.* Bridport: Prism Press.

Clanny, William Reid (1841). *A Faithful Record of the Miraculous Case of Mary Jobson.* Sunderland: Atkinson.

Combarieu, Jules (1909). *La musique et la magie.* Paris: A. Picard et fils.

Conan Doyle, Arthur (1930). *Edge of the Unknown.* New York: Putnam.

Cornillier, Pierre-Emile (1921). *Survival of the Soul.* New York: Kegan Paul.

Crabbe, John (1980). *Hector Berlioz.* London: Kahn & Averill.

Crabbe, John (1982). *Beethoven's Empire of the Mind.* Newbury: Lovell Baines.

Crabtree, Adam (1993). *From Mesmer to Freud.* Yale University Press.

Critchley, Macdonald, and R.A. Henson, eds. (1977). *Music and the Brain.* London: Heinemann.

Crookall, Robert (1960). *The Study and Practice of Astral Projection.* London: Aquarian.

Crookall, Robert (1964). *More Astral Projections.* London: Aquarian.

Crookall, Robert (1966). *The Next World— and the Next.* London: Theosophical Publishing House.

Crowe, Catherine (2000). *The Night Side of Nature.* London: Routledge.

Crowell, Eugen (1875). *The Identity of Primitive Christianity and Modern Spiritualism.* Vols. I and II. New York: Author.

Crowther, Patricia (1981). *Lid off the Cauldron.* London: Muller.

Cumes, David M. (2004). *Africa in My Bones.* Claremont: New Africa Books.

Daily Chronicle. (1905). London, May 4.

D'Angelo, James (2000). *Healing with the Voice.* London: Thorsons.

Dannemann, Monika (1995). *The Inner World of Jimi Hendrix.* New York: St. Martin's Press.

Dening, John (2000). *The Restless Spirits of Langenhoe.* Lavenham: Lavenham Press.

Deutsch, Diana (2019). *Musical Illusions and Phantom Words.* New York: Oxford University Press.

Devereux, Paul (2001). *Stone Age Soundtracks.* London: Vega.

Dewhurst-Maddock, Olivea (1993). *Sound Therapy.* London: Gaia Books.

Dingwall, Eric J. (1947). *Some Human Oddities.* London: Home and van Thal.

Dingwall, Eric J., and Harry Price, eds. (1922). Facsimile edition of *Revelations of a Spirit Medium* by A. Medium. St. Paul Minnesota. London: Kegan Paul, Trench and Trubner.

Diserens, C. (1926). *The Influence of Music on Behavior.* Princeton: Princeton University.

Dodds, E.R. (1951). *The Greeks and the Irrational.* Berkeley: University of California Press.

Dossey, Barbara, Lynn Keegan, Cathie Guzzetta, and L. Kolkmeier (1988). *Holistic Nursing: A Handbook for Practice.* New York: Aspen.

Downes, Wesley (1993). *The Ghosts of Borley*. Essex: Wesley's.

Downes, Wesley (2009). *Memories of an Essex Ghosthunter*. Newbury: Countryside.

Drinker, Sophie (1995). *Music & Women*. New York: Feminist Press, City University.

Drury, Nevill (1996). *Shamanism*. Shaftesbury: Element Books.

Drury, Nevill, and Gregory Tillett (1997). *The Occult: A Sourcebook of Esoteric Wisdom*. New York: Saraband.

Druskin, Mikhail (1883) *Igor Stravinsky: His Life, Works, and Views*. Martin Cooper, trans. Cambridge: Cambridge University Press.

Duchen, Jessica (2016). *Ghost Variations*. London: Unbound Digital.

Edmunds, I.G. (1978). *The Man Who Talked with Ghosts*. Nashville: Thomas Nelson.

Englebert, Omer (1951). *Lives of the Saints*. Philadelphia: David MacKay.

Estep, Sarah Wilson (1988). *Voices of Eternity*. New York: Fawcett Books.

Eubanks Winkler, Amanda (2006). *O Let Us Howle Some Heavy Note*. Bloomington: Indiana University Press.

Everett, Lee (1997). *Celebrity Regressions*. London: Foulsham.

Farrar, Janet, and Stewart Farrar (1990). *Spells and How They Work*. London: Hale.

Fischer, Tobias, and Lara Cory (2015). *Animal Music Sound and Song in the Natural World*. London: Strange Attractor Press.

Flaherty, Gloria (1992). *Shamanism and the Eighteenth Century*. Princeton: Princeton University Press.

Flammarion, Camille (1921). *Death and Its Mystery*. New York: The Century Company.

Flammarion, Camille (1923). *Les Maisons Hantées*. Paris: Ernest Flammarion.

Fodor, Nandor (1934). *Encyclopedia of Psychic Science*. London: Arthurs Press.

Foote, Samuel (1805). *Memoirs of Samuel Foote Esq*. London: Richard Phillips.

Forman, Joan (1982). "Old Soldiers Never Die." *The Unexplained* 68. London: Orbis.

Forman, Joan (1985). *Haunted East Anglia*. Norwich: Jarrold.

Freedland, Nat (1972). *The Occult Explosion*. London: Michael Joseph.

Friedlander, Shems (1992). *The Whirling Dervishes*. New York: State University of New York Press.

Galston, Arthur, and Clifford Slayman (1981). "Plant Sensitivity and Sensation." *Science and the Paranormal*. New York: Scribner's.

Gardner, Edmund G., ed. (1911). *Dialogues of St Gregory*. London: Philip Lee Warner.

Gardner, Gerald B. (1982). *Meaning of Witchcraft*. New York: Magickal Childe.

Gardner, Gerald B. (1999). *Witchcraft Today*. Thame: I-H-O Books.

Gardner, Kay (1997). *Sounding the Inner Landscape*. Shaftesbury: Element.

Godwin, Joscelyn (1987a). *Harmonies of Heaven and Earth*. London: Thames and Hudson.

Godwin, Joscelyn (1987b) *Music, Mysticism and Magic*. London: Arkana.

Godwin, Joscelyn (1989). *Cosmic Music*. Rochester, Vermont: Inner Traditions.

Godwin, Joscelyn (1992). *Harmony of the Spheres: Source Book of Pythgorean Tradition in Music: Source Book of Agorean Tradition in Music*. Rochester: Inner Traditions Bear and Company.

Godwin, Joscelyn (1995). *Music and the Occult*. New York: University of Rochester Press.

Goldman, J. (1996). *Healing Sounds*. Shaftesbury, Dorset: Element Books.

Gouk, Penelope (2000). *Musical Healing in Cultural Contexts*. Aldershot: Ashgate.

Grahame, Kenneth (1997). *The Wind in the Willows*. London: Folio Society.

Green, B., and W. Gallwey (1986). *The Inner Game of Music*. London: Pan.

Green, Celia (1967). *Lucid Dreams*. London: Hamish Hamilton.

Green, Miranda J. (2005). *Exploring the World of the Druids*. London: Thames & Hudson.

Griesinger, Wilhelm (1867). *Mental Pathology and Therapeutics*. C.L. Robertson and J. Rutherford, trans. London: New Sydenham Society.

Guiley, Rosemary Ellen (1994). *Encyclopedia of Ghosts and Spirits*. Enfield: Guinness.

Guiley, Rosemary Ellen (1999). *The Encyclopedia of Witches and Witchcraft*. New York: Checkmark Books.

Gurney, Edmund (1880). *The Power of Sound*. London: Smith, Elder & Co.

Gurney, Edmund, Frank Podmore, and Frederic W.H. Myers (1886) *Phantasms of the Living*. London: Trubner.

Haining, Peter (2008). *The Mammoth Book of True Hauntings*. London: Constable & Robinson.

Hamilton, Margaret (1969). *Is Survival a Fact?* Essex: Psychic Press.

Hamilton, Mary Abigail (1896). *X Rays*. Hamilton: M.A. Dodge.

Harding, Rosamond E.M. (1967). *An Anatomy of Inspiration*. London: Frank Cass.

Harries, John (1974). *The Ghost Hunter's Road Book*. London: Rupert Crew.

Harrington Edwards, John (1904). *God and Music*. London: J.M. Dent.

Haynes, Renée (1976). *The Seeing Eye, the Seeing I*. London: Hutchinson.

Haynes, Renée (1982). *The Society for Psychical Research 1882–1982*. London: Macdonald & Co.

Helmholz, Hermann von (1895). *On the Sensations of Tone as a Physiological Basis for the Theory of Music*. Translated from original 1863 German edition by Alexander J. Ellis. London: Longmans, Green.

Hemenway, Priya (2008). *The Secret Code*. Lugano: Springwood.

Heywood, Rosalind (1978). *The Infinite Hive*. Middlesex: Penguin.

Hill, J. Arthur (1918). *Man Is a Spirit*. New York: Doran .

Hines, Terence (1988). *Pseudoscience and the Paranormal*. New York: Prometheus.

Hippisley Coxe, Antony D. (1973). *Haunted Britain*. London: Pan BooksLtd.

Hoffman, J. (1995). *Rhythmic Medicine*. Leawood: Jamillan Press.

Holt, Henry (1914). *On the Cosmic Relations*. 2 vols. Boston: Houghton Mifflin.

Home, Daniel Dunglas (1864). *Incidents in My Life*. New York: A.J. Davis.

Horden, Peregrine (2000). *Music as Medicine*. Aldershot: Ashgate.

Hutton, Ronald (1996). *The Stations of the Sun*. Oxford: Oxford University Press.

Hyslop, James Hervey (1919). *Contact with the Other world*. New York: Century Co.

Iamblichus (1818). *Life of Pythagoras or Pythagoric Life*. Thomas Taylor, trans.. London: A.J. Valpy.

Inglis, Brian (1985). *The Paranormal*. London: Guild.

Inglis, Brian (1987). *The Unknown Guest—The Mystery of Intuition*. London: Chatto & Windus.

Inglis, Brian (1990). *Trance*. London: Grafton Books.

Ingram, M. V. (1961). *Authenticated History of the Bell Witch*. Rare Book Reprints.

Innes, Brian (1996). *The Catalogue of Ghost Sightings*. Leicester: Brown Packaging Books.

Iremonger, Lucille (1957). *The Ghosts of Versailles*. London: Faber & Faber.

Jack, Albert (2007). *Albert Jack's Ten-Minute Mysteries*. London: Penguin Books.

Jacolliot, Louis (1919). *Occult Science in India*. London: Rider & Co.

Jaffe, Aniela (1963). *Apparitions and Precognition*. New York: University Books.

James, Jamie (1995). *The Music of the Spheres*. London: Abacus.

Janis, Byron (2010). *Chopin and Beyond*. Hoboken: John Wiley and Sons.

Jaynes, Julian (1976). *The Origin of Consciousness in the Breakdown of the Bicameral Mind*. Boston: Houghton Mifflin.

Khan, Hazrat Inayat (1996). *The Mysticism of Sound & Music*. Boston: Shambhala.

King, Francis X. (1987a). *The Magical World of Aleister Crowley*. London: Arrow Books.

King, Francis X. (1987b). *Witchcraft and Demonology*. Middlesex: Hamlyn.

Klimo, Jon (1987). *Channeling: Investigations on Receiving Information from Paranormal Sources*. Los Angeles: Jeremy P. Tarcher.

Knight, David, ed. (1969). *The ESP Reader*. New York: Grosset and Dunlap.

Knowles, David (1961). *The Fire of Love*. Richard Rolle. New York: Harper & Row.

La Vey, Anton Szandor (2003). *The Satanic Witch*. Los Angeles: Feral House.

Lamont, P. (2005). *The First Psychic: The Peculiar Mystery of a Notorious Victorian Wizard*. London: Little, Brown.

Lang, Andrew (1894). *Cock Lane and Common Sense*. London: Longmans, Green.

Le Mée, Katharine (1994). *Chant*. London: Rider.

Legg, Rodney (1969). *A guide to Dorset ghosts*. Bournemouth: Dorset.

Linahan, Liz (1997). *The North of England Ghost Trail*. London: Constable.

London Dialectical Society (1871). *Report on Spiritualism*. London: Longmans, Green, Reader and Dyer.

MacKenzie, Andrew (1983). *Hauntings and Apparitions*. London: Granada.

MacKenzie, Andrew (1987). *The Seen and the Unseen*. London: Weidenfeld and Nicolson.

Magliocco, Sabina, and Holly Tannen (1998). "The Real Old-Time Religion:Towards an Aesthetics of Neo-Pagan Song." *The Journal of the Folklore Studies Association of Canada* 20, no. 1: 175–201.

Manning, Matthew (2007). *Your Mind Can Heal Your Body*. London: Piatkus.

Matthews, John (1991). *The Celtic Shaman*. Shaftesbury: Element Books.

Matthews, Rupert (1993). *Haunted Edinburgh.* Andover: Pitkin.

Maynard, Nettie Colburn (1917). *Was Abraham Lincoln a Spiritualist?* Chicago: Progressive Thinker.

McCarthy Draper, M. (2001). *The Nature of Music.* New York: Riverhead.

McCue, Peter, and Alan Gauld (2005). "Edgehill and Souter Fell: A Critical Examination of Two English 'Phantom Army' Cases." *Journal of the Society for Psychical Research* 69.2. no. 879: 78–94.

McEwan, Graham J. (1989). *Haunted Churches of England.* London: Robert Hale.

Mead, Robin (1994). *Weekend Haunts.* London: Impact Books.

Medhurst, R.G. (1972). *Crookes and the Spirit World.* London: Souvenir Press.

Melechi, Antonio (2009). *Servants of the Supernatural.* London: Arrow Books.

Michell, John, and Robert J.M. Rickard (1983). *Phenomena.* London: BCA.

Miller, Leon K. (1989). *Musical Savants: Exceptional Skill in the Mentally Retarded.* Mahwah: Lawrence Erlbaum.

Mitchell, John V. (1996). *Ghosts of an Ancient City.* York: St. Peter's School.

Mithen, Steven (2005). *The Singing Neanderthals.* London: Weidenfeld & Nicolson.

Moberly, Charlotte Anne, and Eleanor Jourdain (1948). *An Adventure.* London: Faber & Faber.

Monsaingeon, Bruno (2001). *Sviatoslav Richter: Notebooks and Conversations.* S. Spencer, trans. Princeton: Princeton University Press.

Montaño, Mary (1995). *Loving Mozart.* Albuquerque: Cantus Verus Books.

Moses, William Stainton. (1928). *More Spirit Teachings.* Reprinted from early issues of *Light,* Cordelia Grylls, comp. London: Fowler & Co.

Moses, William Stainton (1954). *Spirit Identity, Psychic Book Club,* London (reprint from 1879 book).

Moses, William Stainton (1976). *Spirit Teachings.* New York: Arno Press (reprint from 1924 edition published by London Spiritualist Alliance).

Moss, Peter (1977). *Ghosts Over Britain.* London: BCA.

Mowbray, Major C. H. (1947). *Transition.* London: L.S.A. Publication.

Muldoon, Sylvan (1946). *The Case for Astral Projection.* New York: Aries Press.

Murphy, John C. (2010). *Secrets of the Snake Charmer.* New York: Bloomington.

Murray, Margaret A. (1931). *The God of the Witches.* London: SampsonLow, Marston and Co. Ltd.

Myers, Frederic W.H. (1903). *Human Personality and Its Survival of Bodily Death.* 2 vols. London: Longmans.

North, Anthony (1996). *The Paranormal.* London: Blandford.

Ockelford, Adam (2007). *In the Key of Genius: The Extraordinary Life of Derek Paravicini.* London: Hutchinson.

O'Dell, Damien (2009). *Paranormal Hertfordshire.* Stroud: Amberley.

O'Donnell, Elliott (1939). *Haunted Churches.* London: Quality Press.

Oesterreich, Traugott Konstantin (1930). *Possession: Demoniacal and Other.* London: Kegan Paul et al.

Olcott, Colonel Henry S. (1875). *People from the Other World.* Hartford: American Publishing Company.

Ortiz, J. (1997). *The Tao of Music.* Dublin: Newleaf.

Ostrander, Sheila, and Lynn Schroeder (1973). *PSI: Psychic Discoveries Behind the Iron Curtain.* London: Sphere Books.

Out of this World. (1989). London: Macdonald & Co.

Owen, A.R.G. (1964). *Can We Explain the Poltergeist?* New York: Garrett Publications.

Owen, Robert (1860). *Footfalls on the Boundary of Another World.* London: Trubner.

Palmstierna, Erik (1937). *Horizons of Immortality.* London: Constable.

Panati, Charles (1974). *Supersenses.* London: Jonathan Cape.

Parker, Derek and Julia (1975). *The Power of Magic.* London: Beazley.

Parker, John (1993). *At the heart of darkness.* London: Sidgwick & Jackson Ltd.

Parrott, Ian (1966). *The Music of an "Adventure."* London: Regency Press.

Parrott, Ian (1978). *The Music of Rosemary Brown.* London: Regency Press.

Parsons, Stephen, and Callum Cooper (2015). *Paracoustics. Sound & the Paranormal.* Hove: White Crow.

Payne, Jessie K. (1995). *A Ghost Hunter's Guide to Essex.* Norfolk: Ian Henry.

Pearsall, Ronald (1973). *The Table-Rappers.* London: BCA.

Penfield, Wilder, and Theodore Rasmussen (1952). *The Cerebral Cortex of Man.* New York: Macmillan.

Pepper, Elizabeth, and John Willcock, John (1994). *Magic and Mystical Sites*. Michigan: Phanes Press.

Playfair, Guy Lyon (1985a). *The Haunted Pub Guide*. London: Harrap Limited.

Playfair, Guy Lyon (1985b). *If This Be Magic*. London: Cape.

Playfair, Guy Lyon (2011). *This House Is Haunted*. White Crow.

Playfair, Guy Lyon, and Scott Hill (1978). *The Cycles of Heaven*. London: Souvenir Press Ltd.

Podmore, Frank (1902). *Modern Spiritualism*. Vol. I. London: Methuen & Co.

Poole, Keith B. (1995). *Britain's Haunted Heritage*. Leicester: Magna Books.

Price, Harry (1925). *Stella C*. London: Hurst & Blackett.

Price, Harry (1936). *Confessions of a Ghost-Hunter*. London: Putnam.

Price, Harry (1940). *The Most Haunted House in England*. London: Longmans, Green.

Price, Harry (1945). *Poltergeist Over England*. London: Country Life.

Price, Harry (1946). *The End of Borley Rectory*. London: Harrap & Co. Ltd.

Price, Harry (1993). *Poltergeist*. London: Bracken Books.

Prince, Walter Franklin (1928). *Noted Witnesses for Psychic Occurrences*. Boston: Boston Society for Psychical Research.

Ralls-MacLeod, Karen (2000). *Music and the Celtic Otherworld*. Edinburgh: Polygon.

Ralls-MacLeod, Karen, and Graham Harvey (2000). *Indigenous Religious Musics*. Aldershot: Ashgate.

Randall, Edward C. (1917). *The Dead Have Never Died*. New York: Alfred A. Knopf.

Randles, Jenny, and Peter Warrington (1980). *UFOs. A British Viewpoint*. London: BCA.

Reik, Theodor (1958). *Ritual*. New York: International Universities Press.

Reisberg, Daniel, ed. (1992). *Auditory Imagery*. Mahwah: Erlbaum.

Rettalack, Dorothy (1973). *The Sound of Music and Plants*. Santa Monica: De Vorss.

Reuter, Florizel von (1931). *A Musician's Talks with Unseen Friends*. London: Rider & Co.

Révész, Erwin Nyiregyházi (1970). *The Psychology of a Musical Prodigy*. New York: Greenwood Press.

Robbins, Rossell Hope (1959). *The Encyclopedia of Witchcraft and Demonology*. Middlesex: Hamlyn.

Robertson, Paul (2016). *Soundscapes: A Musician's Journey Through Life and Death*. London: Faber & Faber.

Robinson, William Ellsworth (1898). *Spirit Slate Writing and Kindred Phenomena*. New York: Munn & Company.

Rochas, Albert de (1900). *Les sentiments, la musique et le geste*. Grenoble: Falque & Perrin.

Rogo, D. Scott (1970). *NAD*. New York: University Books.

Rogo, D. Scott (1972). *NAD. Volume 2*. New York: University Books.

Rogo, D. Scott (1986). *Life after Death*. London: Guild.

Rogo, D. Scott (1990). *Beyond Reality*. Northants: Aquarian Press.

Rogo, D. Scott, and Raymond Bayless (1979). *Phone Calls from the Dead*. Englewood Cliffs: Prentice Hall.

Roney-Dougal, Serena (1991). *Where Science and Magic Meet*. Shaftesbury: Element.

Rouget, Gilbert (1985). *Music and Trance*. Chicago: University of Chicago.

Ruland, Heiner (1992). *Expanding Tonal Awareness*. London: Rudolph Steiner Press.

Sacks, Oliver (2007). *Musicophilia*. London: Picador.

St. Aubyn, Astrid, and Zahra Hanbury (1996). *Ghostly Encounters*. London: Robson Books.

Schimmel, Annemarie (1993). *The Triumphal Sun*. Albany: State University of New York Press.

Schoen, Max (1927). *The Effects of Music*. New York: Kegan Paul.

Schonberg, Harold C. (1970). "Mysticism and Melancholy, Scriabin and Rachmaninoff." *The Lives of the Great Composers*. New York: W.W. Norton.

Schopenhauer, Arthur (1818/19 and 1969). *The World as Will and Representation*. E.J. Payne, trans. New York: Dover.

Schullian, Dorothy M., and Max Schoen (1948). *Music and Medicine*. New York: Henry Schuman.

Scot, Reginald (1972). *The Discoverie of Witchcraft*. New York: Dover.

Scott, Cyril (1969). *Music: Its Secret Influence Throughout the Ages*. London: Aquarian.

Scott, Sir Walter (2001). *Letters on Demonology and Witchcraft*. Ware: Wordsworth Editions.

Shah, Idres (2009). *The Book of Power*. Master Aptolcater, author, Coleman Rydie, ed. and pub.

Shankar, Ravi (1992). *Ravi Shankar. My Music. My Life.* New Delhi: Vikas.

Singer, André and Lynette (1995). *Divine Magic.* London: Boxtree Ltd.

Smith, Susy (1965). *The Enigma of Out-of-Body Travel.* Garrett Publications.

Solomon, Grant, and Jane (1999). *The Scole Experiment.* London: Piatkus.

Specht, Richard (1913). *Gustav Mahler.* Berlin: Schuster and Loeffler.

Spencer, John, and Anne (1992). *The Encyclopaedia of Ghosts and Spirits.* London: Book Club Associates.

Spicer, Henry H. (1863/ 2018). *Strange Things Among Us.* Carindale: Black Books.

Spintge, Ralph, and Roland Droh (1985). *Music in Medicine.* Basel: Roche.

Stead, William Thomas (1892). *More Ghost Stories.* New York: Review of Reviews.

Stead, William Thomas (1921). *Real Ghost Stories.* New York: George H. Doran.

Stebbing, Lionel (1971). *Music and Healing.* London: New Knowledge Books.

Steiner, Rudolf (1984). *The Essential Steiner.* R. McDermot, ed. San Francisco: HarperCollins.

Stemman, Roy (1975). *Spirits and Spirit Worlds.* London: Aldus Books.

Stevenson, Ian (1988) *Cases of the Reincarnation Type, Vol. 1, 10 Cases in India.* Charlottesville: University of Virginia Press.

Stewart, R.J. (1987). *Music and the Elemental Psyche.* Wellingborough: Aquarian.

Stewart, R.J. (1988). *Where Is St George?* London: Blandford Press.

Storr, Anthony (1992). *Music & the Mind.* London: HarperCollins.

Sturge-Whiting, J.R. (1938). *The Mystery of Versailles.* London: Rider & Co.

Summer, Lisa (1996). *Music—The New Age Elixir.* New York: Prometheus.

Summers, Montague (1965). *Witchcraft and Black Magic.* London: Arrow Books td.

Suso, Henry (1865). *The Life of the Blessed H. Suso.* T. F. Knox, trans. London: Burns, Lambert and Oates.

Tabori, Paul, and Peter Underwood (1973). *The Ghosts of Borley.* Newton Abbot: David & Charles.

Tame, David (1984). *The Secret Power of Music.* Wellingborough: Turnstone Press.

Tame, David (1994). *Beethoven and the Spiritual Path.* Wheaton: Quest Books.

Tandy, Vic (2000). "Something in the Cellar." *Journal of the Society for Psychical Research* 64, 129–140.

Tandy, Vic (2002). "A Litmus Test for Infrasound." *Journal of the Society for Psychical Research* 66, 167–174.

Tavener, John (1999). *John Tavener. The Music of Silence. A Composer's Testament.* London: Faber & Faber.

Tavener, John, and Mother Thekla (1994). *Ikons.* London: HarperCollins.

Thelmar, E. (1909). *The Maniac.* London: Rebman.

Thurston, Herbert (1952). *The Physical Phenomena of Mysticism.* London: Burns & Oates.

Thurston, Herbert (1955). *Surprising Mystics.* London: Burns & Oates.

Tomlinson, Gary. (1993). *Music in Renaissance Magic.* Chicago: University of Chicago.

Tompkins, Peter, and Christopher Bird (1973). *The Secret Life of Plants.* New York: Harper and Row.

Treffert, Darold (1989). *Extraordinary People: Understanding Savant Syndrome.* Revised ed. Lincoln: Universe.

Trimingham, J. Spencer (1973). *The Sufi Orders in Islam.* London: Oxford University Press.

Trubshaw, Bob (2011). *Singing Up the Country.* Avebury: Heart of Albion Press.

Tubby, Gertrude Ogden (1928). *James H. Hyslop—X, His Book.* York Publishing Company.

Tweedale, Charles (1940a). *Man's Survival of Death.* London: Grant Richard.

Tweedale, Charles (1940b). *News from the Next World.* London: Werner Laurier.

Underhill, Evelyn (1955). *Mysticism.* Boston: E.P. Dutton.

Underwood, Peter (1971). *Gazetteer of British Ghosts.* London: Souvenir Press.

Underwood, Peter (1983). *Ghosts of Cornwall.* Bodmin: Bossiney Books.

Underwood, Peter (1984). *This Haunted Isle.* London: Harrap Limited.

Underwood, Peter (1993). *The Ghosthunters Almanac.* Orpington: Eric Dobby.

Underwood, Peter (1996). *Guide to Ghosts & Haunted Places.* London: Piatkus.

Vaughan Williams, Ralph (1987). "The Letter and the Spirit." *National Music and Other Essays.* Oxford: Oxford University Press.

Vaughan Williams, Ursula (1964). *Ralph*

Vaughan Williams: A Biography. Oxford: Oxford University Press.

Watson, A., and N. Drury (1987). *Healing Music.* Dorset: Prism.

Webster, Sam (2001). *Modern Pagans.* San Francisco: Re/Search Publications.

Weisberg, Barbara (2005). *Talking to the Dead.* New York: HarperCollins.

Williams, Leonard (1980). *The Dancing Chimpanzee.* London: Allison & Busby.

Willin, Melvyn J. (1996a). "A Ganzfeld Experiment Using Musical Targets." *Journal of the Society for Psychical Research,* 1996, 61 (842), 1–17.

Willin, Melvyn J. (1996b). "A Ganzfeld Experiment Using Musical Targets with Previous High Scorers from the General Population." *Journal of the Society for Psychical Research* 61 (843): 103–108.

Willin, Melvyn J. (1999). *Paramusicology: An Investigation of Music and Paranormal Ohenomena.* PhD thesis. Music Department. University of Sheffield.

Willin, Melvyn J. (2004). *Music in Pagan and Witchcraft Ritual and Culture.* PhD thesis. History Dept. University of Bristol.

Willin, Melvyn J. (2005). *Music, Witchcraft and the Paranormal.* Ely: Melrose Press.

Willin, Melvyn J. (2011). "Music and Death: An Exploration of the Place Music Has at the Time of Human Death, with Special Emphasis on the Near-Death-Experience." *The Paranormal Review* 58 (April).

Willin, Melvyn J. (2019). *The Enfield Poltergeist Tapes.* Guildford: White Crow.

Wilson, Colin (1981). *Poltergeist! A Study in Destructive Haunting.* London: New English Library.

Wilson, Colin (1988). *Beyond the Occult.* London: Transworld.

Wilson, Ian (1987). *The After Death Experience.* New York: William Morrow.

Wolman, Benjamin B., ed. (1977) *Handbook of Parapsychology.* New York: Van Nostrand.

Wosien, Maria-Gabriele (1974). *Sacred Dance.* London: Thames and Hudson.

Younghusband, Sir Francis (1935). *Modern Mystics.* London: John Murray.

Zeitschrift für Parapsychologie (1933). "A Pious Girl." March.

Index

Numbers in **bold** indicate main entries;
numbers in ***bold italics*** indicate pages with photographs